Yamasaki I1

ISSEI, NISEI, SANSEI

Three Generations
of Camp Life
Pu`unene, Maui, Hawaii

by
Donald Y. Yamasaki

D & S Publishing Company

D & S Publishing Company
Kahului, Maui
Hawai`i 96732

Distributed in America and the World
by D & S Publishing and Amazon

Issei- Nisei- Sansei – Three Generations in the Pu`unene, Maui Camps
D & S Publishing Co.
Kahului, Maui, Hawai`i

ISBN-13: 978-1482361995

Includes photos and sketches

1. Japanese Life in the Sugar Plantation Camps – Non-Fiction 2. Pu`unene, Maui Camp – Non-Fiction 3. Maui, Hawai`i – Non-Fiction 4. Three generations of Maui Camp Life
5. H.C.& S

TABLE OF CONTENTS

Acknowledgements--1

Preface--5

Introduction---9

Sansei Generation--------------------------------------21
Part I
Chapter One

Issei Generation--41
Chapter Two

Nisei Generation---------------------------------------85
Chapter Three

Sansei Generation------------------------------------119
Part II
Chapter Four

Conclusion--241

Resources---247

Contract, Photos, and Sketches--------------------249

.

ACKNOWLEDGEMENTS

To my Grandfather, who so willingly supplied all information about his life.
January 29, 1887 - March 24, 1979

To my Mother, who so willingly supplied both information about her life, my Grandfather's life, and my earlier years.
July 16, 1922 - January 30, 2013

To my Father, who supplied some essential information and some that I picked up during our lifetimes together.
August 11, 1919 - December 16, 1966

To my Wife, who gave me the time to write this book. Without her, this book would not have been possible. She also served as editor.

To my granddaughter, Dayna Yamasaki, who designed the book cover, and provided technical computer assistance. Dayna is currently a sophomore class president at Henry Perrine Baldwin High School.

To Wayne Moniz, a Maui playwright and publisher, who gave me many suggestions and helped with endless hours of editing.

To my acquaintances, from the camp days, several of whom I am still in contact with. These people have always cared and helped me both in times of trouble or advice. Many of them share similar stories and have lived through comparable trials and tribulations.

To those who have passed on, this book is dedicated to you as well because you were the cornerstones that made this book possible. Many have taken their experiences to the grave. You came from Japan and experienced the harsh life of daily plantation work through your own eyes and aching bodies. Your memories were never recorded on paper but buried with you in six-foot graves, forever forgotten. If only someone had recorded your stories to be passed on through generations, then your rich lives would never have been forgotten.

To those who have given me useful information through written and taped interviews and to those who have passed away or still alive, I promise that I have written this book in the truest way so that everyone will know what life in the camps of Pu'unene was really like. Hopefully, in time, future generations will realize that past generations did not live their suffering lives without notice or in vain.

Let me describe one example of what suffering was like among the early generations. One day, I listened to my aunty for about a half-hour as she unveiled stories of the camp life. She shared incidents in a way as if it had happened yesterday. I felt her every emotion. My aunty finally broke out in tears. I knew first hand how much she had suffered. She had raised her children basically by herself. She had lost her husband by suicide early in her marriage. His misery ended after drinking a full stomach full of gasoline.

Another lady I interviewed told me not to publish this book until she died. She said that it would bring back many bad memories, considering the suffering she went through. She also cried in front of me as I interviewed her. She was of the *Nisei* Generation when things had never really changed that much. It was a generation that many never finished schooling. Many dropped out between the sixth grade and eight grade. Many were still under the strict guidance of the *Issei* Generation.

I admit that a few of the people I called to have an interview refused to share their experiences. They were trying to forget about the past and live for the future.

I can understand those feelings because I suffered through sixteen years of my life in the camps. I lived it first hand! Please, do not think that my sufferings after the camps were any better than the sufferings while living at the camps. What continued beyond them was the discrimination inflicted on me, and many of my friends. Please read on – you will see how racism affected our lives in and after plantation days.

Finally, as I mentioned earlier, I promised a particular woman that I would not publish this book until after she died. Although she was still alive, I nevertheless started writing it at the age of forty on an old Mac, ending up with 148 pages. Well, my promise was kept. That lady had since passed on and, now, after some twenty odd years, you can finally read about the three generations: *Issei*, *Nisei*, and *Sansei*.

Being that there were three plantations: Pioneer Mill Sugar Company, Wailuku Sugar Company and Pa'ia Mill Sugar Company, all having homes build around each mill, I can not and will not describe immigrant conditions of living there. I believe all were different and I will not get into it. This book is only stories and events that happened in and around Pu'unene, nothing else.

That was my goal: To tell the truth, whether it hurt or not.

Thank you very much.
Donald

PREFACE

I chose the title for this book because of the following: My grandfather was of the generation of *Issei*, born in Japan and immigrated to Hawai'i. My mother is the generation of *Nisei*, she was born in the same family as first generation in Hawai'i. I am a *Sansei*, born the second generation in Hawai'i, born in the same family. Being from the same family was important to the first generation (*Issei*).

The first-born male bears the tradition of carrying the family name that the previous generations are very proud of. That first-born male inherits everything from the parents, including the house and most of the fortune (whatever it might be) and must take care of their parents until they die. One disadvantage to this is that the daughter-in-law must live with the husband's parents. If you are lucky, some parents are good, if you are unlucky, then some in-laws could make a daughter-in-law's life very difficult.

In writing this book, I have written stories from the *Issei* Generation, *Nisei* Generation and the *Sansei* Generation to show the readers how things have changed in three generations. To make it clearer, I've provided a list of the first generation to the fifth generation.

The Generations of Japanese from the immigrants to the present:
> *Issei*- First generation arrives from Japan to work in Hawai'i.
> *Nisei*- Second generation is born first in Hawai'i. All siblings.
> *Sansei*- Third generation is born in Hawai'i. All siblings.
> *Yonsei*- Fourth generation is born in Hawai'i. All siblings.
> *Gosei*- Fifth generation is born in Hawai'i. All siblings.

Siblings refer to brothers and sisters of the same family of Japanese decent.

Here is a brief history of Japanese Emigrants who traveled to Hawai'i. This document is from a word for word one-page leaflet that was handed to me while visiting Japan. It's from: *Japanese*

Emigrants to Hawai'i, Yamaguchi-Ken, Japan.

In the first recruitment of emigrants to Hawai'i, more than twenty-eight hundred people (boys and men) were selected, a number that highly surpassed the six hundred who applied for emigration. The City of Tokyo, the ship boarded by the select nine hundred and forty-four emigrants arrived in Honolulu on February 8,

1885 after two weeks voyage. They spent several days in quarantine and completing other procedures at the Depot of Immigration Station (In Japan, those who immigrated were called emigrants and those who arrived here in Hawai'i were called immigrants. After that, they were dispersed among a total of 30 sugar cane plantations, where they were a part of a three-year contract labor force.)

Here is the breakdown of the plantations:
Hawai'i Island:	*16 Plantations*
Maui:	*6 Plantations*
Kaua'i:	*6 Plantations*
Oahu:	*1 Plantation*
Lana'i:	*1 Plantation*

In Oshima-Gun, the population had increased dramatically since mid-Edo period. It was usually for the residents to migrate as carpenters, masons, or sailors because they could not make a living in some parts of the islands. A nationwide recession followed by natural disasters forced the residents on the verge of starvation to take advantage of a plan for emigrants to Hawai'i. Because the Yamaguchi Prefectural Government knew the situation in Oshima, it placed great emphasis on recruiting emigrants in Oshima.

Boys and men from Oshima-Gun made up of one-third of all the government-contract labor emigrants, and about three thousand Oshima residents emigrated to Hawai'i. Oshima-Gun had been called the Sweet Potato-Eating Island, and later as the Emigrants Island.

6

Yearly fiscal statistics of the Government Contract Labor Emigrants showed that Yamaguchi Prefecture on Oshima-Gun had eleven-thousand, one-hundred twenty-two from Hiroshima, ten-thousand four-hundred, twenty-four from Yamaguchi, four-thousand two-hundred forty-seven from Kumamoto, two-thousand one-hundred eighty from Fukuoka, and five-hundred fourteen from Niigata.

The following is the breakdown by year depicting the amount of emigrants and their origins:

Year	Group Number	Number Of Emigrants	Yamaguchi	Oshima
1885	1-2	1,934	420	305
1886	3	877	490	305
1887	4	1,446	637	281
1888	5-7	3,286	1,611	814
1889	8-11	4,072	1,919	781
1890	12-14	2,736	651	240
1891	15-20	6,950	2,228	493
1892	21-22	2,113	703	177
1893	23-25	4,146	1,271	316
1894	26	1,546	494	105
Total		29,084	10,424	3,913

Pioneers of Japanese emigrants to Hawai'i were a group of one hundred forty-eight people called Gannenmono (a person who emigrated in the first year of Meiji Period-1868).

The sugar industry had rapidly developed since the mid-nineteenth century in Hawai'i it needed a labor force from abroad because of decrease in population of Hawaiians.

Because the emigrants program was carried out under government control, it was called Government Contract Emigrants. Until 1894, when the government entrusted an authorized company with emigrant work, twenty-six groups of

7

emigrants were sent, and approximately twenty-nine thousand Japanese crossed the ocean.

INTRODUCTION

I would like to give you information about what happened during the time I lived in the camps. I do not have any information available prior to 1902. This information is word for word, nothing left out. The following are excerpts from the *Maui News* that will help the reader understand the time line. Feel free to refer back to them. Ironically, we could not afford the ten cents to purchase the *Maui News* during the camp days.

Saturday, February 1, 1902
A trial test of the Pu'unene mill was made on Wednesday, January 29, 1902 at 10:45 A.M., which the machinery ran till Saturday evening, and will be closed on Sunday, February 2, 1902 and to start on Monday for the next season run.

HOW CANE IS PRODUCED:
Cane is brought to the carrier in cars (train) and is unloaded by two Gregg's Improved cane loaders. Passing through the rollers, the steam of the juice is pumped to the third floor where it first passes through a series of sand filters, after which it is carried to the lime vats to be clarified. From there it is carried to a Octule System of Exibles Lillie Evaporators on the first floor, and from there to be crystallizing pans. Pu'unene Mill may claim to be the best as well as the largest mill on earth.

March 7, 1903
One Hundred Japanese Laborers were shipped from Honolulu to Kahului Thursday morning to work on the Pu'unene Plantation.

March 17, 1906
Attempts of Recruiting Japanese:
In the North East of Japan are women and children starving and freezing to death. There are thousands of families unable to obtain food to maintain life and unable to protect their shrinking bodies from the cruel cold of an unusually severe winter. Snow covered grounds where the able body would work if they could and these, together with the aged, the crippled, the women and the children – from twenty-five to forty-thousand – suffer, all

9

having no hope but that the human charity that always is ready to respond to real suffering will be informed of their dire need. The spectacle of the single woman, a single child, freezing or starving to death, if close at hand, would be enough to melt the heart of anyone seeing it. Enough to stir him to the most earnest, even frantic efforts to give relief. Living in a hole dug out of the hillside, about 7x6 feet, four and a half in height, a little lean-to roof or kitchen 8x6 feet. The whole family huddled together in this hole.

In nearly all cases finds a child hanging on to the mother's breast, the poor mother, still full of smiles, giving her very life to feed her child.

Saturday, August 10, 1908
Sometime during the latter part of the week, the new Pu'unene Store at Kahului will be opened for business and as the store is the finest building and most tastefully arranged and will carry a complete line of such goods as will meet the requirements of the trade it is certain that the new management and assistants will make this one of the most popular stores in the territory.

Saturday, September 5, 1908
While the British statistics for the year 1907, show 2,445 Japanese and 126 Americans born in Hawai`i. These Japanese born will grow up with the right of citizenship – the right to vote. The figures are the culmination of several years of increase by leaps and bounds in Japanese births here. The growing generation is enough to vitally affect our politics. It is easily seen that in about twenty years, unless some different tide of immigration sets in, the birth percentage can hardly change unless otherwise-Hawaii will be thoroughly Japanese. The proportion of births in the year 1907 was 2,445 Japanese, 674 Hawaiians, 30 British, 37 Germans and 388 Chinese, 591 Portuguese, and a few Spaniards and Puerto Ricans compared to 126 Americans.

The Japanese children growing up in the territory and in many aspects, the privileges of voting, will eventually swamp the electorate, get all the offices, and shape legislation antagonistic

10

to American interest. Statistics of the last census show that Japanese residents compose, roughly speaking, about two-fifths of Hawaii's population.

School statistics of the latest date show that the Japanese children makeup about one-fifth the total attendance in the public schools. Assuming that all these children who grow up under American influence and education, elect to accept the duties of citizenship, and assuming that these Japanese-Americans will combine to defeat the American government, under which they are educated, we should still find the Japanese in a hopeless minority.

The statistics of arrivals and departures of Japanese children go to prove that it is the established policy of the Japanese to send their children back to their home country.

Saturday, June 25, 1910
Haole Camp Pool:
A concrete swimming pool, three to eight feet deep, seventy feet long by thirty feet wide, is being constructed for employees of the Pu'unene Sugar Mill near the Pu'unene Club House. It will be filled with filtered water.

Saturday, May 18, 1912
Opening New Theater:
The new Pu'unene Theater which has been under construction for sometime, will be opened next Thursday, May 23, evening, with the first class vaudeville show.
Besides the moving pictures, Thursday evening, the Italian Saxophone Quartet, which has had such a successful run at the Bijou Theatre, in Honolulu, together with the Qaldstein Trio of fancy roller skaters. Waldstein, Sr., is one of the oldest fancy skaters in America and executes over 200 figures on the little wheel.

Saturday, March 8, 1913
Patients Were Easily Moved:
Patients who had been inmates of the old Camp 1 Hospital at Pu'unene, (Camp 1 was never in Pu'unene, Spreckelsville,

11

maybe!) were all transferred to the new hospital which is now complete. The Pa'ia Hospital ambulance carried serious cases in comfort in it. Private individuals also donated their automobiles and that way; the patients were all transferred in easy manner. The new hospital is an up-to-date one and is equipped with the latest medical apparatus.

Saturday, April 11, 1914
Picture Bride Troubles:
The woman had been married at the Immigration Station, in Honolulu, upon her arrival in Hawai`i. She had never seen her prospective husband, and knew nothing about him till she found herself fettered to a drunken brute that brought her to Maui, and then, after a few months, deserted her. The practice of importing some Japanese women was for the purpose of building up a citizenship through the natural birth rate.

The picture bride business began to flourish. Thousands of young women have reached these islands during the past few years and, while some of them have been lucky in their choice of haphazard husbands, many, in fact, have simply waited a short time before securing a divorce on any possible grounds.

The Japanese women are a superior class of female, and it is only through their decency that they are not forced into prostitution. Alone in this country, with no work and unable to speak the English language, the women stand but little show, and a large number of them fall victims to the pimps who originally instigated them to leave Japan for Hawai`i.

Friday, September 22, 1916
The Japanese American
The belief that Japanese cannot be Americanized is almost certain to be soon shattered by American born citizens of that race – the Japanese of the second generation in these Islands, whose custom and convictions have been reversed from that of their parents by the enjoyment of a liberal, American public school education.

The Japanese American citizenship would be found fighting

against the country of their parents for America, if necessary should even require. Individuals have been heard to make similar statements with convincing conviction.

Racial pride is as strong with the Japanese as that of any other race, and race prejudices are probably just as deeply implanted. But both sentiments are balanced in the Japanese character with steadfast principles of citizenship –principles of patriotism – which tends to make them loyally true to the country to which they owe their livelihood, protection and fealty.

"By little things you shall know men." The American raised and the American educated Japanese find many of the customs, points of view and beliefs of his elders just as anciently amusing.

Friday, January 31, 1919
Camp 1 Theater Burned in Sunday Morning Blaze
The moving picture theatre at Camp 1 was destroyed by fire at an early hour last Sunday morning. When the blaze was discovered about 1 o'clock the building was a mass of flames and it was impossible to save any of the furnishings or equipment. The show had been given the night before, and it is supposed that an overlooked cigar or cigarette butt in some waste paper basket was the origin of the blaze. Among those were 8 reels of film, the projector apparatus, and a piano, the total value of between $700.00 and $800.00.

Friday, April 2, 1920
HC&S Company to Be Greatly Improved
The Pu'unene Dairy is soon to be augmented by the addition of a new concrete milking barn, large enough to accommodate fifty cows at a time, and equipped with the latest thing in pneumatic milking machinery and other adjunct. The dairy will supply between 12,000 to 14,000 quarts of milk a month; practically all of which is used on the plantation, although a considerable supply is going to help the schools combat the malnutrition among the pupils.

Monday, January 29, 1923
New Pu'unene Theater Opened; Pleases all.

Pu'unene's new theater was opened on Saturday, January 27, 1923, with a capacity attendance, estimates running as high as 600. Everyone was delighted with it. Built by the plantation, conforms to safeguard audiences from fire, designed for the comfort of its patrons, is modern and thoroughly attractive.

Saturday, December 4, 1926
Very Watchful of Child Life
Child life is vital matter on the HC&S Plantation and much of the health activities of that organization centered in the care of the child from birth until it passed through the schools. There are many women at work on the plantation and every morning sees the mother going to the 12-day nurseries of the company to leave her child while she performs the duties of the day.

Located at Pu'unene in a modern and up-to-date hospital that is capable of accommodating 100 patients. This structure composed of eight wards and 7 private rooms was constructed in 1912 and since that time every modern piece of equipment for the conduct of the hospital has been added to its furnishings. There is an x-ray; a splendid operating room and fine airy wards is a feature. 3 physicians, a staff of 4 trained nurses in addition to the District Nurse. Every day there is a clinic at the hospital in Pu'unene and a clinic is also maintained every afternoon at Camp 5 except Saturdays.

Wednesday, April 30, 1930
New Store Building Nears Completion
On Saturday, May 10, 1930, Central Camp Store will replace the old Camp 5 Store in all but name. Combined with it is a filling station and H. J. Fujiyoshi will be in charge of it as he is of the present Camp 5 Store. The new building is surrounded on sides and back by a galvanized iron fence and either side it has been grassed so that it will have a setting of green lawn. Leading to it and to the filling station is a macadamized driveway. For the benefit of those not acquainted with the location, it may be added that Camp 5 is reached by continuing on out Pu'unene Avenue beyond the clubhouse and past the meat market and theater and new gymnasium.

Saturday, May 7, 1932
Talkies showing Spreckelsville Theater Tonight
With the inauguration of talkies at the Camp 1 theater tonight, will boast the latest in sound equipment. Hush-Money is billed as the opening show at the
Camp 1 theater. Talkies are now been shown in Wailuku, Kahului, Pu'unene, Spreckelsville, Pa'ia and Ha'iku.

Wednesday, June 1, 1932
Pu'unene Dairy Add
Effective May 29, 1932, Grade AA Raw Jersey-Holstein milk will be:

    Per quart------------18 cents
    Per pint---------------9 cents
A discount of 2 % is allowed on quantity orders (2 quarts or more).
Deliveries limited to HC&S Plantation homes including the town of Kahului.
Cream prices: quart-$1.00; pint-50 cents; half-pint-30 cents, and quarter pint-20 cents.

Saturday, May 9, 1936
New Pu'unene Sport Plant Opens Sunday
Pu'unene's new recreation center built by HC&S for its employees at the cost exceeding $65,000 will be opened

Sunday, May 10, 1936.
The new athletic layout includes facilities for all field sports, such as football, baseball and soccer. There is a fast quarter mile cinder track and provisions for high jump, pole vault and broad jump pits. Permanent bleachers accommodate a large crowd.

A championship size swimming pool, complete with two low spring boards and a 10-foot board, is the most modern in Maui County. Adjoining it are bathhouses and locker rooms for men and women. Space is provided for spectators. Lighting is provided for night swimming by floodlights mounted on high towers. An attractive high bamboo fence that affords privacy encloses the entire pool area.

Near the swimming pool is a tennis layout, also enclosed by high bamboo fence. There are 3 double courts and seating accommodations for spectators. The surface is comprised of a new composition variety that is easier on bare feet then the clay or concrete courts.

Saturday, November 14, 1936
Ma'alaea Now Unsuited To Modern Planes
Plans for a new airport in Central Maui, the site recommended will be about a mile beyond the end of the pavement o0n the Camp 5-Camp 6 road between Camp 6 and Kihei.

Plans call for a full size field, 3000 feet long and 500 feet wide. Ma'alaea airport has been declared unsatisfactory by the Department of Commerce because of its location. The department will not approve an airport located within 5 miles of mountain and hills. The Ma'alaea field is less than 5 miles from the West Maui Mountains. A concrete runway will also be built.

The new airport is necessary because of the large planes being brought to the islands by Inter-Island Airways and the Army. Because the land is virtually level, little grading will be necessary and estimated that the job will be completed in less than 2 months of actual working time. It is believed that the Ma'alaea Airport will be abandoned as unsuitable for the use of the new larger airplanes that are being put into service in the islands.

Wednesday, June 16, 1943
New Airline Building Opened
Hawaiian Airlines, Ltd. Dedicated a new Hawaiian Airlines building last Friday, June 11, 1943, at the Maui Airport. The future of air transport in the Territory, nearly all inter-island travel one day would be by air at greatly reduced rates.

Wednesday, July 7, 1948
Nationwide Publicity For Dream Town
Des Moines paper's amusement that plantation labor's living in a company town could afford to own automobiles. That the wage scale for agricultural labors in Hawai'i is much higher than it is

16

in the deep south of the mainland, and that our company towns would put company towns on the mainland to shame. 2 big Maui companies-Hawaiian Commercial & Sugar Company and the Kahului Railroad- got together to plan a town to house sugar plantation workers who are now scattered through 25 different settlements.

A program of development for the next 25 years, for a community of 4,000 or more homes, where now there is only a small village surrounded by rolling hills.

In the first 18 months, a beginning will be made: The first of the streets, water and sewer mains will be put in. 200 homes for sale and rent will be built, and lots made available for sale to those who want to build on their own. In 1948-50 some more streets, homes, and part of the business district will be built.

The assumption is that these plantation laborers living in the company town are thoroughly in the automobile age. The new city and the street patterns is based on the automobile – wide belt and radial streets and narrow residential streets, in a pleasing semi-circle facing Kahului Harbor.

The houses are to be 3 bedroom-and one-bath bungalows, with wide windows and a built-in carport, on lots 70 to 80 feet wide, 120 to 140 feet deep. Parks, playgrounds and schools are spotted in advance, so that everyone can readily access it. And yet, the new development is to grow slowly, over a period of years, with opportunity to keep plan up-to-date as time goes along.

Saturday, August 6, 1949
Commission On Maui For Airport
Transferring Maui Airport there from Pu'unene to N.A.S.K.A. with indications that the Territory will receive from the Navy a revocable lease to the entire property at N.A.S.K.A.

The use of Kahului is created both from the viewpoint of its superior facilities and public convenience, and also in order to give passengers to and from Maui relief from the constantly bad flying weather off McGregor's Point and 'Ulupalakua. At

17

Kahului, planes would fly windward and avoid the current bumps that have given Maui Air and inequitable reputation with all air passengers.

Saturday, February 11, 1950
Mill, Tournahaulers in operation At HC&S Company
It was the start of tournahaulers operations. These giant trucks have replaced the miles of railroad tracks and rolling cars that were formerly necessary to carry the harvested cane to the mill.

Almost all evidence of the past road system have been removed from the mill yard. Now 40-foot roads have been built for the Tournahaulers, service trucks and cranes, while a service station for the Tournahaulers has been constructed. A 14x65 foot truck scale with a capacity of 100-ton weights each loaded Tournahaulers as it enters the mill yard.

A 25-ton railroad type crane painted a bright blue is being used to unload the Tournahaulers. After the huge vehicle comes into position, the crane hooks on to one side of the chain net that lies under the body. The net is raised to unload the cane.

Notes about the proceeding *Maui News* Chronology:
These above dates and occurrences have been taken from microfilms from the rare documents room at the Kahului Library. These are word for word transcripts as compiled by the *Maui News*. Nothing has been deleted or added.

In this book, if I have not experienced it, did not get the facts directly from *Maui News* articles, documents from the library, culled it from residents of the camps, received it from my relatives, or pamphlets listed on my reference page, then you will not see it.

You should realize, while reading it, that some of the things written in the *Maui News* were either exaggerated, left out, or untrue. Whoever wrote the articles looked at the facts superficially or simply decided to write whatever they felt like writing. Perhaps they were urged to write it a certain way. I do not have evidence of what was on the agenda of particular

18

newspaper reporters or their editors.

There is an old adage, "You have to be there to experience what happened." You cannot write a truthful article if one had not experienced the situation first hand. A good reporter should not exaggerate. He or she has to be open to information from all sides.

I know for a fact that the only persons that can support my story are people who lived in the camps and experienced it with first hand knowledge.

SANSEI GENERATION
Part I
Chapter One

It is said that every one of us who are born to this world chooses their parents before they are born. If this is so, we are predestined to become whomever we decide to become. Is this not so?

Before I specifically look at my grandparents' life in the camps, my parents' life in the camps and my own life in detail let me share with you some items that deal with camp life.

December 7, 1941, Japan decided to attack Pearl Harbor during the early morning hours. I understand from my parents that they could see a glow coming from one of the islands in the Hawaiian chain. They were wondering what was happening. Because of this incident, lives changed.

Marshall Law was enforced and everyone on the Island of Maui was under curfew. People were not allowed in certain places, and the American military kept a constant check of homes during the night with their flashlights. They made sure that every curtain was drawn so there were no lights showing throughout the house. If there was light showing from a house, there was a stern first warning, no more, no less.

I was born on June 22, 1944 at Pu'unene Hospital. I was told years later that the day after I was born, both my mother and I transferred to a makeshift hospital on the outskirts of Pa'ia Town, about seven miles away. My mother and I were taken by a plantation truck, and stayed for five days.

Because it was during the war years with Marshall Law in effect, no one was allowed to travel on the road at night except military vehicles and emergency vehicles. My dad worked during the day so no one came to visit my mom and me.

21

After five days, my mom and I returned to our home in Pu'unene on the same plantation truck that first took us to Pa'ia from the Pu'unene Hospital.

My parents lived in an average sized camp. The camp was first called Sam Sing Camp because the first immigrants to Hawai'i were the Chinese. Working for the sugar cane company, they were isolated at this camp for many years. As time went by, some of the Chinese died or moved to the mainland with money they had saved.

To make it more confusing, there was a camp near to the Pu'unene Hospital called Camp 4. Because the hospital was right across the street, the sugar company later called it Hospital Camp. As I said before, because Sam Sing Camp lost most of its Chinese population, the sugar company decided to change Sam Sing Camp to Camp Four.

Planners of the camps worked for the sugar company. Guess what camp is the oldest? Obviously, Camp 1. Camp 2 followed this. On and on it went until the sugar plantation decided to name camps by names.

Anyway, my parents told me in later years that I was a very lazy kid. I did not walk until the age of two. Because I was a huge kid, my uncle made my parents a small cart with wheels just to pull me around, instead of carrying me. I have a picture of my grandmother *opa-ing* (carrying a child) me by the hip, with one of my legs in the back of her and the other in front of her, and her hands on my back so I wouldn't go backwards. One picture showed her carrying me on her back with a struggled look. She was bent over from carrying me because she was a mere ninety pounds or so.

My first adventure out of Camp Four in Pu'unene, as I remember, had to be riding on the bus to Camp Three in Sprecklesville to visit my other grandparents (mother's side). My parents and I would catch the bus owned by Kahului Railroad Company, in front of the Camp Four Store. My father would buy tokens for our round trip fare from the bus driver. We placed the tokens in the coin hopper, asked for three transfers, and then sat down in the closest empty seats.

We would get to the end of the stop right next to the Kahului Theater, walk across the street to the Kahului Bus Terminal, and transfer to a bus bound for Camp Three in Spreckelsville.

After about a ten-minute ride, we would reach the outskirts of Camp Three. To the left of the entrance of Camp Three were pigpens, where we smelled the overwhelming stench from the pigs, especially when the winds were blowing from the south. The odor that drifted throughout the camp was something one could never forget.

Past the pigpens to the right was a big bougainvillea tree covered with clusters of purple colored flowers. After the bougainvillea tree were homes to the right, known as Upper Camp Three. There was one business there known as Matsui Fish Market. There were a couple of businesses to the left of Camp Three: Sam Sato Store, Kitagawa Gas Station and a photo studio. There might have been another store. I don't quite remember because I never visited it.

I remember being dropped off by Matsui Fish Market. Then we crossed the paved macadam main road that separated Lower Camp Three and Upper Camp Three. To the left were homes. An irrigation ditch ran parallel to the main road. A bridge wide enough for vehicles ran across the irrigation ditch near the middle of Lower Camp Three. This is what we crossed to get into Lower Camp Three.

None of the roads in Lower Camp Three were paved. Its red dirt was forever present. The red dirt along the side of the road was a fine powder. The trade winds would blow from the Northeast and stir up small whirlwinds, kicking up the fine dirt to settle on anything and everything. It settled on the clothes of people, laundry hanging on clothes lines, on the cars parked outside or community garages where more than three or more cars were parked, on the screens and windows, on the roof tops, on the sides of houses, and in the houses of the residents, as well as their nostrils. There was an old saying: "Never wear a white shirt when the wind is blowing in Lower Camp Three." That red dirt caused a lot of headaches for the residents of that camp.

Past the bridge and down a slight hill on the road, a little to the left, there stood a house bordered by a fence. Watermelon papaya trees lined the inside of the fence. It got its name because the papayas were as big as watermelons. In the yard was a garden full of string beans, eggplants, corn, long green onions and a tree from Japan called *shisho*. This plant is very important to the Japanese. The matured leaves were used in the pickling of ginger, young green peach (better known as *ume*) and even fresh vegetables. The *shiso* has a very special taste to it. When used in preserving, the smell is very unique, not unpleasant, but distinctive. A similar scent is the smell of mint, very unique, not unpleasant, but distinctive. When the mint leaves are used in salads, it's a scent never to be forgotten.

Beyond that garden stood a long chicken coop that housed about fifteen to twenty chickens. The roof's frame was made of wood. Wire mesh completely surrounded the structure and the underbelly of the coop. What's interesting about the chicken coop was the little chute my grandfather devised so that when the chicken laid an egg, it rolled down to the front where my grandfather could easily gather them. My grandparents had a very consistent supply of eggs, so many that I occasionally stole some of them. I cracked a small hole at the points of the egg and sucked it raw into my mouth. It might sound gross to some but they tasted so good at the time. The yellow part of the egg has a sweet taste to it; the white part is like *hana-butta* (mucus from the nose).

Behind the chicken coop was my grandparents' home, nestled at the rear of the lot. As one faced the property, on the left side was a long driveway, where one passed papayas, the garden, and the chicken coop.

The sugar company had smartly laid out all of the homes. Each had a down slope to avoid flooding during the rainy season that sometimes could be torrential. In planning on a decline, the water from the heavy rains would flow downhill. No house ever flooded from the bottom up. Rainwater always ended up at the lower base of the camp, flooding a dirt road, a ditch, a cane field or any type of drainage available.

My grandparents' home had three bedrooms and a kitchen with a dirt floor. In the kitchen, there was a kerosene stove and two benches without backs on either side of the table. The living room was quite simple with a few *goza* (straw mats) with *zabuton* (cushion-about fourteen inches by fourteen inches and two inches thick), with no television or other furniture. The three bedrooms had a bed or two, depending whether more than one were sharing it. Some bedrooms had dressers, if the family could afford it. My grandparents couldn't afford such luxuries; they had eight kids to care for. With my grandfather's minimal salary, things were hard. My grandmother never worked a day in her life for pay as far as I knew.

Along side the driveway of my grandparents and the neighbor's driveway, right smack between them, close to the road, was a small building that was called the outhouse or toilet.

No one can ever forget the outhouse. Two families shared it. The outhouse was divided with a partition with separate entry doors. Within each partition, a hole was cut into a piece of wood with a toilet seat attached by hinges. The seat was elevated a foot and a half from the dirt ground. A hole was dug beneath the toilet seat about five feet down. When the holes were almost filled, they would be covered up and new holes would be dug close to or near the vicinity of the last toilet. I am guessing that the residents dug the hole and not the sugar plantation workers. I heard rumors that once the holes were covered, vegetables that generated deep in the soil, such as carrots, grew at a record-breaking size. I heard that one carrot weighed over three pounds and many other vegetables grew so big that they amazed the residents.

There were no children around when these outhouses were built. These outhouses and camps were probably constructed way before the time when the picture brides from Japan started to appear. They needed a home to live separately from other couples and where they could eventually raise their children.

25

A small child had a slight probability of falling through the hole and wading among human waste and critters of all sorts or possibly die if the waste was deep enough. The holes were cut in the wood intended for adult use only. There was never a consideration for children. With numerous cockroaches, centipedes, spiders, earthworms, and other unknown creatures residing in the hole, occupants of the outhouse could sometimes feel them crawling where the sun don't shine when sitting on the toilet!

I remember one incident that happened to me when I was around the age of six. I went to the toilet with my father. He couldn't come in with me because the enclosure was very small. Being a young kid, I sat at the edge of the toilet, not because I was afraid of falling inside but for comfort's sake. I suddenly felt something crawling up between my legs. I spotted a centipede. I yelled to my father, "There's a centipede crawling up between my legs." He swung open the door and told me, "Don't move!" Of course, when those numerous legs are crawling on you, you tend to get an itch. My father rolled up newspapers and tried to hit the centipede. He failed in his attempt to kill it or brush it away. I got a bite on my leg from the critter and it just hurt. Of course, my leg swelled up as expected, but I recovered in the healing process.

As I mentioned, my father used a rolled up newspaper to try and kill the centipede. In those days, there were no such things as toilet paper as we know it today. My parents and grandparents scrambled for paper to use in the toilets. Any mail including Sears Roebuck catalogues, telephone books (especially the Yellow Pages), envelopes and letters from Japan, newspapers, both the *Maui News* and *Hawai'i Hochi* published in O'ahu, and what ever they could get from the stores including box wrapping, were saved to be used as toilet paper.

These outhouses were extremely smelly. Sewage piled up in both holes. It was so bad that when a resident was finished with business and went into the house, the other residents knew that someone had used the toilet. The smell even lingered on the clothing. The outhouse could be smelled a mile away. A little exaggerated but nevertheless pungent.

It must be mentioned that running water or lights did not exist in these outhouses. Mosquitoes bred and lay their larvae in stale and still water left in open containers such as cans, soda bottles, buckets left outside of the homes. Rains filled them with water (clean or dirty), particularly in outhouses. During the night, swarms of mosquitoes would attack toilet users. One could have as much as twenty-five bites like I experienced when I once visited my grandparents.

My grandparents' house seemed extremely scary after dark to a youngster like me, especially on windy nights. Behind my grandparents' house was a small ditch, pine trees, and a sugar cane field. At night, I could hear the sounds of wind whistling through the long needles of the branches of the pine tree, accompanied by the crackling sounds of sugar cane hitting each other. It sounded as if a stranger was walking in the cane fields. To a kid, it was the stomping of a giant with big feet trudging in the cane field that made the night eerie. When I heard these sounds, my youthful mind imagined ghosts, witches, and every evil lurking out there in the darkness. Everything and anything seemed possible during those dark windy nights, especially after ghost stories had been shared earlier in the evening. Before radio and television, family conversations were the prime source of information and entertainment. Ghost stories often evolved from these conversations.

On our return trip home to Camp Four, we would often make a brief stop at Kahului, before transferring on the bus to Pu'unene. There were a few stores in Kahului town such as Ooka Market, Hollister Drugs, Maui Dry Goods and some small shops. I could not afford to buy anything. Just visiting these stores was a treat to me. My parents were careful not to buy a lot. They were limited to necessities. I could buy gum and candies from the Camp Four Store that was only a few houses away from where we lived. My father felt bad when he had to deny me gum and candy, but I understood the situation.

27

I would wait for the bus by Kahului Theater at the intersection of Pu'unene Avenue and Ka'ahumanu Avenue, to get home. Most of the time, we'd wait only for a few minutes but sometimes longer when the bus was late. Besides the bus terminal in Kahului, there was also a train terminal in the building that also included a post office. The Kahului Railroad train carried passengers, supplies, and equipment to the cane fields and traveled on as far as Ha'iku, about twenty or so miles away.

When our bus arrived, we'd get on it and traveled along Pu'unene Avenue. The bus would turn right into McGerrow Camp (Hey, a camp with no number attached to it.), stop at a few places, then get back on to Pu'unene Avenue, (passing the sugar mill, movie theater, bakery and the Pu'unene Hongwanji Mission to the left and to the right a gym). About a mile away from McGerrow camp, we'd go over a bridge (under the bridge was the ditch that carried water to various parts of the cane fields), and make a right turn in to Camp Five. The driver would pass the Pu'unene Mercantile Store and a service station, again making a few stops. The bus would continue by turning around, retracing its route, (passing Hamada Saimin Store) and heading half way down toward Alabama Camp. There it turned right and maneuvered through Alabama Camp, (passing the Filipino Club House to the right), where it made a few stops. It then crossed over the Tournahauler road with two stops at Spanish B Camp and finally to Camp Four and its store, my final destination. All of the main roads that the bus traveled were paved macadam roads including the Tournahauler roads.

Living in Camp Four was an experience never to be forgotten. I could go from house to house at an early age and not fear getting lost. If I went to the wrong house or played in someone else's yard, I was ushered back to my house. Everyone knew each other. "That's the kid who lives three houses from the Camp Four Store. His mother works for Maui Pineapple Company and his father, Mala (nickname for Masamitsu), is the tractor driver for HC&S (Hawaiian Commercial & Sugar Plantation)." Everyone knew who I was because of the closeness of the people in the camp. Everybody lived together. Filipino, Japanese and Chinese all intermingled together and shared what they had when they had enough to give. Sometimes residents from other camps, farmers with a supply of vegetables or fishermen with an abundant catch, shared their bounty. Some Filipinos who were watermen, grew their vegetables in the cane fields – sharing their harvest of squash or sweet potato. There seemed to be a spirit of giving all through my camp, that I'm sure was happening in all the others in Pu'unene.

Actually, everyone knew each other because most of the people in the camps either worked at Maui Pineapple Company or at the Hawaiian Commercial & Sugar Plantation. Few had other jobs at retail stores, offices, or government establishments such as the United States Post Office.

As a child, everyone seemed to me to be concerned for each other; the residents didn't seem nosey, there appeared to be no animosity among camp people, just the feeling of family. Each had a different kind of love, the love of mankind in its truest sense of the word, that old fashion feeling...caring. Everyone was part of one big family, or so I thought. Later, I came to realize the truth that some were not all that loving. When you are young, a lot is kept from you, I suppose because children are too young to know the difference. I found out eventually that there were cliques among the community as a whole.

The best way to describe the layout of Camp Four is to say that the homes were built extremely close to one another. Homes were built in rows, up hill rows, and down hill rows. At the top of the camp (the highest point of an incline), there were cane fields followed by a dirt irrigation waterway called Spanish Ditch (about eight to ten feet across), parallel to a dirt road. Eleven homes flanked by a park led to a dirt road on the other side. The next row of homes consisted of twelve more, again traced by a paved macadam road, followed by another twelve homes in a row. The last row consisted of twelve more homes, with a dirt road running parallel to it. A row of chicken coops ran along about half of the last of homes. Last, but not least, were plots of gardens and coops assigned to every home in the camps.

To my knowledge (except for McGerrow Camp), there were

29

never camp-assigned plots to plant vegetables. In those camps, residents planted vegetables and fruit trees, generally mango trees of different varieties, star fruit, lemons, or oranges in their own yard, vegetables if there was any space left.

There is another side to Camp Four. There is a four-way shaped road, ninety degrees paved with macadam (as described in a previous paragraph, one side splitting the camp in half). At the ninety-degree angle of the macadam road, one part of the road was a dirt road that crossed over a bridge over Spanish Ditch and led to the cane field. Another part of the macadam road that's part of the ninety degree led out of   Camp Four and connected to Hanson Road.

There was another part of the four-way dirt road that ran to the other side of Camp Four. There are two homes on the top of the hill below the same Spanish Ditch. Then there were six in the next row. These were followed by three homes, a separation, and then another five homes in the last row. It included a very tiny Chinese restaurant, the Camp Four Store, and a clubhouse with pool tables across the store.

They were many people living at Camp Four that didn't know about the Chinese restaurant. The restaurant was so small that there were only about six seats in the place. I distinctly remember it because my father once took me there.

Most or the camps that were owned by the sugar plantation were surrounded by sugar cane fields. Those camps that were not surrounded by cane fields were lucky; they did not have to deal with the smoke from burning and dust from the clearing of cane fields.

As was mentioned before, the sugar plantation owned all of the homes. Because of the strikes, some privileges were taken away. Residents of Pu'unene, in time had to pay rent, some more than others, depending on the size of their home, but all had to pay. One would think that because the houses had been built for the plantation workers that the housing would be free. I remember my father telling me that he had to pay $35.00 a month to live in the house.

I also wondered why all of the homes weren't clustered together as one community, but separated with a limited number of homes in each camp. I understood that HC&S built camps, as they were needed. Some of the smaller ones were hidden from view because the cane fields totally surrounded them. Since the camps were scattered in earlier years, the sugar plantation made it a point to pick up employees from the various camps to transport them to their work sites and return them back to their respective camps.

The one reason for the separation of the camps was brought to light by a family friend's opinion. The sugar plantation was willing to spend money in building separate camps scattered around Pu'unene because they wanted to separate the employees from unifying, and therefore denying employees from rallying against the company.

Exceptions to the rule, not all homes were built the same. Some of the homes had a porch considered large and there were some smaller. The partitions inside of homes were also different. The configuration of each home was different. Some of the homes were larger than others. I can only describe homes that I've seen in Pu'unene. I do not know about other plantation homes scattered throughout the island.

Homes within the Pu'unene camps were built on square concrete blocks that angled to the top on four sides making the block smaller at the top, perfect for perching a 4x4 post no longer than a foot-and-a half.

Our home and all others in the camp were made of wood, single wall construction, open beam ceilings, and partitions to separate generally two bedrooms on either side of the house with the living room in the center with a step down to the kitchen. All walls were constructed using Tongue-and-Groove lumber. Homes were constructed in an L- shaped figuration with the kitchen being one part of the configuration. In earlier years, kitchens were completely separated from the house, mainly to

31

prevent fire because wood, delivered by the sugar company, was used for cooking the meals. When electricity was introduced to the residents, kitchens were later attached to the homes or torn down and rebuilt.

The roofing was made of very thin roofing paper and equally thin wood shingles. One could see the roofing paper from inside the house. After time and wear from windy conditions and rain, the roof would leak so much that pails, pots, pans, and even bowls were needed to catch dripping water. Some houses had so many leaks, that one had a hard time finding a dry place to sleep at night.

Electrical wires were exposed in the homes. The wires were stapled to the sidewall and on the rafters. There were light switches in every room. The light was a simple light bulb screwed into a porcelain fixture that, in turn, was screwed to the rafter.

Each window had a screen and a four-sectioned pane that came in two pieces. Both the top and bottom section of the window were made to slide up and down, between the window-frame. Unlike the windows today, the windows in the camps had wood-to-wood contact. Windows had to be constructed precisely to make sure each section would slide up and down. Each window was held in position by a spring-bolt attached to the windows. Holes, a size for the spring-bolts were drilled into the jam of the window at the resident's desired open position.

There is a disadvantage to this type of window, especially on rainy days. Wood tends to swell on rainy and high humid days and prevents the windows from going up and down properly. Because of this problem and the fine dust entering the homes of the Pu'unene residents during cane harvest, some of the residents nailed shut their windows permanently. Remember, some of the camps were surrounded by sugar cane that caused the trade winds from the northeast to kick up a lot of fine dust including the small whirlwinds that raised havoc to residents. Dust was a devil of a problem to all of the camp residents.

I am now describing my second home. There were two to four doors of entry to the house. At the front of every plantation home were at least two or three steps to get on to the porch. There were two doors to enter the house from the porch, one entry led to the living room and another to the kitchen. The living room entry had a step up. There was no step up to enter the kitchen because the kitchen and the porch were constructed on the same level. The kitchen also had an entry door with one or more steps at the front left. Very few of the homes had a fourth door entry to the home. Some residents added a fourth door as an entry way to the bedroom on the far right of the house, with a few steps to climb. Some of the residents only had one entrance to the front of the house. The other entry was at the side or back of the house.

The interiors of the homes were simply furnished. The living room had a couch made of *koa* or bamboo covered with cushions. Other pieces of furniture included one or two matching koa or bamboo chairs. The floor had a small rug by the couch or was covered with vinyl. *Goza* mats with thick or thin cushions (*zabuton*) on the floor completed the furnishings. Some homes in Pu'nene were not furnished at all. Some did not have the finances to purchase any of the furniture. Then again, some of the residents had a small home and there were only a few furniture items that could fit in a limited space.

Most of the beds either had a *futon* (Japanese comforter) or just a bottom sheet with a blanket. All the materials for the *futon* was purchased here or imported from families in Japan and sewn here. They were too bulky and costly to send so they never came from Japan. The *futons* were very pretty with the traditional Japanese designs with bright reds, oranges, blacks, and blues on a white background. The comforters were never washed, but on a bright, sunny day, *futons* could be seen swinging on the clothesline to be aired out. In my younger days, I remember families growing cotton trees, so the fibers could be used to fill the *futons*.

My parents' bedroom consisted of one double bed and a dresser or *tansu* (Japanese furniture to hang clothes, made of wood with two doors, and a few drawers for personal items).

33

In the other room, on the opposite side of the house was the bedroom for the children and/or another adult. These were, generally, small rectangular sleeping quarters. Only two single beds could fit in it with one dresser shared by the occupants. If there were three or four children in that home, beds were shared with more than one sibling on one bed. Sometimes one or two slept in the living room, one on the floor, and one on the couch. Some families had a good rotation system to avoid territorial tensions among the children. The more children you had, the more you shared. Families became very close in this manner. Although many had to give up a lot when sharing, they also learned a life of giving and the most important thing – LOVE. Of course, some big families had children who complained about sharing things, but I also saw some children move to their nearby grandparents' home so that they could have their own bedrooms.

Most kitchens simply housed two benches on either side of a table close to the window, a stove (electric or kerosene), a very small refrigerator, a tiny freezer within the icebox (which had to be defrosted constantly due to icing), and a very small sink. The sink had a faucet with cold water only. Hot water that was needed to wash dishes was boiled on the stove. A Bull Durham bag (a small tobacco sack) hung from the faucet. It had a draw- string on the top to tie the bag around the pipe. This Bull Durham bag was used to filter all impurities. Occasionally a tadpole made its way into the water system and into the tobacco bag. It was always a good idea to check the homemade filter every so often, especially after a big rain. When the pouch darkened with the sediments, it was replaced. It seemed that the water in those times came from the ditches and that explained how tadpoles and other foreign items appeared in the bags.

After the loose tobacco was purchased and smoked, the bag was saved. We got our supply of bags from my grandfather who rolled his own cigarettes. I watched him tap the tobacco onto the paper and lick one end of it to seal the roll. He usually rolled a few more cigarettes for future use.

Although we later got an electric stove, many of the resident kept their kerosene stove, thereby avoiding the high cost of electricity. Kerosene stoves were made of cast iron and lasted a long time. My grandmother had one for years.

I always saw an extra glass gallon bottle of kerosene with a small opening on the top with a screw cap near the stove. There was also a gallon of kerosene turned upside down on the left side of the stove. Whenever a burner was turned on, the fuel was fed through a pipe to the burner; a valve controlled the amount of kerosene entering the burner.

There were many downsides to owning kerosene stoves. The smell permeated the inside and outside of the house. There was always the possibility of leaving the stove on, setting it ablaze, blowing up the kerosene bottle, causing a fire in the kitchen, or worst yet, the destruction of the entire house.

Some of the other camps had community garages, but all other homes had single dirt floor car garages, that were attached to the house. It was very difficult to get in and out of the car considering how small the garages were. It was a general practice that all of the passengers got out of the car to allow the driver to park the car closer to the wall on the opposite side so the driver could get out easier.

House lots were very small. The measurement of a house with a kitchen was no more than four hundred square feet. There was a six feet buffer yard between homes, and the front yard was no more than six feet, fifteen to twenty feet wide. The kitchen was always forward of the living area. The back yard was about ten feet plus from the next house. People in Camp Four who lived on the last bottom row of the camps had very big back yards.

To use the toilet and the washroom at Camp Four, the residents had to go outside to a separate building. The toilet and bathroom were built like those in an ordinary home in a rectangular fashion with the toilet situated in the middle of four homes, separated by four partitions. There was a roof but there was no ceiling to cover the partitions. One could actually hear neighbors talking as they took a bath.

There were lights in the bathroom but, again, each of the electrical wires were exposed and stapled to the partitions. The light was attached to a board that ran in the middle, across each bathroom. A small porcelain fixture, similar to the one in the house, held a light bulb.

The toilet and the bath area were joined together with separate doors. There was one door to enter the washroom and another room to enter the washbasin and in the back a toilet separated with a door. This was not so in the adjoining units. Some had a bathtub near the entrance and a toilet in the back separated by a door.

We were very lucky; we had two separate entrances. One was opened to the washbasin and enclosed toilet in the back. The second entrance was only for the *furo* (Japanese type bathtub).

Each bathroom had a *furo* and/or a shower. The square tub, *furo*, was made of redwood and/or cement. If one could get or steal the redwood and the copper sheet from the sugar company, he could build a *furo*. The bottom of the redwood ones was lined with copper sheets (used to retain the heat). Each *furo* was about three by four feet wide and about three feet deep, just enough so that when one sat down, the water rose to the bather's neck. There was a cover on all the *furo* to maintain the heat. There was always a pan, a small scrub towel, *ha-ke* (a small brown scrub brush imported from Japan) and a very small stool made of wood.

The proper way to bathe was to use the pan to scoop hot water from the *furo*, add cold water from the faucet over the *furo* to get the desired temperature, and pour it on his/her head. Once done, the bather would wash his/her head with Fels-Naptha (a brand of soap used widely by the camp residents to wash all of the body and clothing). A small scrub towel was employed to wash the face and body, the *ha-ke* to scrub the bottom of feet to rid them of the red/brown dirt. The process was repeated with more hot water from the *furo* and a cold water rinse from the tap. Before soaking in the *furo*, one had to remove all excess dirt because the tub water was not changed every day. The water was changed when it needed to be changed. The water from the *furo*, when drained, went down a pipe and ran directly into the cement ditch of the toilet.

Upon submerging into the Japanese style tub, all troubles and problems seemed to melt away. It felt as though the bather had not only cleansed his/her body but their soul as well. The best time of the year to bathe was during winter, or on a very cold or rainy day. In Japan, soaking in one of their famous mineral hot springs, it always brought back memories of the *furo*.

The *furo* was created with a small outside hole/tunnel that ran directly under it. This hole/tunnel was used to burn firewood and, every so often, there was a need to clear out the ashes. Once the sugar company stopped supplying the wood, my father had to strip wooden boxes or ax his own *kiawe* mesquite wood that was prolific. To make the *furo* very hot and fit the wood in the hole/tunnel, my father gathered wood of a certain size and dryness. If the branches were too young, green on the outside, or white inside, they were judged difficult to burn. Perfect pieces were thin tree branches that could be broken by hand, or wood with bark that was peeling. The ideal size or perfect piece of wood was about three to five inches thick. A couple of months' supply of wood could fill a trailer if it was stacked and lined up properly. Sometimes, the heap was so high that my father had to tie a rope to prevent the wood from falling off the trailer.

The supply of wood was piled under the bathroom rafters, away from the rain and close to the pit. If the wood got wet from the rain, starting the fire would definitely be a problem. A bit of kindling from small branches, a little bit of paper, and a match under the three to five inch branches, started the fire. I often had to check if there was a fire, to see if more wood was needed, or feel the temperature of the water by hand. Sometimes I got burnt testing the scalding water.

The condition of the toilets in the camp was different than an outhouse. In the commode, a door separated the toilet from the sink area. The floor was paved with cement. Below the toilet was a cement ditch with walls about three feet down, a board covering the whole opening (a hole), with a toilet seat screwed onto the board.

There was a constant flow of water in the ditch, not because of the draining from the *furo* but from a source somewhere upstream. It must have been a pipe because the flow of the water was constant. It was amazing that the toilets never clogged up. It must have been designed the same way as the buildings. Water always flowed downhill. Where it ended up, I never found out.

A broom was used to scrub the sides of toilets. Sometimes it got so soiled that, once in a while, a pail or two of water from the sink pipe was used to clean the edges of the toilet.

There was a sink beside the toilet. The sink was not only to wash hands but also to scrub the laundry. There were no washing machines at that time. A scrub board with grooves was a very handy thing to have considering the condition of my father's clothes when he came home from work. He was covered with dirt from head to foot. Besides taking a bath with Fels-Naptha, the soap also was used for washing clothes. Fels-Naptha, a grooved washboard and a *ha-ke* were used to scrub off the dirt from my father's white shirts, denim jeans, and white under wear. Fels Naptha had a very distinctive smell that I can recall to this day.

When I was about five years old, a frightening thing happened to me. A friend of mine and I were fighting and pushing each other on one of the bridges. Brown irrigation water was flowing underneath. He shoved me and I shoved him back. When we got close to the edge of the bridge, because I was bigger and a few inches taller then he was, I realized my strength and leverage. I shoved him hard. Off the bridge, he went, into the water. I heard the splash; the flow of the ditch swept him under the stone span. I ran to the opposite side of the bridge, anticipating his surface. I waited and waited. It seemed forever although it was only a minute or so. I still couldn't see him. My heart pounded as I ran in search of the closest adult, a company employee working parallel to the ditch, not far away. I told the man what had happened. We raced back to the bridge. When we arrived, he immediately jumped into the dirty water and submerged under

38

the bridge groping for my friend. The man emerged at the other end of the bridge a minute or so later, claiming sadly that he did not feel or see anything under the bridge.

I was so scared I ran all the way home crying, believing in my mind that I had just killed my friend. It was all because of a silly argument. I had gotten mad and shoved him over the bridge and into the water, and now he was probably dead. I tearfully shared the misfortune to my skeptical dad. After some stern scolding and lectures, he waited to hear the real story from my friend's parents.

Later in the day, my father brought me the good news. I found out that while I had gone hunting for adult help, my friend had drifted down stream, climbed out of the ditch, and ran all the way home.

After that incident, whenever I got into an argument with someone, I always tended to back away. If I could avoid a fight, I would. I was always afraid of hurting someone else because I was taller and bigger than other kids my age. If a fight was brewing, all I had to do was remember the situation on the bridge when I almost killed my friend. As time passed, I learned to avoid arguments that could lead to a fight. I never let things escalate to a situation where I would get mad or let that person hit me. I always tried to walk away. Later in life, rules and situations changed.

From here on in, I must note that my grandfather had moved to an adjoining camp called Spanish B Village by the time I initially interviewed him. I actually had spoken to him at least three times regarding his knowledge of the past. Our first conversation was when I was nine years old. Later, I talked to my mother about her generational side also a number of times.

ISSEI GENERATION
Chapter Two

In Japan, in earlier times, the loyalty to the Lord was more important than to the individual's family. Japan's feudal society considered women as fragile as an inferior human. Women never fought in war and were considered only the background of an entire picture. Women were seen but not heard.

During the Meiji Restoration Period, the new government was under the control of the emperor for fifteen years. In 1869, the emperor moved to the great Shogun Castle of Edo, renamed Tokyo or Eastern Capital. The Meiji Government persuaded the old feudal domain to return land to the emperor. The *samurai* (well trained swordsmen) relinquished their special privileges for nine years, whereby, Japan began to make great advances in education and individual achievements flourished.

Banking systems were created, and the *yen* (Japanese currency) was established as a monetary unit. Railroads were built and silk production improved with new machinery from private funding.

Foreigners were sent to Japan and new students went abroad to learn new technologies, to help improve the government.

To maintain a working budget, the Meiji Government started a series of tax reforms to increase income for expenses. The farmers were targeted for these tax reforms. Because of the fluctuating market conditions and the high price of rice crops, the farmers paid two times the tax compared to other businesses. The farmers were forced to raise other crops besides rice, in case the price of rice fluctuated. Silkworm was the alternative crop. Silk was in demand not only in Japan, but in China as well.

In 1872, Japan's common people were ordered to pay government taxes. Fluctuating rice prices and poor harvest left people of Japan in an odd position. This resulted in debts owed to village moneylenders. Lacking food to eat, many starved to death. The desperate ate tree bark, roots, wild animals, and insects. Overpopulation, drought, storms, and lack of food were burdens faced by the Japanese population.

There are so many mountains in Japan that only one-fifth is level enough for agriculture. Narrow valleys and long forest hills left little agricultural land to grow rice, vegetables, and fruits.

In Honshu, mountains reach heights of up to ten thousand feet. Mount Fuji, Japan's most famous volcanic cone is twelve thousand, three hundred eighty-nine feet high. The last volcanic activity on Mount Fuji was in 1717.

Autumn and winter are generally dry seasons. Because there are many mountains in Japan, there are between forty to one hundred and twenty inches of rain per year. Japan never runs out of fresh water throughout the year. There are fresh water and hot mineral springs all over the country.

The construction of homes allows cool air in the summer and prevents cold air in the winter. Summers in Japan are very humid and hot. Mountains are the cause of the high humidity; temperatures in Japan sometimes reach over one hundred degrees, making it very uncomfortable to be out and about. Humidity makes you sweat and the heat makes it uncomfortable.

During the winter months, snowfall on the mountains covers its peaks. Snow is dominant all over Japan. The northern coastal region of Honshu has five to six feet of snow in most areas, making it the heaviest snowfall in the entire world. Winter is very cold all over Japan with winds whipping down from the mountains that cause extremely low temperatures.

During winter, one means of heating was to use a *hibachi* (container to keep charcoal in one central area but generally used for barbecuing) to keep the rooms warm. Another method was to have the *kotatsu* (a sunken heated pit) in the floor of the living room where residents could warm their feet. Everyone would gather around the hole and cover their legs with a *futon* to keep him or herself warm, have dinner at the table, and/or converse

42

with one another. Some of the farmhouses had the luxury of a *furo* to keep their bodies warm.

Late summer and autumn is typhoon season. The typhoon attacks the land at wind speeds exceeding one hundred miles per hour from the sea and devastates the terrain so badly that major repairs need to be made.

Japan also has problems with earthquakes that devastate buildings and property and create hardships for the people. Earthquakes can happen anytime, day or night. There are often no warnings.

In early Japan, the knowledge of agriculture came late, about two or three centuries before Christ. China was believed to be the homeland of East Asian civilization. Wet rice farming fields were developed in the south of ancient China. By the second century A.D., the crop was planted by creating small water filled pieces of land. Man-made ditches brought water from the mountains. Rice seeds were planted in bed containers with water and soil. Later, these were transplanted in fields to produce more seeds thus increasing production. This type of planting produced a high yield and also made it possible to plant multiple crops within a year. The southwestern half of Japan grew rice in the summer and grains and vegetables in the winter. The Japanese farmers used practically every inch of land to feed the enormous population.

Harvesting rice in old times was a tedious job for the farmers. First, the farmers had to dry up the field, pull the dried plant from them, prevent the rice from falling from the plants, tie them in bundles and carry them to the waiting wagons driven by a horse or mule. When the farmers took the bundles of rice to the barn, the farmer had to hit the rice over a large mat on the ground to separate the rice from the plant. After all was done, he would carry it outside sometimes into stiff winds. The farmer used a straw basket to heave the rice in the air to get rid of the pieces of branches from the plants and the rice covered husks. The farmer then had to fill the rice into a cloth sack to the desired weight. Later, machinery was used to plant and harvest the rice, and separate the branches and the husks from it.

43

Night soil or honey wagons carried the human waste to the fields. The honey wagons would suck up the waste from individual homes and dump the human waste into the fields that the farmer ordered ahead of time. The use of honey wagons was a very big business in the old days. There was money to be made. However, the population looked upon the owners of these wagons as inferior. Human waste yielded bountiful crops. Every type of plant and vegetable grew to enormous size. That practice was later replaced by fertilizer.

Rice, the staple food of Japan, is eaten three times a day and consumed in great quantities. The Japanese word for rice in Hawai'i is *gohan*. In Japan, the word is *shokuji*. Another by-product of rice was the making of *sake* (rice wine) with its contents between fifteen and twenty-per cent alcohol. Men drank the very popular drink cold or warmed.

In old Japan, cattle were used primarily for pushing wagons and for plowing farm fields in preparation of planting new crops. They were never to be consumed. The early Japanese were non-meat eaters because Buddhism taught that the taking of an animal's life was unacceptable.

The Japanese got their protein from the sea by eating fish, shellfish, sea squirts, abalone, crab, *ika* (squid), and *tako* (octopus). The people also ate *konbu* (large sea kelp which is softer than the American variety). It was dried and used when needed in soup or other dishes. Algae (harvested commercial or taken from the sea shore) was used in soup or the making of *nori* (flattened and dried) used, in turn, to make sushi. Rice was rolled around ingredients such as fried eggs, ginger, carrots and, later, canned tuna (prepared with sugar and soy sauce), the *nori* held it all together. This was a very special treat, especially on holidays.

Soybeans were imported from America. Later, the Japanese grew their own soy beans because it included many of the following by-products: Japanese *shoyu* better known as soy sauce, *tofu*, made with soy bean curd and eaten by everyone in Japan and now the world, and *miso* (fermented bean paste) used mainly as a soup base with added ingredients such as green onions. *Daikon* (white radish) was also eaten along with *konbu*, *nori*, *kamaboko* (Japanese fish cake) and, some times clams from the can.

The Japanese meal consisted of *gohan*, *takuwan* (pickled *daikon*), *tempura* (grounded up fish), *gobo* (deep fried), and vegetable *tempura* (fried separately) using *nasubi* (egg plant), cauliflower, string beans, broccoli, sweet potato, or yams. A batter was made and the tempura cooked to a crispy yellow (depending on how many eggs are used) or a light brown. Sometimes stir-fried meat dishes with vegetables and clear gravy were served. If one was lucky, *sashimi* (raw filleted fish sliced thinly and topped with thinly sliced cabbage) rounded out the meal.

I talked to my grandfather a number of times in his long life. I tried to remember all that he had said. If I forgot some of that information, I'd ask a family member or go straight back to him to get further information.

I once sought more information from my grandfather so I could write an essay as part of a school project. In 1957, I was only thirteen years old; my grandfather was seventy years old. After thinking it over for a couple of days, I decided not to submit any of my grandfather's history but kept this information for future use.

Here is the story told to me by my grandfather:

"I was born on January 29, 1887; my name is Sadazo Hongo. I grew up on the plains of Kumamoto, Southwest of Japan, on the province called Kyushu. Our village was called Itoda Machi, Kumamoto Ken Kamasi-Go, an area used mainly for farming. Living close to the mountains with my parents were my two brothers, a sister, and I.

My father was a farmer and raised rice as a staple and silkworms as an alternative crop; he grew whatever was in demand at the moment. He had to make a living to support his wife and the children. With the high taxes from the government, living conditions were very hard.

45

Houses were made of whatever wood we could gather, tied together to form the framework of the house. Dried tall grass grew everywhere and since my father could not afford to buy material to build a house, he gathered as much as he could. He tied the grass in bunches and tied these bunches to the wood. We all lived in a one- room house. My father even made an attic. In those days it was very important to have a snake in the attic of the house. The snake represented good luck for those living in the house.

Coming from a very poor family, I received a limited amount of education. Because my father needed help on the farm, education was never a high priority. I left school when I was able to handle a hoe, around the age of ten.

Being the eldest of four children, I was left with the burden of helping my father on the farm. A day of work started at the crack of dawn. As soon as my father could see the land, we would start working. We worked and worked until dark, without lunch or a break. When I first started to help my father, I developed blisters on both hands. After that, I used gloves. During the summer it was humid and hot. In the winter the temperature fell down to the teens.

Sunday was the only day of the week my father rested. We would rest on national holidays, during *bon* (the services honoring the dead), New Year's, and when there was heavy rain or snowfall.

Although my family was poor, we were close-knit. We would help each other in the time of need. Sometimes we would get frustrated because of lack of food, but eventually we'd remember that no one else had things better than us. Positive thinking was equal to survival in Japan at that time.

Every so often, a stranger from a different place would come to our village to recruit young gentlemen to do available *dekasegi-rado* (temporary work) away from home, somewhere else in Japan, to help supplement the income of the family. As soon as the families got financially stable, those with *dekasegi-rado*

46

would return home. This type of practice had been going on for years, especially in regions without work.

Then one day, the agents from the emigration companies started appearing in the poor regions of Japan. The duty of these agents was to recruit laborers to work in the sugar plantations in Hawai'i. The bosses from the emigration company related stories about the people in Japan that were so poor that they were starving and dying daily.

A number of agents of the emigration companies were *shizoko* (men of stature). They did not have enough money to start a business, but they made more money than farmers by recruiting laborers as emigrants to Hawai'i. The emigration company agents searched for farmers (*nonin*) based on their skills or profession. Therefore, the company never needed to train the laborers. These agents went from village to village recruiting men. They were very good talkers, spoke about a paradise called Hawai'i, even though none of them had ever been there. The only way they knew about it was from reading papers issued from the emigration company itself.

Some of my friends heard about these agents. I was curious enough so I attended one of those meetings. It was 1904 and I was seventeen, feeling old enough to make up my own mind.

During the meeting, recruiting agents insisted that we all sign a contract that would give us a day off every seven days after working ten hours a day in the hot sun. This sounded better than working from early morning until the sun went down; I would have more days off than the few I had with my father.

The following was a typical recruiter's presentation: 'Hawai'i is a beautiful place. No winter. Spring all year around. After three years, your contract will be over and you'd be able to return to Japan a very rich man. With the money that you'll save, women will be all over you. What you make here in a whole year, you can make in a month working on the plantation.'

That night I couldn't wait to tell my father all that was said earlier in the day. I finally told him that I was thinking of leaving Japan to seek my fortune in a far and distant land called Hawai'i, where everything is totally different and the climate was warm year round. Money could be made so quickly without laboring long hard hours as here in Japan. In three years, I would return with a lot of money to help the family.

I showed my father the book handed out to all who were interested in working in Hawai'i. *Kata-To-Bei-Ammi* was a popular book given to all emigrants-to-be with step by step instructions on the proper way of handling oneself on the hard questions asked by foreign emmigration officials and custom inspectors. Included was a list of items needed to travel abroad to Hawai'i, common English words used in Hawai'i (translated into Japanese), and a simple English lesson.

After telling my father all that was presented to me by the agent of the emigration company, I asked his permission to leave Japan. My father told me, 'I heard from a friend of mine that you did attend the meeting today. He said that the look on your face showed him that you were very interested. He warned me that you might come and ask my permission to go to Hawai'i. Remember son, you are the oldest and I cannot let you go to Hawai'i. Here in Japan the oldest stays home, takes care of his father, and inherits the land and the house. This tradition has been going on for centuries. I am sorry, but I can't let you go that far away for such a long time. I'm sorry but my answer is no.'

I felt so discouraged with my father's answer that I felt that I had to convince him that Japan was not the place for me and that life here was miserable. I always had respect for my father although, at times, I didn't like what he said or did. He was my father and that was that.

Tradition in Japan is very hard to break. The elderly are so set in their ways that they refuse to change them. Whether right or wrong, the tradition and the words of fathers came first and foremost. Call it brainwashing, but that's the way it was.

Knowing how discouraged I was, one day, a few weeks later

48

before dinner, he sat next to me and told me something I will never forget. He said, 'I feel that you have reached the age where it's up to you as to how you want to live your life. Your mother and I have talked it over and decided that life is hard here and that if you could find a better place and make money, then go – follow your dream. Since you asked my permission, which I thank you for, go, son, and make your fortune in that far away place called Hawai'i. Japan has always been an isolated country with little or no knowledge of the world outside.'

I thanked my father and mother for their decision to let me leave them for at least three years. Thoughts crossed my mind as to whether I would ever see them alive, considering how long I would be away. I will certainly miss my brothers and my sister who had been so close to me. After thinking everything over, I decided that to leave would be very sad. I had lived seventeen years with my parents and my brothers and sister through thick and thin and, now, I was leaving them. I was so engrossed with the idea of moving that I never thought beyond it. Was it a good or bad decision?

I gave all necessary information to my father as to the situation of my plans to leave Japan. I told my father that the agent had returned to our town and that I was going to tell him that I was interested in going to Hawai'i as an emigrant. The agent told me later that the main office of Kumamoto Emigration Company was preparing the necessary documents (permits, passports, and other official documents), both in English and Japanese, to assure my safe passage to Hawai'i. As soon as the documents arrived, I would be able to review with the agent all the necessary documents, enabling me to emigrate.

I made up my mind that I would leave that place of suffering and misery for three years and return home a very rich person with money in my pocket to help the family's financial burden, which was heavy. I would make my father proud of me. I would buy land to feed the family. This was my wish and dream. I said it proudly to myself over and over again. It took a couple of weeks after signing with the recruiting agent before I knew that I was leaving Japan. The agent in Japan gave us a woven willow basket as a farewell gift. I had to fit all my belongings in that willow basket.

I was so bewildered. I had never left my village. I do know that I traveled by train but don't even know the name of my ship or the port of departure.

As we left the harbor for the open sea, I knew that this was going to be a very long and uncomfortable journey. The constant rolling of the ship made almost everyone sick. Most of us had never been on a ship before. This was a totally new experience. If a passenger did not get sick from the rolling sea, he'd get sick from the constant heaving of others. The smell carried throughout the ship. However after about a week, everyone adjusted to the ship.

The bathroom was a wooden box with a hole cut in and a pail on the bottom to collect the waste. The contents of the pail had to be thrown over board and the pail scrubbed and replaced.

After bathing every day in Japan, it was rough to go without a bath for fourteen days. Fleas and bugs bit everyone on board. Passengers developed sores all over their bodies from scratching. Some passengers were so badly bitten that they developed infections. Green pus oozed from their bodies, taking months to heal, resulting in permanent scars. The bodies of those who died on the way to Hawai'i were kept in a separate room and stored.

On board, we were served the same staple food day after day: black beans, chopped dried turnip stir fried with canned salmon. You could barely taste the *miso* (bean paste) in the watery soup. We had no more than two tablespoons of rice.

Because of the length of the voyage, gambling was a way to pass the time, usually by playing *hanafuda* (Japanese playing cards). Many of the passengers lost the money they brought with them and some had to borrow cash to continue playing. Those who brought out their own cards were professional gamblers. They knew how to shuffle to their advantage. Many passengers were taken advantaged of by their own people before arriving in Hawai'i.

After fourteen days at sea, the sight of the islands totally consumed the eyes of the immigrants on the steamer ship. A gleam shown in their eyes as they viewed the lush valleys, hillsides, waterfalls, green pastures, all surrounded by the blues of the ocean and the sky, highlighted by a few scattered clouds. The temperature of the air was comfortable, with its warm trades. Everything I could see had a brilliant color. Everything that the recruiting agents from the Kumamoto Emigration Company had mentioned and promised seemed true. I thought that this was the place where fortunes would be made and that I'd be able to return to Japan in three years with that fortune.

I must explain something here. When in Japan, those who decided to work on the plantations here in Hawai'i were called emigrants in Japan. Upon arrival here in Hawai'i, they were called immigrants. I do not know the reason why.

Upon arriving on land on the island of O'ahu, we were taken over a long walkway that led to the Sand Island Immigration Station. It was a desolate place with little vegetation composed of coral with a muddy shoreline.

Sand Island Immigration Station consisted of a large building that accommodated hundreds of immigrants at once. Next to the large building, in a smaller one, quarantined immigrants were held. In a nearby brick building with a large chimney, the dead bodies from the steamer were burned.

At the Sand Island Depot, agreements in both Japanese and English language were printed out. The contracts that we signed were very different from the contracts that we signed in Japan. Those contracts that we signed at the Sand Island Depot Immigration Station demanded a lot more of us as far as work hours and pay. Since we were here already, we had no other choice but to sign. We were told that if we wanted to return to Japan, then we would have to pay our own way. Since all of us had little or no money, that was impossible, and the Sand Island Depot Immigration Company knew this.

We asked for the previous contracts that we signed and were denied. Our understanding became real when a person who had been here for a while told us that the contracts we signed in Japan were left there. The agents from Japan were not aware of this. All of us had been double-crossed by the companies here in Hawai'i.

As part of the necessary processing procedures, forced upon us, other documents needed to be prepared. Questions were asked with an interpreter present, translating both in English and Japanese. We answered all the questions but we started to doubt if the interpreters were asking the right questions and if the persons who were documenting them were actually putting down our answers. We also questioned whether the companies had paid off the interpreters.

To the Japanese, a daily bath was a must. Cleanliness was of utmost importance. After the long voyage from Japan to Hawai'i, the first welcoming experience was a shower with fresh cold water. We washed our dirty clothes by hand by scrubbing them, with or without the use of soap. We also had to hang clothes wherever we could.

I remember an embarrassing procedure when I had to give a sample of our *unko* (bowel movement) to the nurse to check for any disease we might be carrying from Japan. I remember asking a friend whom I had met on the ship to give me part of his sample because I had already relieved myself a short time before. I guess everything was all right; the doctor cleared me.

Immigrants, who had settled on O'ahu, made and sold *geta* (sandals made of wood, cloth, and nails). Underneath the sandals were two pieces of nailed wood about an inch high, about an inch away from the front and the back across the bottom that became the base of the slipper that made the sandals hard to walk on. Two pieces of V shaped cloth were nailed to the top and sides to fit between the big toe and the others toes. When someone with *geta* walked on concrete or a hard surface, the sound could be heard prior to the wearer's arrival. The sandals made a crackling sound. *Geta* was not safe to walk on because there was a good possibility that one could slip, fall, and possibly break an ankle or arm.

In Japan, men and women used sandals commonly. Men used the sandals at home while the women wore the *tabi* (similar to cloth shoes-white only) with the *geta* as formal footwear about town with their *kimono* (very expensive and colorful clothing). Rich women often had more than one in their *tansu*, or cabinet to hang clothes.

In the old days, women always walked behind the men as respect and honor to the man of the house. Women never talked back to the husband in public places. They lived with the husband's parents, cooked all meals, cleaned the house, and took care of the children in an orderly fashion. Women were seen but not heard, raised this way from childhood.

Immigrants like us who arrived at the Sand Island Depot from southwestern Japan such as Hiroshima, Yamaguchi, Kumamoto and Fujioka were healthy, accustomed with the outdoors, and well suited for work in Hawaii's plantation fields.

We stayed at the Sand Island Depot Immigration Center for about a week. There we were assigned to the different islands. My friend on the ship was assigned to the Big Island of Hawai'i while I was assigned to Maui. Before we left for our assigned island, I said goodbyes to the friends I had made on the steamer and at the Sand Island Depot Center, I also vowed to a friend that I had become close to that we would visit each other's island sooner or later. Of course, it never happened. We were probably blowing smoke in the wind and we understood deep in our hearts that this was true.

As we boarded the *S.S. Kinau*, a ship owned by the Inter Island Navigation Company, the voyage lasted overnight. We crossed the channel named Pailolo and the island of Moloka'i; rough seas made some of us seasick all over again. Despite our weakness from being sick, we were ordered to gather our belongings and prepare to leave the ship.

53

At our destination, ladders were lowered on to the dock. There, one by one, we came off the ship. At the far end of the pier, horse driven wagons awaited our arrival to transport the immigrants to the assigned plantations here on Maui.

We were loaded on wagons and headed to the camps. Along the way to the plantation, I looked up and saw the splendor of Haleakala towering in the background, Mount 'Eke and Mount Pu'u Kukui to the right. I have not seen such tall mountains before. I lived near a mountain in Kumamoto but I had not seen mountains so beautiful and green. This was to be my home for the next three years of my contract. I really couldn't wait to return home and tell my family how beautiful a place can be, so far away from Japan.

Upon arriving at the plantation homes, we were herded into a single house where six families lived together, partitions separating one from the other. I was given a space to sleep on the floor and a shelf above my sleep space for my willow trunk. I was given a blanket and a pillow, without a sheet to place under my back on the floor. We found out the bathroom was in another very small building that the residents called the outhouse. It was very smelly, without windows, and very hot.

After seeing our living quarters, we were taken to a warehouse to get our supply of clothing. We were to get a pair of shirts, pants, shoes, socks, and a hat. We were told that this was the one and only time we would be supplied with clothing and shoes. Thereafter, we had to buy our own with our own money.

After that, we were taken to a train depot where the *luna* (boss of assigned people in a group) boarded all of us on a train bound for the field that was presently being harvested.

After arriving at the harvesting field, we were all told to carry bundles of cane harvested by other employees to the train and load the cars in a fashionable form (in rows). We were told to follow the others who were more experienced. It seemed the day would never end. We worked from the time we got there, which was about noon, until it was almost too late to see anything.

Each cane bundle from the field to the train car became heavier and heavier as time went by. We also had to walk farther and farther from the fields to reach the train cars.

After returning home from the gruesome work, some of us talked to the residents of the building we were housed in. We were told that we were considered lucky to be here at this camp.

They also told us that the earlier immigrants at various plantations, including this one, had several hundred people living in a large dormitory size house. Their sleeping area consisted of rough wooden planks (six feet long and twelve to fifteen inch wide). The same size planks also comprised the walls that separated one living quarter from another. Separation height between each living area was about four feet high, four rows high and eight partitions long. The unfortunate sleeper on the top berth had to climb all the sections to the top with his belongings. In the building, the rows and partitions ran completely around the building. The living quarters were crowded, lacked privacy, and had poor sanitation facilities.

Many of the residents fell from their perch. Some broke legs, arms, or both. In extreme cases, some died from hitting their head as they fell to the wooden floor, depending how high the person was situated.

The bathroom was outside; an outhouse without lights. The floor was not wooden, but dirt. We used our own toilet paper and soap. Some of the immigrants were too lazy and urinated outside of the building at night, creating an awful smell when the weather was warm. I guess it was better then trying to use the outhouse toilet in the dark.

Next to the bathroom was also a long sink with faucet of cold water for the residents to wash their face and their clothes. After doing their laundry, they hung their clothes to dry on a rope stretching from one tree to another. If I was late in washing my clothes, and if there were no lines available, I had to hang my clothes on branches of trees. This sometimes invited unwelcome guests into clothing: centipedes, spiders, scorpions and fire ants, all numerous in the islands. Bites or stings resulted if clothing wasn't checked.

Tired or lazy residents would steal freshly washed clothes from the line in the wee hours of the morning, forcing some of the victims, in turn, to use or steal another person's clothes. The cycle caused conflict among some workers.

I heard rumors that after three years of my contract, I could keep on working at the plantation with a raise, work somewhere else in Hawai'i, or return to my homeland.

I wanted to find out as much as I could about my new home in Hawai'i. I felt that to get more information, the very person I had to see was an elder of the group. He told me that he had been here for over three years and had not made much money. He, too, naively believed in the stated contract. In fact, he told me that I should forget about returning to Japan after my three-year contract was up. He also told me that he would be lucky if he had saved a hundred dollars in his three years there. I felt so discouraged. I felt that a few fellow countrymen had betrayed me.

He passed on some conversations and stories that circulated among immigrants of the first ship, the *Scioto*, that arrived in Hawaiian waters on May, 1868, and was the first ship to send Japanese immigrants as contract workers. The success or failure of the voyage determined whether more Japanese immigrants would be allowed in to the Hawaiian Islands.

Planters were attempting to solve their labor problems under the Master & Servants Act. There weren't enough Hawaiians to service the jobs needed by the plantations.

With worsening conditions in Japan, this was the perfect opportunity to solve the problem by importing immigrants from Japan to work in their fields. King Kalakaua made his first journey to Japan, the first Hawaiian to touch Asian soil. As an Ambassador of Hawai'i representing the Sandwich Island plantations, he visited Japan to encourage its laborers to work in

Hawai'i at the sugar mills.

Earlier, in 1852, Chinese were shipped to the islands as laborers. When they reached their quota, Portuguese immigrants were welcomed. It was expensive to send Portuguese. (They refused to be separated from their families). In 1868, large numbers of residents from the island of Madeira sailed from Europe to Hawai'i, alleviating the fear of an influx of Chinese immigrants to the sugar plantations. Adding to this racial mixture were Norwegians and Germans, not to serve as laborers on the plantation, but to be bosses.

The terms of the contract for the first immigrants from Japan included four dollars a month based on a three-year contract. Each laborer would receive ten dollars in advance before leaving Japan. Food and passage was provided on board the ships. Another two dollars, after working out the contract, would be given to worker, from his earlier deposit. Of course, the ten dollars was never given to the laborer before he left Japan. Later, the laborers found out that the ten dollars had been deducted from their wages.

An agreement with the Filipino Government to send laborers to Hawai'i began in 1906. Filipinos arrived to work the plantations, glad to be employed by the sugar companies. In the Philippines, their wages were so low that they, like the Japanese, had a very hard time feeding their families. Their work ethic was very different from the other nationalities that came to Hawai'i. They worked slowly, but they lasted the long hours because they conserved their energy.

At seventeen, I most desperately longed to be with the younger immigrants I had traveled with from the village of Kumamoto, on the vessel to Hawai'i, at Sand Island Depot, and aboard the S.S. *Kinau* bound for Maui. I'm sure they had the same longings. However, I listened to all who told me their life stories and struggles in Japan and about their parents, brothers, sisters, grandparents, relatives, friends, their dreams of a better tomorrow, and their future with the help of the sugar plantations. These friends that I had made earlier had been scattered to different plantations across the territory. I often wondered how they were doing. I hoped their lives were not as bad as my suffering.

Here on Maui, although the weather was beautiful, we were in the hands of the plantation managers and *luna* whose temperaments varied from day to day. Hawai'i became another place of suffering and unreasonable burden. In the fields we were abused, called *Japs*, scolded, punched, shoved, slapped on the head and even whipped.

I want to clarify something here. There were a few *luna*, and I mean a few, who did nothing to the laborers until the managers showed up. Those *luna* scolded us, slapped us, and, from the order of the manager, whipped us, not with his full strength but with a lashing that still hurt. Workers had welts but not cuts. The fair *luna* knew that his laborers would work their hearts out for him and try not to cause any trouble. He trusted in them and they trusted in him. In fact, there was more work done by these groups than any other sections of the field harvest gangs.

The whipping caused shirts to be torn, created welts on the body and, in some cases, bleeding. We were whipped from our necks to our legs. Many of the cuts and the welts would not go away for weeks. Returning to work daily did not help the situation for the workers. The lesions were exposed to dust stirred up when cane was carried to the rail cars and further irritated from standing and bending for long hours at work.

Medicinal products were ever so present. Immigrants brought part of the traditional medicines from Japan to be used by the Japanese community. Those medicines, brought or sent, eased the pain only temporarily. Those medicinal ointments did not completely heal the welts and cuts on the bodies. Many of the cuts got infected. Some turned to gangrene, requiring the removal of limbs that sometimes resulted in death.

Whenever a person had a fever, a heat plaster was cut and placed on the forehead. The plaster was called *Jin-Tung*, a Japanese product used for sore throat. Whenever someone had a cold, this equivalent of Vapo Rub, was applied by coating the chest and throat, after a bath in the *furo*.

Often, without the proper medication, plantation workers resorted to drastic measures. One way to deal with wounds was to place them over a fire to burn the blisters and cuts that would not heal. Some sufferers, desperate to heal the wound, sometimes got a piece of charcoal and placed it on the injury. The sound was like meat sizzling over an open fire. Later, they'd wash their wounds with soap and water, apply ointment, and wrap them with cloth strips, ready for the next day's work.

I witnessed workers who cut themselves accidentally on the leg or arm while planting sugar cane stalks in the ground. Many got slit when they were cutting the stalks in sections. Others got sliced while cutting the tops and bottoms of sugar cane stalks during harvesting. The cane knife was so sharp that when the worker followed through, and an arm or leg happened to be in the way, accidents occurred. Their wounds were so severe that co-workers made tourniquets from cane stalks and kerchiefs, to stop the bleeding. On rare occasions, the supervisor took the injured person to the hospital. The answer most of the time, was a impassionate, 'He'll live.' What was worse was that the person had to return to work, immediately.

Most of the earlier immigrants had scars all over their bodies. Ashamed to show the scars, and because a sense of embarrassment, they rarely took off their clothing in public. Whenever I saw those scars, I called them Wounds of the Work.

If a worker had to stay home because of sickness or pain from cuts from the whipping, the laborer was not allowed to recover in his bunk bed without a doctor's certificate. If this was not retrieved, camp police armed with whips came and forced the employee into submission. They escorted him forcefully back to his work place to continue his chores for the rest of the day. Wages were deducted from the employee for hours not worked.

Plantation doctors who were hired by the company were infamous for sending sick and hurt employees back to work regardless of their condition. Some of the doctors eventually admitted they felt sorry for the patients whom they had to send back to work. They admitted it later, but the apologies came too late for those who died because of those doctors' inhumane practices.

Because I was single, I paid another immigrant's wife two dollars and fifty cents to cook my meals and another dollar to do my laundry. I saved the remainder of the money or sent a small portion to my father in Japan. Doing laundry by hand with a brush and a scrubbing board was hard work for these women, but doing necessary chores by immigrants provided them with good money for the month. If that housewife hustled, she could, in some cases, possibly make more than her husband.

With the blast of the plantation siren at half past four in the morning, the day started. Another plantation siren went off at eight in the evening to signal the end of the day. Better known as curfew, no one was allowed to roam the camps or leave their lights on. Before electricity, candles, kerosene lanterns lit plantation homes.

In the early morning hours, villagers heard roosters crowing and dogs barking as wives packed lunches for their husbands. Some wives who had to cook *gohan* (rice) got up earlier than usual, aroused by a loud ticking clock. Other wives woke up earlier than their husbands, some before the four thirty wake up call, to burn firewood.

Before electricity, women cooked the family breakfast by the glow of candlelight. The meal consisted of a very simple array of food: *miso* soup, *gohan*, pickled vegetables called *tsukemono* or another pickled vegetable called *kon-kon* (pickled turnip, including the leaves), and *ocha* (hot tea). All were prepared prior to the morning siren and before the husbands or single men got up. Breakfast was simple but filling. Some families were so poor that they only had tea for breakfast. *Gohan* was available but rationed and saved only for dinner.

The laborers carried their *kaukau* (Hawaiian for food) tin (two-tiered, lunch container with round basins about five inches in diameter) to the fields. One tier contained rice and the other *okazu* (main dish). The rice was always on the bottom layer because it was hot when scooped into the tin and kept the main dish warm. I also had a pair of *hashi* (chopsticks) to eat with. *Kaukau* tins were carried in used cloth rice bags with sewn on straps. The rice bag kept the food warmer for a longer period.

Some of the workers never ate any breakfast or lunch. Those who brought lunch felt sorry for those who could not afford noon meal and shared their food with them. That is how it was in those days. The habit was mutual. If you helped someone, later on that person would help you immediately, or perhaps later in life. Some shared their lunches without thinking about the future. To many, today was the future; there was nothing to look forward to.

The cloth rice bag had many uses besides carrying the *kaukau* tin. It was used to make shorts, shirts, sheets for the bed, and blankets. Many used the bags for freshly caught fish. They were heavy because they were stitched on both sides, on the bottom and at the top. The top was sewn with string making it possible to untie. It had to be unraveled at one end and pulled to open. These rice bags were readily available since rice was a staple food and a very important part of the daily diet.

It is important to store rice properly. Generally, rice was stowed in containers because of two reasons. First, once the rice bag was opened, the rice could topple and scatter all over the floor. Second, during poor weather, especially the rainy season, the rice could get damp and become moldy. At that point, the rice had to be thrown away. Some residents did not have the luxury of having a container so, when the rice became moldy, they simply cleaned it the best they could, cooked it, and ate it. Sadly, many couldn't afford to buy a new bag of rice until they got paid. A third reason to store rice properly was because small black bugs made their way into the opened bags.

The rice came with doused powder that prevented the grains from sticking together. This powder needed to be rinsed off before cooking. During the rinsing, the black bugs would occasionally surface. The preparer had to make sure that all of the bugs were gone, and then proceeded to add clean water to steam the rice. There's a simple method to measure the amount of water needed to steam the rice. The whole hand, flat, is placed on the rice in the pot. The water should be slightly above the hand to properly steam the rice.

Use of the stationary steamroller was an advancement of preparing the fields for planting. Yet manual labor was still needed for stripping the leaves from the cane stalk called *holehole,* cutting seeded cane to pieces, planting, watering, fertilizing, *hoe hana* (weeding), cutting, and loading the cane by hand on to the railroad cars (*hapai ko*).

Endless rows of sugar cane awaited laborers. If anyone slowed down in their work or rested, the Portuguese or Hawaiian *luna* (foreman) would swear and threaten the laborers in English or inflict lashes with their black whip. The new arrivals of Japanese and Filipino workers did not understand the *luna* because English was not their native tongue. The laborers were always misunderstood and punished unnecessarily because of the communication barrier. Because of the constant pushing and whipping by the *luna*, a few of the workers purposely cut their legs with the cane knife (a long flat wide metal with a handle, sharpened at one end) so they could take a break from the fields and go to the hospital for stitches. Unfortunately, they were forced by the doctors to return back to their work location to finish the day's labor.

The wounds would not heal fast, but, despite that, a laborer had to return to the job the next day or the managers would take a few goons to the house to 'encourage' the person back to his work place. Also, if the laborer did not show up for work, even if he was really sick, the enforcers would be sent to drag the ill person from his house and drag him back to his place of work to finish the day.

The Portuguese were chosen to be *luna* because they looked like the managers of the plantation. They were of fair skin and many of them tall. The Hawaiians were also hired as *luna* because of their size. Most were young and muscular in stature and could beat up the smaller Japanese and Filipinos. What's really a shame was that they were forced to do it; there was always a manager on a horse, making sure the *luna* worked their way. Some *luna* were sadistic and loved beating up laborers. Those few refused to come near the camps of the common laborers because they knew what would happen to them.

The *luna* who refused to do the beatings worked alongside the laborers. Those were the very ones that the laborers looked up to. These exceptional *luna* had the courage to say that they refused to beat up the workers. Some of these *luna* were comfortable living among the laborers, and, in some cases, suffered along with them. Because some of these former *luna* suffered as much as the laborers, they were a part of that world, and the burden of injustice was lifted from their shoulders.

Some of the Japanese knew the art of *karate* (self-defense method of fighting), and many other self-defense tactics, such as *aikido*, *judo*, and *kung fu*. In the old teachings of the Japanese, *karate* was not used as an offensive form of fighting, but as self-defense. I'm sure there were a number of Japanese who could have shown a couple of *luna* what it felt like to be hit by a person knowledgeable in the art of *karate*, including, as part of the training, the breaking of bones.

Bango (badges made of brass) numbers were the form of identification used by the plantations administrators. A worker had to carry his plantation identification number wherever he went, including to the store; he needed it to charge things that he bought. Generally, most of the stores trusted the immigrants and allowed them to charge things because they didn't have money to purchase items immediately. Later, when the laborer got paid, he returned to the store to pay off the debt and buy more things.

The *bango* or the plantation identification number was to catch runaways who escaped their camp because of the misery inflicted on them by plantation bosses. They'd flee for miles under the cover of darkness to a new life at other plantations or by assisting independent farmers with growing their crops. Some plantations would return the laborers back to the original plantation where they would be punished. Most of the non-plantation farmers kept their new hired laborers without notifying the plantations, sympathetic because they too had emigrated from Japan. These fortunate individuals continued their profession in a new land.

At half-hour lunch breaks, laborers would gather around in a circle and eat their lunch. The lunch, upon availability, included: salted dried salmon, dried cod fish, cooked beans (*nimame*), or vegetables cooked in soy sauce and brown sugar called *nishime*, a very popular dish from Japan. Each person had a bottle of *ocha* (brewed tea). As said earlier, those who did not have any lunch shared with those who had a lot or were willing to share regardless of how little they had.

From sunrise to sunset, after hours of grueling field labor, the laborers rushed back to their living quarters hoping to use their precious private hours. The employees worked twelve to fourteen hours a day, seven days a week, cutting cane, *hoe hana*, *hapai ko* or working in the mills. For most laborers, the new land of promise and dreams had turned to bitter suffering pain.

Many plantation owners considered workers as nothing more than beasts of burden. Workers were cruelly pushed, verbally abused (called *Japs*), and physically harmed by some of the plantation bosses. The feeling among many Japanese was that they were treated no better than animals. In fact, many believed that animals were treated better; at least they had food to eat.

In Japan, many laborers believed that goodwill and human brotherhood awaited them at the sugar plantations. It was an illusion. The camps were initially and, purposely, ethnically segregated, starting with the Chinese, and followed later by the Japanese and the Filipinos.

The camps later became multi-ethnic communities. When people of a specific race died or someone moved out to seek better opportunities, a person of another ethnicity moved in. People also left the camps because, as the family grew, they looked for a bigger house to live. So, eventually, Japanese, Chinese, Filipinos,

64

Hawaiians, and a few Portuguese all became neighbors. Those camps that were multi-ethnic got along much better than pure race camps. They all had the same goal in mind – to work as one and to help each other in times of need. This feeling of togetherness was what I witnessed growing up. We didn't have to lock our doors nor did we have to hide precious items. No one took anything from anyone because every one trusted each other.

What was not to be trusted were introduced species. Some of these pests were introduced into the Hawaiian Islands for the purpose of killing off the former pests introduced previously by plantation companies. One good example was the mongoose that was imported in 1883 as a means of getting rid of rats. In 1887, mosquitoes were introduced to the Hawaiian Islands. These aliens probably hitched a ride on ships. They sucked blood from a person's skin, caused itches, and sometimes carried disease. African snails were introduced in 1936 to rid other small snails. They multiplied at an alarming rate and created a greater problem. They ate all the vegetation that the laborers grew around their home. Other useless pests introduced were yellow jacket bees, scorpions, and centipedes. They stung people, caused welts on their bodies and, for a few, serious infections that resulted in hospital treatment.

Stings and bites had to be combated by using specific clothing. The laborers needed a variety of protective clothing against stinging insects, rainstorms, and the sharp razor like sugar cane leaves. Because women also worked in the fields in later years, they created their own style of work clothes. Aprons were made of denim (*ahina*) because of its thickness, strength, and durability. For footwear, *tabi* from Japan were used. A knee-to-ankle leg wrapping (*kyaban*) went around the *tabi* and pants along with a cummerbund (*obi*) circled the shirt and pants area. There was also an arm cover (*oi*) around the gloves and the long sleeves. Straw hats (*papale*) and kerchiefs around the neck to prevent sunburn, cuts from the cane leaves, and insect bites and stings.

Men's work attire consisted of *ahina* pants, a t-shirt, denim jacket during inclement weather, a denim apron to protect the clothes from getting dirtier, *tabi* or shoes if they could afford it, round rimmed hats (*papale*), gloves and a kerchief worn around their necks or tied around their heads to prevent sweat from dripping into their eyes. Mill workers who worked inside only needed denim pants, a t-shirt, shoes, and a denim jacket.

During its later years, sugar plantations decided to burn the sugar cane before harvesting to get rid of the leaves. The burning and hauling of the charred cane, the dirt, and blackened soot soiled working clothes so badly that they had to be boiled in five gallon cans over a fire pit to try and remove the soil and ash stains.

Every evening, women and men washed their underwear when they took a bath to save water. Many had only two pairs brought here from Japan. Eventually, these were replaced by hand made rice bag cloth underwear. Since under garments were not seen, both men and women wore the rice sack version, a simple solution for those with limited income.

Both men and women wore their plain robes (*kimono*) at home. The kimono was made simple and looked exactly like a bath robe but with added Japanese designs for the woman's version. Men's robes had simple designs such as stripes with colors of black and grey on a white background. Sometimes these were black and red with a gray or white background; black was always traditionally included in the design. All of the kimono cloth was thin but not transparent.

Sunday was the only day to do laundry, if and only if the harvesting season was completed. Camp residents tied a rope from tree to tree and hung their wet clothing on it to dry under the warm Hawaiian sun. Later that Sunday evening, after all the dried clothes were gathered, an iron filled with charcoal was used to press wrinkled items. Later that night, those who didn't own a sewing machine took time to patch ripped clothing by hand. Camp residents wore a good amount of hand-me-down clothing, including those from the recently deceased.

Some were fortunate enough to acquire a sewing machine. It was the model that required foot pressure to pump the threaded needle up and down. The machine was used to sew work clothes, casual home wear, torn pants, shirt and jackets, among others.

Many railroad tracks ran from field to field, and to the main processing mill. Cane was hauled to the mill for processing on train cars. To unload the cane from the cars, two cane loaders were used to speed the process.

In the mill, the cane stalks passed through rollers. The steamed juices from the cane were pumped to the third floor, passed through sand filters and carried to the lime vats to be clarified. Then it was further carried to an Octicle System of Sexibles, little evaporators on the floor, and from there, to be crystallized. The final result was raw brown sugar. The sugar went through a chute, was loaded onto railway cars, transported to the pier, pumped into waiting ships through large port holes, shipped to Baghdad and Crockett, California to be refined and processed. The result – the white sugar we are familiar with.

A mosquito netting (*kaya*) was sent from Japan and used to keep mosquitoes, centipedes, cockroaches, bees, scorpions and occasionally red ants away during the night. The *kaya*, tied to a rope, hung from the rafters to completely cover the bed.

Nearly all of the immigrants sent whatever they could afford to their parents in Japan. They heard from their parents through letters and other workers talking, that life in Japan was described as worsening. They described floods, cold winters and storms that plagued the countryside. One letter in particular described a family of ten who starved and froze to death in a grass shack.

With what little income they made, the immigrants had to make do with what they had. Just as their parents did back in Japan, the immigrants believed that by not doing anything intentionally wrong, by working hard, by not complaining, and by following Buddha's teaching, The Enlightened One would take care of them.

The main religion of Japan was Buddhism so most of the Japanese camp residents were Buddhist. Many brought or bought

67

small shrines (*hotoke-sama*) for worship. These were placed in the middle of a cloth-covered table in the house. Often, one or two flower vases decorated this shrine. The *hotoke-sama* housed a statue of the Buddha, as well as an area to place fruits, food or beverages (beer, soda or *sake*) as offerings to those who had passed away. Outside the *hotoke-sama*, in separate containers, were a candle, incense, or *sennen ko* (joss sticks), a bell, and an incense bowl. In front of the altar, on the floor, was a cushion for kneeling. The worshiper bowed his/her head and clasped hands together in prayer. Some use a *ju-zu* (beads strung together, used for chanting or reciting mantras), between the thumb and fingers of both hands, while praying.

Buddhist immigrants attended the *hotoke-sama* every day. They prayed to Amida Buddha in the early morning for the deceased, a good day of work as well as for the relatives back home, hoping they were safe and with ample food. After taking a bath, prayer was said in front of the *hotoke-sama* again, this time to insure a good day without incident. Another prayer was said before going to bed, wishing the dead, family and ancestors a good night.

Sadly, the *hotoke-sama* had another purpose. The altar was used before and after a funeral. The ritual changed as the first incense stick was lit; the members of the family knew that one of their own had passed away. The burning of incense continued night and day until the deceased was buried. It continued to be lit because it was believed that the deceased needed light to find his/her way into the next world. Family members took turns staying up all night to keep vigil and maintain the incense burning.

Because of the absence of actual churches of Shinto Buddhism, Zen Buddhism, general Buddhism, and religions of Japan, ruthless opportunists roamed the camps posing as ministers, preaching religion, and asking for large sums of donations in return. Japanese immigrants, who could afford the request of these impostors, contributed willingly to these wandering ministers. In fact, many of them worked as laborers, then pretended to be a minister of Buddhism during the weekday, afternoons and weekends. There were no documents to prove the

68

difference between an authentic minister and a fake. Sadly, however, as soon as one fake was exposed and expelled, another impostor would appear.

These ministers preached damnation and death, an eventuality that even plantation administrators could not deny. The sugar company carpenters constructed coffins for the dead. No more than a pine box, these coffins very simply made and stored at the carpenter's shop. These boxes were available only when the shop was open, on weekdays. If a person died during the weekend, the body was left on the bed of the deceased, covered with a white sheet until the weekday.

The procedure went as follows: a family member or a good friend notified the sugar company that the employee had died. That very same day, or on Monday, if death occurred over the weekend, a coffin was delivered to the deceased's residence. Prior to horse driven wagons, taking the casket to the burial site, people of the camp carried the coffin to the burial site after the six-foot hole had been dug. Sometimes friends did the digging; sometime workers were hired by the family to perform the task. Some graves were a distance from the camps, and some camps shared graves. Since residents carried the coffin to the gravesite, burials were another ordeal for families.

After the person died, there were services by a legal minister bedside and at the grave. Then the body was laid to rest and the hole covered up by the people who dug it. A wooden marker was stuck in the ground near the head of the buried. On the marker were the person's name, date of birth and the date of death, all in Japanese. Later, a head stone replaced the marker only if the family could afford a head stone.

The sugar plantation company hired immigrants who had been sheet metal welders, tunnel diggers, and carpenters in Japan to work in those capacities for the plantation company. Those carpenters built houses for the immigrants, as well as warehouses, storerooms and other necessary buildings for the company. Later, plumbers, electricians, and workers with other skills were hired.

For entertainment, camp residents listened to the radio. KMVI hosted a Japanese show, *The Yamato Program*, every afternoon. The Yamato's delivered the news from Japan, happenings around the world, and local news. They also played Japanese music. Some residents were fortunate to own phonographs (*chi-kon-ki*). Some were originally imported from Japan to play Japanese music. Some of the 78 records were played so many times that there were serious scratch marks on the records that resulted in sound deterioration. The poor quality of imported phonographs added to the poor sound. Many residents borrowed the phonographs of others to listen to records they had brought over from Japan.

The music was needed relief from the grinding work. I had done hard labor for two years, but, finally, luck struck. A friend of mine who came on the same boat to Maui suggested that I try for a job as a waterman. I applied and got the position because the *luna* approved of my transferal to another department. My primary job was to open and close the gates in the ditches as soon as the fields had been irrigated. I walked long distances to check the end of the ditch to make sure that the water had gone to the end. Sometimes I had to run back to close the gate before the water overflowed. I did this for a couple of years. Although the job was fairly easy, I didn't like it because it was a lonesome job; I had no one to talk to.

After a few years, I heard that an apprentice carpenter's job was available because of a death of an employee. I was fortunate to be hired as go-for carpenter. Whatever they needed, I built. For a while, I helped repair plantation home roofs, construct new homes for new campsites, and build community *furo*.

I had a very good supervisor; I learned a lot from him. He was more than willing to teach me the tricks of the trade. Although he was much older than me, we were of the same nationality and got along very well. He was so knowledgeable about carpentry that he not only answered my questions, but explained the processes and the reasons why the job had to be done a certain way.

70

My construction of *furo* made me an expert on the subject. Community *furo* were made for the many residents of the camps. After a hard day in the fields, residents soaked their weary bodies in hot water to ease their pains away. Because the *furo* were communal in nature, someone had to maintain them. That person from the camp charged a ten cents fee to cover the cost of the heating of the water, its cleanliness, and the soap. The sugar company sometimes supplied firewood.

Furo, enclosed in a wooden building, had concrete floors, concrete block walls on four corners (two and a half feet deep), and enough space to rinse the soap off before entering it. There were two entrances, one for women and one for men. Both used the same water, but were separated by a partition both across the washing area and directly above the water level. Men would often go under water to spy on bathing women. Of course, it resulted with screams from the women. Often, the person in charge of the *furo* would kick the dirty minded out.

Women who took a bath in community *furo* were, at times, abused. Although they were separated by a partition, men would sometimes reach under the partition and touch women's legs. A woman could not accuse anyone because the partition prevented one from seeing who the culprit was. At times, women refused to take a bath in some community *furo*. Many would wait until the late hours of the night, after the men had finished, before taking a bath themselves. At those times, the water was not hot. Girls who were single as well as married women had to be especially worried about seduction from single and married males. These female late night bathers were thankful for the person in charge of the *furo*. They served as bodyguards to the young women, keeping vigil with a candle until ten at night.

The down side of the *furo* was that there were no toilets. So, if someone wanted to urinate, they simply did it in the hot water. Often the families bathed together, including small children. The infants didn't know better, so some would have bowel movements in the water. The hardened feces would float on the surface. Mothers tried to catch and conceal the excrement by putting them in washcloth to deposit, washing their hands with

71

soap later. The problem is that if a child had the runs, everyone in the bathhouse would smell the bad odor. The person in charge would have to chase everyone out of the *furo,* drain all of the water, scrub the walls and floor, and replace it with cold water. Should it happen at night, the *furo* would be closed for the night. The *water* would take too long to heat again.

Many felt that the price of the use the *furo* was too high; those who had no money to own a *furo* resorted to using a big pan (*oki*). After boiling the water over an open fire, the hot water would be poured into the *oki,* and then cold water added to attain the desired temperature. From the *oki,* one would scoop the water to wash their bodies. The problem was that the pan was too small to soak in.

Another problem with the *oki* system was the pecking order. The father of the family always took a bath first, the mother and smallest child next. The rest of the family then took turns. That meant that by the time the last of the family took a bath, there was not enough water. It was also cold and had to be re-boiled again.

As mentioned earlier, there were women in the camps who cooked and washed for their husbands and for single men. Many men came as single immigrants first. They observed the conditions of plantation life before they committed themselves to marriage. I heard reports that a thirteen year old had faked his age to come to Hawai'i. Life was unpleasant because men sorely missed girlfriends they left behind. Many asked them to come to the island, to live with them, where they later got married.

Many of my neighbors and friends sent letters and pictures to their parents requesting that a woman from Japan be their bride. If the couple did not know each other previously, many letters and pictures were sent back and forth. This was known as *shinpai* marriage (arranged marriage). The reason why this happened was because if the parents of the man knew or heard of a family who had a daughter of similar age, they requested her hand in marriage with their son. If this were agreeable, the woman's name would be placed in the man's family registry. The family filled out the necessary papers thereby releasing the woman to make the trip to Hawai'i. The marriage would take place after the woman's arrival. Not everyone could get married right away because some were under age. (Some had lied about their age when they came to Hawai'i.) I was seventeen when I arrived here in Hawai'i.

There was another type of marriage besides an arranged one. It was better known as a picture bride (*shaskin-kekkon*) marriage. A bride is selected from a picture of a man sent to the family. A lot of elderly men in desperation asked good-looking younger men for pictures of themselves that they could send back to Japan. Although devious, a youthful picture would make it easier for them to attain a bride. Younger and handsome men agreed to the proposition for a price. A go-between agency, for a price, also searched for a bride. The agency would show a picture of the man to the parents of the bride to be. If agreed upon, necessary documents were signed, and the woman, often ignorant of the trickery, would then travel to Hawai'i to get married.

With that in mind, possibilities of a successful marriage loomed heavy in the minds of Japanese. The traditional idea of divorce was totally unheard of in Japan. In most cases, the family would disown that family member in disgrace if one divorced in the old country.

The woman had everything to lose. First, she didn't have any first-hand knowledge of the conditions in Hawai'i. She did not know anything about Hawai'i, except in conversations with her parents. Second, she had nothing to do with the decision of marrying a person in Hawai'i. What ever the father decided had to be followed. In the Japanese household, father ruled. Third, she was leaving a place she had known all her life. In Japan, she was comfortable and accustomed to her every day life. She had family and friends there and was happy. She came to Hawai'i, a stranger in paradise.

She had so many doubts about her future in The Sandwich Isles. What were the living conditions like? What was the weather like? Where would she be living? And, most important of all, who was the man she was about to marry? Was he a kind man? A well learned man? A tall man? A handsomer man than the picture indicated? All of these questions bothered some women to a point that they requested to their fathers that they remain home. In all conditions, the father always had the last word.

It needs to be clarified that if the gentleman was honest and sent his own picture, everything worked out fine. If an elderly, short, or not-so-good looking gentleman sent a picture of another person who was young and handsome, the woman, upon arrival here in Hawai'i, would be totally shocked to see someone totally different waiting for her. Without any money to return home, she had no choice but to try and make the marriage work.

In the picture-bride marriage, there was always a go-between, either an agency or individual. Both in Hawai'i and Japan, the go-between worked together in finding a woman for the gentleman. The gentleman looking for a bride had to pay both sides lots of money.

Ads were used in Japan to lure women to marry a man from Hawai'i, and live a life of comfort and luxury on the plantations. Both the gentleman and the woman had to write a little history of themselves as part of the application.

The go-betweens in Japan decided on matching the couples based on both histories, nothing else. The go-between might decide that because they had similar histories they would make a fine match. On another day, the go-between might say that the intended couple should wed because their names sounded good together, and that made them compatible as husband and wife. Decisions were rarely based on love or personality.

Here is a little story I heard. Some of those who decided to meet their wives at the Sand Island Immigration Station and married there, found that place poorly managed. I overheard that because of the language barrier even brothers and sisters were married by mistake. At times, the intimate ceremony of marriage was done with insensitivity. Fifty couples were married at one time.

74

Because they were natives of Japan, many requested a Buddhist ceremony when exchanging vows. Instead, they were joined in holy matrimony, by exchanging Christian vows. It all depended if a Buddhist minister or priest was available at that time. The immigration station management was arrogant. Why would they have a priest there when they knew the couples were primarily Buddhist? Eventually, the situation was solved because of the many immigrants' complaints. Sand Island Immigration Station eventually hired Japanese and English interpreters to clear up the confusion.

In Japan, as it was in Hawai'i, many men believed that a woman's role in the family dictated that she obey the head of the household, the man. Sometimes, at all cost, this attitude allowed beatings and verbal abuse. The husband was, of course, the one who brought home all of the money. He worked hard for it so he felt he should get a little respect. Many men practiced this at home. Some were even proud of this practice. In ignorance, they bragged all over the camp, 'We are men!'

Not all picture bride or *shin-pai* marriages were pleasant. Because of the unpleasant conditions at work, many men used their wives to release frustrations. Their husbands abused some unfortunate women, especially after the male drank a lot. A number were beaten to near death and, in some cases, to death. Worst of all, these outdated notions were imported by the Japanese men. Why wouldn't they? They had seen it happen back in Japan where the mother would be beaten after the father got drunk.

Those who were constantly beaten had no place to go. Even if they did have a place to go, perhaps to a friend's house, the husbands would find them, drag them home, beat them, and verbally abuse them again. To conceal pain and verbal suffering, these women hid from the public eye: cuts, swelling, bruises and even scars, the results of previous beatings.

With these deceptions, the chances of a successful marriage dwindled. Many ended in divorce, due to the lack of love, the embarrassment of being seen in public with an old man, or the shame in the eyes of the families back in Japan. Wives wrote back to their parents and told them of the deception and lack of love for that person. These women could not return home to Japan after a divorce because of the disgrace to the families involved.

On the other side of the coin, many men failed to obtain a bride through go-betweens or the *shin-pai* system. Some tried year after year with futility to obtain a wife; they eventually gave up and remained single for the rest of their lives. A few ended up marrying formerly divorced women. The bright side was that the fortunate ended up finding a mate right here in Hawai'i.

I, too, sent a letter with a photo to my parents in Japan, requesting them to obtain a picture bride for me. I waited impatiently for a reply. After many exchanges of letters, I received one from my parents that a woman had been selected for me. She had been selected from the Shimazu household. She came from an adjacent prefecture, a place called Kosa-machi-Itoda, a farming community close to the mountains, no more then ten miles from where I once lived. Her father, like my father, raised rice and silk worms and tended a persimmon orchard. A persimmon is a seasonal fruit tree that grows in cold climate. I am familiar with two types. One is elongated and needs to be cured before eating. Another is flat and can be picked from the tree and eaten immediately like an apple.

My bride-to-be came from a town close to where I lived and grew up with her parents, a brother and sister in a well-to-do family. Her name was Koto Shimazu and she was born September 20, 1887. She was the same age as I was. A photograph enclosed in a letter pictured her as a very pretty woman. Because I was taller than most Japanese, some five feet, eight inches, she was amazed, as she was a mere five feet tall.

I guess Buddha was looking after me that day. I overheard that a couple was moving to a bigger house in a different camp. It was an opportunity to have a home of my own. I approached the couple to assure me that they were planning to move. They said that it was true.

The very next day, I made it a point to go to the main office of the sugar plantation where they handled housing, and explained my situation to the office personnel, although I had an apprehension from past experience that I would probably be turned down. After begging with the supervisor for a while, I realized that the person I was talking to had visited my residence a number of times. She happened to be the sister of the lady who served as my cook and laundress. She finally acknowledged who I was. I explained to her that I sent for a wife back in Japan, and she would be arriving as soon as she could complete the paperwork. I also told her that I couldn't possibly let my wife live in the same home with a couple of single men. With that, I was assigned another home in Camp Three. It's whom you know that sometimes helps.

Although it was no different than other homes in Camp Three, the new house was very special. It was my first. This is the home my wife and I could share and raise children. I was fortunate to have a home almost identical to the one that I was leaving.

The home was built on concrete blocks about a foot and a half off the ground. The walls were single wall construction (Tongue-Groove). The roof had roofing paper and thin shakes. The bedroom and parlor floors were wooden.

The kitchen was attached to the house with a dirt floor portion for making a fire pit to burn wood to cook meals. Fifty-five gallon drums cut in half with a hole cut totally around the barrel in the bottom and a hole cut on the side was used to burn wood. On top of the drum was a grill. The kitchen also had two benches, a rectangular table, and small sink with an old Bull Durham bag tied to the faucet.

There was no refrigerator. To keep things cold, blocks of ice were delivered to the camps and placed in a box with a lid that lasted for a week. The Japanese were so good at carpentry that carpenters created these iceboxes that were totally sealed with a cover. Even when the ice melted, there were no signs of leaks from the box.

As soon as the family moved out, I immediately began repairs on the house. Because I was a carpenter, I knew how to fix and repair homes. I even helped construct some of these homes. Repair was a simple task for me but this house had lots of needed work. Some of the wood on the walls, doors, portions of shingles on the roof, windows and floorboards had to be replaced because of termite damage. Wood needed to be exchanged where it became paper thin due to insect infestation.

Termites came with the importation of people to the islands. There are two types of termites. One is the flying termite that ate wood in the home like they had a daylong appetite. The second kind of termite is the ground termite. They traveled in hoards underground, and have a particularly voracious appetite, especially in hot weather. Ground termites could devour a home in days. Indications of ground termites are the telltale mounds of dirt along the wood of the home.

Finally after four months, my wife-to-be came from Japan. Because we were not married yet, she remained at a friend's house. We got married as soon as we could. Happily, we both got along very nicely.

The initial expression on her face told me that she didn't seem to care for the place with its red dust and different nationalities. She wasn't accustomed to some of her primary obstacles; she must have thought a lot about returning to the Japan that she had left. She assured me, however, that she would make the best of the situation and circumstances.

Life for her was very hard for a couple of months. She had to adjust to camp life by waking up early in the morning, by making my breakfast and lunch for the day, and, of course, adapting to my temperament; my likes and dislikes took some getting used to.

Not knowing anybody else did not help. Who were these strange people? They didn't look like Japanese. In fact, they have very dark skin. She later found out that they were Filipinos and that they all were very friendly.

She eventually got to know the Japanese women in the community and they became very good friends. They got along well because they all had shared experiences. They really helped her in transition by giving her the scoop of plantation life and the conditions they all had to face. Even in time of need, they helped her along. She eventually got used to living here in Hawai'i and in the camps in particular.

Our honeymoon consisted of moving into the home that I fixed while waiting for my bride. Since no one had any money to run off to spend a little private time together, we settled in our house to celebrate our marriage. Our renovated home was our honeymoon.

At first, my wife was paranoid about using the outhouse. There were occasions when she went to use the outhouse and someone else was on the toilet on the other side of the partition. She felt a lack of privacy. She neither liked the smell of the outhouse nor the creatures that lived within its confines. She never got used to it. Whenever she used the outhouse at night, she'd fearfully always insist that I go and guard the front door. I would have gone with her anyway, since I was concerned about her safety. We always took some kind of light whenever we went to use the bathroom.

Originally, candles were used for lighting. Oil lamps came later. Both made the houses look dim. Brighter kerosene lamps replaced earlier illumination. During night hours, it was very hard to read anything because of the flickering lights. Much later, electricity came into use.

Mail and Japanese newspapers were hand delivered by one or two mailmen that worked for the company. They carried a large sack of mail on their shoulders and delivered mail from house to house in the camps.

There were also vendors who delivered food to the camps but poor people ate anything and everything in order to survive. They purchased canned salmon, made salted codfish, or caught fish from the ocean or plantation ditches (imported to kill mosquitoes). If one was resourceful enough, one could make use of wild plants along the mountainside or various seaweeds readily available from the ocean.

Resourceful people even brought their talent from Japan and opened businesses from home. They made food items available to camp residents, using recipes from their homelands. They sold *tofu* (made of soy beans – in blocks), *mochi* (rice-steamed, mashed and made into round flat pieces with either *azuki* beans (small red beans cooked with sugar), plain manju (filling of *azuki* beans, Lima beans or mashed sweet potato). They also sold rolled *sushi* (rice flavored with vinegar, salt and sugar) placed on *nori* (flat sheets of seaweed imported from Japan) with added ingredients of carrots, thinly sliced in strips, and tuna cooked with sugar and *shoyu* (soy sauce), *kampyo* (dried squash), and fried eggs. Rolled with a small bamboo mat from one end to the other, the sushi was generally sold as a whole. After taking rolled *sushi* home, it would be cut into eight pieces and arranged on a plate for consumption. Another type of *sushi* sold was known as cone *sushi* made with *aburage* (fried *tofu*) and cut in triangles. The cones were filled with the same flavored rice as the rolled *sushi*, except the rice was mixed with grated carrots and thinly sliced green beans. Sometimes, the cone *sushi* filled half of the plate. Another food product was *saimin* (homemade noodles boiled and placed in a bowl, added with beef bones soup stock, green onions, and a piece of pork).

Besides selling food items, one cooked so well that they opened up their own restaurants. Other talented individuals cut residents' hair and sewed clothing for a fee. One in particular opened a tailor shop. A few opened fish markets and grocery stores.

These resourceful individuals started with little or no capital and a very big dream. These businesses started from the home, and, with a lot of hard work and perseverance, the entrepreneurs eventually opened their own specialty shops within the camp communities. Generally, stores were converted from a resident's home. The owner of the store lived close by or right next to the shop. In some cases, they lived behind of the store. Many, because of the popularity of the products they sold, became wealthy.

One of the many products sold was ham. Ham was hung in the kitchen where rats or insects would not get at it. It was covered with a cloth and, when a need for ham arose, the chunk would be cut piece by piece. Many a child was tempted to get a chair, climb up, and swipe a piece of ham. Hungry camp youngsters would resort to such tactics and hide to eat the ham. Eventually their parents identified the culprits by their greasy telltale signs. Oil stains would be visible on their shirts.

A lot of people spent their free time and money gambling with a Japanese card game called *hanafuda*. The explanation of the game would take pages and pages to explain. In time, some residents lost their hard earned money either by friendly games or games with professional gamblers who took advantage of the poor people. Some addicted players went so far as to borrow money that they had not yet earned. Eventually, American cards were introduced, and with the same results.

One of the bad traits brought from Japan was bootlegging. Homemade beer, hard whiskey (Japanese moonshine), and *sa-ke* (rice wine) were distilled somewhere on Maui and distributed in the camps. How they got the hops to make beer, I do not know, but, because of these vices, camp life became overwhelmed with sinful deeds. Some of the women went into the prostitution trade. For many single men, drinking and paid sex helped combat loneliness. I was fortunate to have self-control and only drank occasionally.

Although my job as a carpenter had many benefits for supporting a family, I realized that I wasn't making enough money to survive, let alone have any chance of returning to Japan a rich man. So, I decided to transfer to be a cane cutter in another department of the sugar plantation, where I'd be making much more money.

When I first began the job as a cane cutter in the fields, I was

81

amazed at the hard work of the railroad gang. The railroad gang laid tracks wherever the harvesting took place. After harvesting, the tracks were removed and located to another area.

Originally, horses were used to carry the manager to overlook the general operations of laborers in the cane fields. Horses, in later times, were used to carry fertilizer into the fields to help the growth of the sugar cane. They also carried poisons into cane fields to kill weeds." With this, he ended. He must have been tired. So, I said my good -byes and left.

I had to see my grandfather again. The next day I made it a point to do my chores quickly after returning home from school. I hurriedly made the fire for the *furo* and fed the chickens. Within an hour I had finished my jobs, and was on my bike heading to Spanish B Village, where my grandfather lived.

Japanese never go to visit a friend or a relative empty handed (tradition). They always take something, generally food. My mother knew that I was going to visit my grandfather, so she gave me a bottle of *tsukemono* (pickled vegetables) to offer as a gift.

I saw my grandfather sitting on the porch, as if he was waiting for me. There were no telephones then. How could he know that I was coming to see him at this time? Again this funny feeling came over me.... a warm feeling, as if he was waiting for me.

I gave him the package and told him, "I'm sorry that I couldn't come yesterday. I had to go and pick *kiawe* beans with my father. By the afternoon, I was so tired, that I didn't have the energy to go anywhere." After apologizing, I sat next to him.

After a short pause, my grandfather continued with his experience; "After my children grew up and left the house after getting married, I was promoted to a supervisor. At that time, things were changing at the sugar plantations. Administrators finally came to realize that Japanese laborers could be trusted as supervisors. Of course, my stature was an added help. I was lucky because I had a good boss, who helped promote me by giving excellent recommendations to upper management.

Because Camp Three at that time was dwindling in population, remaining residents were asked to move and consolidate into other camps. Each camp member was assigned another home at another village. It was really a sad time for both your grandmother and me. We had to part with the people we had known for such a long time.

For a while, we tried to stay in touch with former camp members. After months went by, we drifted farther and farther apart. When we finally saw each other, we found that we had little in common. There was only small talk, hellos, and good-byes. We were shocked to find out that someone we had known had passed away. 'How is your husband?' 'Oh, he died a month ago.' We were totally speechless, fondly remembering those people who had once been part of our lives."

At this point, grandfather told me about everything he could remember. "You must hear your mother's side of the story and what she went through. She might repeat some of the stories I mentioned to you already, but she might also give you a different viewpoint of some of the stories. Remember, each person sees things, especially the past in different ways." This is how my grandfather ended his story. With that, he stopped.

I've had many conversations with my grandfather. What you read up till now is a combination of stories I put together from conversations between my grandfather and me.

A few afternoons later, I would visit my grandfather to try and get more information from him about his past. Sometimes, my oldest uncle would answer some of the questions my grandfather forgot to tell. In most cases, he would answer the question but eventually ramble on about the past. I remember that a couple of times I had him repeat his answer because he had gotten emotional and talked too fast for me to write the stories down.

As I began to leave, he said to me, "Do you understand everything that I've told you, Donald?" That was the last time he spoke to me about the *Issei* Generation.

The sun was setting so I thanked him for sharing all the details, the stories, and its conclusion. I had to hurry home or I would miss dinner. That night, after reviewing all the notes I had taken, the one thing that stood out the most was the suffering and hardships the immigrants had to go through. I cried that night thinking how people can be so cruel in this world. I thought of how nice this world was, until today. Today, I found out that there are persons who take advantage of other people. I found out, today, that some make this world more unpleasant for those who are already suffering. I found out today that the world itself is okay, but it's these uncaring people that make this world unpleasant.

NISEI GENERATION
Chapter Three

My mother, who came from the first generation born here in Hawai'i, went through a lot of trials and tribulations as she grew up. She knew about the struggles her father and mother went through. She, because of the situation, rebelled by trying to be better in her own way.

It was easy to get the information of her earlier life since I lived with her. I made sure that I wrote down everything she told me. Some of her experiences were similar to my grandfather's, but this is my mother's exclusive story.

"I was born on July 16, 1922. I was the fifth and youngest daughter, second to the last child of eight children. I came from a poor family, even though my father, in later life, became a plantation supervisor.

Because they were poor, my parents raised their own pigs, chickens, rabbits, and vegetables in the garden. The pigpens were generally away from the camps and down wind. When the wind would shift in the opposite direction, everyone could smell the foul order of the sties.

As I grew older, I carried two five-gallon cans attached on each side of a wooden stick with wires. Every day after school, I went around the camp collecting slop. Everyone had five gallons, not often full, of peeled and rotten vegetables or fruits saved for the pig farmers. These cans were left hanging outside the homes. We filled and carried the five-gallon cans at least a hundred yards to the pigpens. Pigs would eagerly wait for me. While they were eating, I would pet the backs of the animals. One of them was exceptionally friendly. That pig had white, orange, black and brown colors. I called him the obvious – Colorful.

One day, as I was collecting slop for the pigs to eat, I noticed that Colorful was missing. I finished feeding the pigs and rushed home to ask my father what happened to the animal. To my horror, my father had killed him and was about ready to shave off his hairs. I was so mad at him that I picked up the first thing I could find and threw that object as far as I could. I don't know what I threw that day but it sure flew far. By the way, I refused to eat a single piece of Colorful.

We wouldn't keep more than five pigs at a time. Every time one of them was born, my father would slaughter the oldest male pig. Colorful was slaughtered shortly after a new pig was born. Many of the neighbors kept up to fifteen at a time. Of course, the more one kept, the harder they needed work; so more slop would have to be collected.

Many camps had a general store that sold all sorts of things. If there wasn't one in the camp, then there was always one close by. Those of us from Camp Three were very lucky because we had a number of stores along the main road.

We had the Sam Sato store that sold general merchandise. It carried basic needs such as vegetables, canned goods, meats, candies, as well as many of the hardware items that the camp people used in their homes.

Kitagawa Service Station was situated next to Sam Sato's. Those who could afford a car bought gas and had their cars repaired at the service station. Kitagawa's originally started as a bicycle shop, and then later became a complete service station.

There was also a photographer. He took pictures of young gentlemen who needed them to show to their picture brides. At that time, he made lots of money. Thereafter, he primarily took wedding pictures and family photos.

Matsui Fish Market stood across and on the corner of the main road in a section called Upper Camp Three. They originally sold fish from their home, then, later, moved their business to that corner location because of supply and demand.

Many peddlers came to our camp to sell merchandise twice a

86

week. Local and imported items from Japan were sold. They included clothing, food, and household wares.

Before refrigerators there were iceboxes. The wooden containers were made by Japanese carpenters with extraordinary skills. A refrigerated container with a cover was a tight fitted wooden box that never leaked. These containers were so well made that a twenty-five pound block of ice would take more than a week to melt. Twice a week, Maui Soda & Ice Works would deliver ice, if needed. Residents would pay for the block of ice upon arrival.

With the importation of vegetable seeds from Japan, those who tended gardens raised lettuce, green onions, round onions, eggplants, string beans, pumpkins (*bo-bula* or *kabocha*), Japanese radishes (*daikon*), burdocks (*gobo*) and *shiso* (both green or red leaves-used for pickling), tomatoes, squashes, and many more vegetables.

The vegetables planted in the gardens were extensively used in cooking or pickling. Eggplants, round onions, and cabbages were some of the items used. Japanese radishes and there tops were used to make *daikon* by the barrel for future consumption. Poor families ate only *gohan* (rice) and pickled vegetables for breakfast, lunch, and dinner.

Besides raising vegetables in the garden for friends and neighbors, residents also raised them in the cane fields. In later plantation years, the employees who watered the cane fields raised these vegetables. It was a very common practice for workers to take advantage of the cane fields to supplement their garden. Sweet potato, squash and small bitter melon (seeds imported from Philippines), and pumpkin, were among the other vegetables planted in the fields.

Chicken or pigs were raised by families and shared with relatives, friends, and neighbors. Eaten sparingly, they helped workers get their protein. Fish, another rare commodity, was eaten only when caught by family, given by relatives, friends or sold at the store. Meat was bought at the stores or from peddlers selling in the camp from their wagons. Every so often, a peddler would stop at a certain place in the camp. There the people would gather to buy their meats and an occasional treat, like candy, for the children.

Grammar school was no more than a half-mile away. After we got to the main road, we walked about a hundred yards to the down hill road that was bordered to its right with elephant ear trees (huge trees with pods that looked like elephant ears with beans inside). Farther down the road were three Portuguese family homes and, to the left, a view of Camp One. Even farther beyond that was Spreckelsville School, kindergarten to eighth grade.

At the two-way road, to the right, was Camp Two where the Japanese School was situated. It was about a half mile from Spreckelsville School.

The left of the two-way road led to Camp One. In the middle of the camp was a general store. The opposite side of the main road was Camp One with homes occupied by Portuguese families. Consequently, this area was known as Portuguese Camp; it included a movie theater within its confines.

There was a four way stop with signs at the end of the road which headed toward the ocean. Straight ahead, near the shoreline, was Stable Camp that was occupied by the rich.

When drivers turned right on this road, they'd approach the English-only school – Kaunoa – about a third of a mile down. This is where the well-to-do children received their education. What's really amusing is that, after the eighth grade, all these privileged students had to attend regular schools like everyone else.

A right turn on the road led one to Pa`ia Town, some three to four miles north. There was nothing really special that Pa`ia had to offer to immigrants. They rarely went there except to visit friends or relatives.

After English School ended, we walked a half-mile to Camp Two to attend Japanese School at the outskirts of this town, near the cemetery. Many of our young Japanese were trapped between Japanese school and English School. My parents felt obligated to Japanese traditions. They insisted that we attend *Jo-Goko* (Japanese school) and finish! Girls, especially, were forced to learn the Japanese language. Because I was forced to study Japanese, I'd pretend to read the Japanese book, but within it, hid the English book.

All young people of our generation believed that the only way out of plantation life was through American ideas taught in public schools. Yet, due to lack of money, many first-born Japanese males who attended public schools had to quit school at an early age to work at the plantations.

Our parents insisted that our hopes would be dashed without proper education; there would be no reward of a prosperous future life. Some of the youth in the family had opportunities to finish high school. A number of men volunteered to join the army to earn the G.I. Bill so they could attend college after their military obligation. Some women who finished high school went on to college, but many could not.

After my sophomore year in high school, I decided to quit formal education because of pressure my parents put on me to attend Jo-Goko. I ran away to a relative's home on Oʻahu. My parents found out where I was, so they later retrieved me and brought me back to Maui. I never returned to school, Japanese or American.

Many of the girls who were no older than thirteen and who didn't have good grades in school, were told to quit school and worked in the cane fields to earn extra money. The majority of them felt robbed of their teen years. Men of the household were favored and paid more than women.

Many girls, at the ripe age of nineteen, were *shin-pai* (promised to a gentleman by her parents) and married off. Both parents agreed to the marriage. Money was often exchanged between both parents but mostly from the boys' father and mother. More often than not, the boy and girl had fallen in love before the actual marriage. Parents just wanted to get their girls married so they wouldn't have to support them.

Many of the girls already knew their mates because they came from the same camp or from nearby camps. Sometimes the *shin-pai* man was not to the liking of the girl. Some men were up in age, unattractive, or shorter than the females.

These women hated the idea of *shin-pai* marriage. They wanted the freedom of marrying a man of their choice, often their boyfriend. They also disliked forced marriages because they felt that they were too young to get married.

Let me tell you a story of one of these *shin-pai* marriages. I met a girl while attending English School and Japanese School. She was my age, and we became good friends. In fact, she and I hung out a lot. I often slept at her house and, in return, she would *tomaru* (sleep over) at mine. Those times were good times. We would talk into the wee hours of the morning about school, what we planned to do in later life, about ourselves, and, of course, about boys.

On one of her visits to my house, she informed me that her parents got her involved in *shin-pai* marriage. She asked her parents not to go ahead with it. They told her that they were very poor and could put the money to good use. Also if she left to live with the man, they would have one less mouth to feed. She had no choice in the matter. What a Japanese father said was the law of the house.

A couple of months later, she was forced to marry. She packed up her things and went to live with the gentleman. I didn't hear from her for a year. I often wondered what had happened to her.

Then, one rainy night, as I was about to go to sleep, I heard a tapping. At first, I thought it was rain falling on metal. Then the tapping became louder. I suddenly realized that the noise was coming from my window. It was a hand. I raised the window and, to my surprise, it was my old girlfriend dressed in a robe, soaking wet, standing outside in the falling, chilly rain. I grabbed her by both hands and yanked her in through the window.

She was on the verge of crying and told me that the past year had been miserable. 'Remember, I told you that I was involved in a *shin-pai* marriage? Well, a couple of months later, I was told to go and live with the man I didn't love. We had a hastened marriage ceremony. I wanted to invite friends, but I was denied. I was told that there wasn't enough money to have a big party. So the only people present were his parents and mine. As soon as both parents left that night from our home, the gentleman ripped off my dress, bra, and panties. He carried me into the bedroom and forced himself on me. At first, I thought it was a game of sorts. When he entered me, I felt this pain between my legs, pain I never felt before. He was on me for quite a while. He was truly enjoying the experience, while I cried through the whole thing. When he was satisfied, he got off of me. I just lay there in shock for a few minutes. When I got up, I noticed lots of blood on the bed. I also felt pain as I walked to the basin to wash myself off. I felt as though he had ripped my insides, that he had put his hand inside and torn out whatever he wanted to take, including my dignity.

I've had conversations with other girls about sex. Most liked it. My mother and I had a discussion about it. She told me that if you liked the guy, then sex is enjoyable. Believe me, this sex was painful.

The following night, the same thing happened. This time, I tried to fight him off. Instead, he slapped me across my face as hard as he could. I tasted blood in my mouth, like the first time I got hit in a schoolyard fight. He yelled at me that he was the man of the house, and that I had to listen and obey whenever he demanded. He gave the same speech whenever he wanted sex.

As time went by, the beatings got worse. After slapping me the first time, he progressed to punch me. I lost a couple of teeth in the process. After a while, he hit me so hard that I passed out. When I awoke, I was naked in bed.

When I said things that he didn't like, he'd also beat me. He'd punch my stomach so hard that I had a difficult time eating for a

91

while. He'd even punch me on my chest. I had such shallow breathing that I honestly wished I would die. I never enjoyed my life when I was living at his house. I honestly believe that my ribs are broken now. When you grabbed both of my hands to pull me through the window, I thought that I was going to pass out from the pain. I'd look so battered that he never invited anyone over nor did he let me leave the house.

One evening my mother came to visit. I hadn't talked to her since I had gotten married; she was worried. She wanted to know how I was getting along with my marriage. In fact, the brute had locked me in the bedroom and ordered me to be quiet while he answered the door. He pretended all was well and never let her in.

That evening he came home drunk. As soon as he came through the door, he went straight to the bed and fell asleep. I immediately left the house, unconcerned about what I was wearing. I didn't care. I went running to my parents' home.

Upon arriving there, I confronted my father and my mother. I lifted up my clothes and showed them my many welts, black and blue bruises, and scars that were inflicted by my husband. They stared at me without feeling and insisted that I was married to him, and that I had to obey him. They told me that it was my fault and that I deserved the beatings. Before I left my parents, I asked them if they still had the money that was given to them from the *shin-pai* marriage. I wanted a part of it. I would take the money and run away. My father told me that the money was gone. After pressing the issue, he finally admitted that he had taken all of the money and gambled it away.

I felt so desperate and frustrated; I didn't know who to turn to or where to go. Then I remembered you and the good times we had together, the times when we would talk for hours and hours. I felt that maybe you and I could talk about the good times together, again.'

I sensed in her voice the need of a friend. 'I was so shocked and frustrated that I had only one choice-to come and see you, my friend.'

At one point, she lifted up her clothes and showed me the welts, bruises, and scars that she had shown her parents. I especially remember the bruises more because they were all over her body. Some of the scars were long. The sight of her abused body made me feel sorry for her. I had to do something so I told her she could stay here for the night. I promised her that we would talk to my father in the morning and see what he had to say.

The following morning when I woke, she was gone. I asked my parents if they had seen her. They said no.

I later found out that she had decided to take her parents advice and return home. Always imbedded in her mind was this feeling of loyalty to her parents. Who else could she trust but the very people that brought her up? She had so much devotion for her parents that she took that loyalty to the grave.

When I found out later that she had died, I immediately asked around to find out what happened. One of my relatives told me that when she returned home, her   husband, the abuser, was waiting for her. As soon as she entered the door, he shoved her around and hit her numerous times all over her body. In retaliation, she ran to the kitchen, grabbed a knife, and stabbed herself repeatedly in the stomach. I guessed that she felt that it was better to die than to receive painful beatings day after day. He no longer had power over her.

I could understand her desperation after seeing all the marks on her body. I might have done the same thing. However, I definitely would not have gone back to the house but would have found a better way to leave this earth with honor. And yet, she probably wanted her husband to see what she was going to do. Enough is enough; what else could happen to a deceased daughter?

I asked when the funeral would be because I wanted to attend. I was told that there wasn't going to be one. Because the parents were so poor, they would merely wrap her body in a sheet and place it in a grave the next day with no funeral service. That was that.

How could they do such a thing? That was their daughter who gave up her life for her parents because she had so much loyalty and love for them. When they refused her the night she ran to them, they lost a daughter. What else could I say?

I asked a *Bon-san* (Japanese minister) to accompany me to the gravesite the following morning. There was no one there. The only evidence of her life on earth was a stick in the ground with her name on it. The minister was so shocked that he promised to replace the insignificant post with something more fitting. After the minister conducted a more complete service for my friend, we both left. I told the minister that I didn't have any money to give him. He told me that money was not the issue during times like this. 'You asked me to come to the grave with you because you felt that your friend deserved more that what her parents gave her, and you are right. I came with you to the grave with my heart.'

True to his word, the next time I visited her grave to decorate it with some flowers and say a little prayer, the minister had placed a stone marker there with her name, date of birth, and the date of her death.

The night she came to visit me she did not ask for help at all. All she wanted was a friend to talk to, a way of reliving a more memorable past, if only for a brief period… a moment in time when things were beautiful, innocent, and happy.

There were many stories like those of my friend throughout plantation life. Like her, some died, while others survived the ordeal by divorcing their husbands. Some who survived still carry the scars of the past. For those, there were no happy endings. Yet, for some, the results included a very happy life with their partners.

Besides death, illness was experienced in the camps. I have seen many people die of various illnesses. Sometimes simple colds led to pneumonia, and pneumonia to death. There wasn't a cure for simple illnesses in the early years.

There weren't any medicines a sick patient could take. Pu'unene Hospital was the only hospital we could go to, and it provided only limited care. To receive any care, residents of my camp had to travel about three miles to the hospital. When we didn't have transportation, we walked there, no matter how sick we were.

Unfairness caused Japanese inter-family frictions. It resulted in hatreds that transcended those times. In my family, one of the older girls had a chance to go to sewing school. The rest were married off through *shin-pai* marriages.

Women suffered from hard work and we did not receive our just rewards that we rightly deserved for all the pain we endured during the years. These injustices inflamed hates that would not go away. I cry when I talk about those times today. And, saddest of all, many took their disenchanted lives and secret sufferings to their graves.

The first-born son, according to Japanese tradition, receives everything from his parents. The first son was expected to carry on the name of the family and was expected to take care of his parents during their declining years. As a result, the first son, my oldest brother, was the privileged one who owned a car.

He was devoted to his religion and would pick up those of his faith and drive them to church every Sunday. Oddly enough, my brother was a Baptist, my father, a Buddhist. I couldn't understand how my father tolerated this.

As time passed, my sisters and younger brothers eventually married and moved out of the house. One of my younger brothers joined the army and later got married. All of us were married through *shin-pai*.

When I first heard about my marriage, I was very apprehensive. The first thing that came to my mind was the memory of my friend with the abusive husband. I pleaded with my father to no avail. I also asked my mother to talk to my father. Again, to no avail. I had no recourse but to marry your father.

I got married to your father, the eldest son, a week before World War Two broke out. The bombing of Pearl Harbor started the whole thing between the Japanese Imperial Government and the United States of America.

I moved into a house across from his mother's house. His mother's name was Mizu. His father, Otokichi, died many years before I arrived there. One night, in 1937, he walked a couple of houses down to drink with his friend. He had a heart attack, fell to the sidewalk, and never recovered. I also heard that my husband's younger brother died at a very young age.

Two sons lived in your grandmother's house. The youngest attended school; the middle son worked for the sugar plantation. I was not accustomed to the ways of your father's family. Whatever your father earned was given to his mother. Your grandmother bought all the food. In order to save money, she bought the same items over and over because they were cheap. There are only so many things a person can make with the same foods before the dish is repeated over and over again. I was sick of eating the same meals. Worst than that, whenever my mother-in-law got mad and decided not to have dinner with us, we had to deliver the dinner to her.

While living with your father's family, I was never given any money to purchase something of personal use that I had seen in the store. My husband knew about their stinginess but never did anything to change it.

The middle brother, who was working at that time, promised me that he would give whatever he could. He eventually not only gave us money to buy food, but he also gave us fish that he caught from the ocean.

After dinner, this brother would visit his friend's house. He had a good friend who sold wood for A&B Commercial Company in the wood department so he knew the kinds of material needed to build a boat. He was a boat owner himself, made them, and sold them to fishermen.

He believed that if a boat was built well and cared for properly, then it could last for forty years or more. If any of the boats he sold needed repairs later, he would gladly re-fix it for free. Of course, that rarely happened. In fact, most people who came to his shop at the back of the house commented about how long their boat had lasted.

Once in a while, my brother-in-law would help his friend fix someone's boat engine. They never charged anything for their labor if that person could find the specific parts of an engine. The very next night, that person would be at the shop with the needed part.

On the weekends, he and my brother-in-law went fishing together and brought home a lot. They brought home *mahi-mahi* (dolphin fish), *paka* (grey in color and long), *onaga* (red in color and long), and my favorite fish – *aku* or *ahi*. *Aku* or *ahi* can be filleted and made into *sashimi*. I used to fry the bones and the head to a crisp and eat the remaining meat with *shoyu* and rice.

During some calm nights, they would go fishing for *opelu* (shiny silvery-round fish*)*, *akule* (shiny silvery-flat fish), and sometimes they netted *ika* (squid). They would often catch so much fish that they had to sell them to the markets, residents, or, with no buyers, give it to anyone who would take it.

One day, his best friend died suddenly of a stroke. My brother-in-law had a very hard time coping with the tragedy. He told us not to bother with him for a while. Even when he came to the dinner table, he barely ate or said anything. As time went by, he came out of it, resigned to the reality that when the time comes and your number is called, it's time to leave this world and go to your maker.

As soon as I arrived at Camp Four, housewives welcomed me to Pu'unene camp life, one different from my past existence. One conversation comes to mind. A lady who had been there for quite a while came to welcome me to the camp. She was quite old;

97

spoke softly, and always smiled. She and I got into a very long conversation about the history of the camp.

She told me that Camp Four was originally divided into two Chinese camps within a camp – Sam Sing and *Pa-ke* Camp *(Pake-* Hawaiian for Chinese). Some Chinese originally owned Camp Four Store, and then called Sam Sing Store. They imported many items from their homeland. Because there were more Chinese residents in the camp than any other nationality, the shelves were filled with Chinese items. Later, a Filipino family owned the store.

There was a community *furo* at this Chinese camp that was constructed by plantation workers and paid for by the Hawaiian Commercial & Sugar Company (notice the change in name). Located in the middle of the camp, the community *furo* was run by a resident designee. Generally, it was a woman who had the time to heat the *furo*, maintain cleaning, supply wash towels, which she also washed, replace soap, and collect fees to use the *furo*. The company furnished all the supplies. All she had to do was to go to the store and buy what she needed for the *furo* and charge the items to the company.

A *tofu* store, candy and pastry store, a barbershop, and a pay phone were located at the front porch of the house near the *furo*. The person in that house was selected by the camp to be the camp manager.

There were two flagpoles in the middle of the camp. One of the flagpoles was of significance to the Japanese community. On April 29th of each year, the Japanese flag was flown for the sole purpose of celebrating the emperor's birthday. Flying the flag signified attachment to their homeland. Individuals still had hopes of returning to Japan as very wealthy men.

Sam Sing Camp homes were originally built with two bedrooms, a living room, and a kitchen, separated from the house. The reasoning behind this was because pits had to be dug into the floor where wood would be burned to cook daily meals. Because wood was burned there, the kitchen had to be kept separate from the house in case of fire.

An open fire was used first. Later, kitchens converted to wood stoves made of cast iron, with wood still supplied by the company. Women had the tedious job of cooking all of the meals. The kitchen was later attached to the house with an electric or kerosene stove. Kerosene furnished by the company was delivered to the homes in large glass bottles, for a monthly charge. Kerosene stoves were much safer that burning wood, such as *kiawe*. Burning pieces of *kiawe* wood could spark, fly and sometimes cause a fire.

Clothing worn by field workers in the cane fields turned black from the soot of burned cane. Clothing had to be boiled in five-gallon cans on the kitchen stove to remove most of the soot. The remainder of the soot left after boiling had to be hand scrubbed with a *ha-ke* (Japanese brush), Fels-Naphtha (soap), and cold water. Denim was used extensively due to the long wear of the fabric. I made my own panties with empty rice bags because I didn't have the money.

Every day at precisely eleven o'clock, Pu'unene Dairy came to the cane fields selling cold milk and hamburgers to the workers. Afraid of carrying and losing their money when they worked, employees who had money often charged their purchases using *Bango* Numbers (Identification numbers) to purchase hamburgers and milk from the dairy.

Gathering around a circle, laborers brought out their *kau-kau* tins from their rice bags. Those who bought food also made a circle. They would talk about anything and everything they could think of.

As time went by, trains on tracks transported workers and cane to the mill. Then the locomotives were permanently removed and replaced by trucks. All workers who worked in the fields were given a designated spot to wait for the plantation trucks to take them to their fields.

With ingenuity, the immigrants devised a bootleg drink called swipe. Because of its availability and low cost, many Japanese immigrants drank the potent alcohol every night. Sadly, a lot of the men went home drunk and beat their wives so badly that women were scarred for life. Without knowing what happened the night before, wives begged their husbands not to drink before coming home. Some ruined their lives by their nightly addiction. They spent so much money on drinking swipe that, at the end of the month, they had no money to pay their bills.

That was the bad, now the good. There were those who used swipe for medicinal purposes. People used the intoxicant for coughs and pains, which, of course, never went away. People used swipe for parties on special occasions and weekends. Sadly, women also drank swipe to relieve their pain. Some of them drank so much that they went home to beat up their husband. But these were rare cases. Some of these women were so frustrated that they felt they had to beat up somebody. Why not their husbands? Unusual as it may seem, husband beating does happen. Perhaps the women who got beat up should have hired these crude women to beat up their husbands, to show them how bad it hurt. Everything was hush-hush, so nothing was discussed in public.

Children observed many of the beatings. These left everlasting memories of sorrow for their mother and a feeling of contempt for their father. This period of unhappiness, until today, is very visible on their faces. Each account of beatings was enough to be etched in every individual that had witnessed such an act. Accounts included picking up teeth from floor that had been dislodged from the punching, wiping up a mother's blood from the floor or dining table, or, worst of all, listening to the cries of a mom at night, moaning from the blows inflicted day after day.

After the last story, the woman said good-byes and left. I remember to this day the last words she said to me before leaving. 'I told you about the history of Camp Four and all of the stories that I remembered. One of these days, someone will be asking you about the history of Camp Four.' True to form, someone did eventually ask me about its history.

After many get-togethers, she never talked about Camp Four. A couple of months after our last get-together, I wondered what had happened to her. We had gotten close. She'd come to my house or I'd go over to hers on a weekly basis.

One day, I saw a friend of hers of the same age whom she talked a lot about. She told me that my friend was in the hospital fighting a disease. The doctor didn't know anything about *gung* (cancer). My friend kept on throwing up blood. It was so bad that she needed a transfusion every few days.

As soon as I found out she was sick, I made it a point to visit her. I went to see her a few times, always bringing something to eat. On one of our meetings, I had this funny feeling that it would be my final visit. Upon seeing her, I felt a difference between her and me, an intuition that we were never going to speak again. I wanted to cry, but I held back my tears for her. When I grabbed her hands, the feeling of death entered my mind; an emotion I never felt before.

I found out from her friend that she had passed away the previous night. She told me that she was present when her friend died. She also said that our common friend felt peace when she grabbed her hand. She was filled with so much consolation that she was not afraid to die.

I went home and cried my heart out. From the very first time that we met, I felt a bond that could never be taken away. Yet, that bond changed me with her death. From that day on, I was afraid to be close to anyone. I felt that if I got intimate with someone like her, the tragedy would repeat itself.

I did go to her funeral a few days after she died. It seems like the whole camp was there. Another person I did not immediately recognize was also there. Remember the minister who did the service for my other good friend? He looked much older than the last time I saw him at my abused friend's gravesite. His hair had receded and the remainder graying. He whispered to me, `Here we go again.' I heartily agreed.

101

After many years of plantation life, I read, heard and I noticed the gradual change of working conditions. During those years, workers became more knowledgeable about how to earn money quickly. Under the *uku pau* system, the harder and faster the laborer worked, the sooner the job was finished. When one was finished with his daily tasks, he could go home earlier.

Short and long term contracts were also implemented. Under the short-term contract, workers were paid according to the work completed. Under the long- term contract, the plantation would plant sugar cane and do the initial watering. From then on, a dozen or more men would take care of about fifty-to-one hundred acres of cane fields until maturity. Pay would be determined by the amount of sugar tonnage produced within the fields.

It was apparent for a very long time that a go-between was needed to help the working relationships between the laborer and the sugar plantations. The go-between would help in soothing laborer tensions, handling mistreatments, interpreting unfamiliar rules set by the sugar plantations, inspecting cramped quarters, and citing unsanitary conditions.

One such go-between was named to the Bureau of Inspection of Japanese Immigrants. With the annual salary exceeding four times the salary of a plantation worker, this man unfortunately, from the very beginning, sided with the sugar plantations. He berated and yelled at workers who visited his office complaining of working conditions. He often lied to immigrant workers and told them that they were under contract and that such treatment was part of their contract. He also told his own workers that the laborers were no more than ignorant individuals. It is rumored that he died at the hands of an immigrant worker.

The mistreatment of laborers was not isolated to Maui. Both the Japanese Federation of Labor and the Filipino Labor Union decided to go on strike on O'ahu in 1920. In retaliation, eviction notices were issued to the plantation protesters involved. They had an option of returning to work or leaving the plantation homes in three days. Thirty-six hours elapsed. Thirty O'ahu families defied the plantation and remained in their homes. They were later evicted. The remaining families who decided to go on strike left their homes and sought shelter with families, friends, churches, halls, or rented low-income apartments.

The rest of the islands did not participate in the strike. They assisted those on strike by sending food, clothing, money, and whatever they could spare. Many of the Japanese laborers did not return to their jobs after the strike. During the strike, many found other jobs that paid more and were less strenuous. Then, three months after the strike, HSPA (Hawaii Sugar Planters Association) trustees raised wages by fifty cents a month and promised bonuses on a month-to-month basis. The planters association also offered social, welfare, and recreational programs to plantation workers on O'ahu, yet the laborers still did not return to their jobs.

During the strike, two significant events occurred. First, a flu epidemic struck an estimated 1,056 Japanese and 1,440 Filipinos and other nationalities. Of the 1,056 infected Japanese, 55 died. Second, the plantations hired Chinese, Koreans, and Puerto Ricans to replace the striking Filipino and Japanese laborers. These strike breakers, better known as scabs, worked at an increased salary of three dollars a day. This was four times the amount the Japanese laborers were receiving and twice the minimum pay that Japanese Federation of Labor was demanding.

Because they paid laborers low wages, sugar plantations netted gigantic annual profits that averaged around twenty-two million dollars a year. Accordingly, a male Japanese laborer in his prime age was paid equal to the lowest paid female on the continental United States.

As time went by, Japanese laborers received little more than eighteen dollars a month, while Portuguese or Puerto Rican workers, doing exactly the same job, were paid more than twenty dollars a month (non- *luna* or supervisor). To add insult to injury, these Japanese laborers lived in single cottages (not homes). Even with a difference of pay, Japanese workers tried to make the best of the situation.

Camp Four and a few other camps were extremely fortunate since their drinking water came from a place called Nahiku, where immigrants had dug a ditch and tunnels that channeled water into pipes that went through a filtration system. It transported water from a place that rained a lot to our camps. The water system was a miraculous accomplishment. Japanese immigrants dug approximately more than forty miles of ditches and tunnels, six feet high and eight feet wide. Those ditches can be still seen along the road to Nahiku in East Maui.

With the water from Nahiku, HC&S created a seven-stage filtration system. Water flowed from one tank to another until all seven stages were completed. Each tank contained sand that was used to filter the water. By the seventh tank, the water became crystal clear. Although no chemicals were used to kill bacteria in the water, the water was far superior to the drinking water in some of the camps.

As I said earlier, I got married to your father one week before a catastrophe that would change the lives of Japanese residents. On that Sunday morning, December 7, 1941, a resident yelling from the top of his lungs shattered the quiet of the camp, `Pearl Harbor has been attacked!' Many ran outside still in their nightclothes or kimonos, shocked to hear such news. Many wept as they returned to their homes, trying to sort out the situation to the best of their knowledge.

Because war was declared on Japan by the United States, no one knew about the future of Hawai'i nor the future of their homeland. No one knew the impact the war would have on each individual, especially members of the Japanese community. Remember, Japan started this war. This left the Japanese communities in an awkward situation. For one thing, it was not the fault of the Japanese in Hawai'i. Did Japan intend to invade the other islands of Hawai'i? What's going to happen to those of us of Japanese descent? All of these questions raced through the minds of Japanese throughout Hawai'i.

The *Issei* generation still believed that they would return to Japan, more financially stable, until this terrible thing happened.

104

They just couldn't believe that Japan had done such a horrific thing.

The *Nisei* Generation believed in their minds that they were Americans first and Japanese second. There was no doubt in their minds to which they were loyal. Even though they had families and relatives back in Japan, their allegiance rested on a place they had lived all their lives – the Territory of Hawai'i and the United States.

Many rules were placed in effect during the war. Everyone was required to carry and wear a gas mask. Whenever sirens would go off, gas masks went on. Wherever I went, I had to carry one.

Curfew was imposed so no one could go out at night after eight. Sirens went off at eight o'clock precisely. Blackouts were enforced throughout the camps. During blackouts, no lights could be turned on after the sound of the sirens, and windows had to be covered with a dark material.

If lights were seen by the Military Camp Police night patrol, the enforcers would knock on our door and demand that the lights be shut off. Because I had to get up in the early morning to make lunches, I used a flashlight to cook. I was very careful not to shine it at the window.

Before the war, there was a dirt road in the middle of the camp. During the war, the road was paved so that military vehicles could enforce blackouts in the camps.

Plantation trucks were used for emergencies. Families had to find and notify a truck driver to pick up the sick or injured who needed transportation to the hospital.

At the beginning of the war, with help of *Nisei* contacts, the Army Counter Espionage Section, Navy Intelligence, local Federal Bureau of Investigation, and the Maui Police Department arrested official representatives of the Japanese government. Among those Japanese considered dangerous, and therefore arrested, included: Shinto priests, Buddhist ministers, Japanese

105

language schoolteachers, *Issei* and *Nisei* Community leaders, and college educated men and women.

The police and FBI came and handcuffed educated Japanese people at all times of the day and night and hauled them away like a criminals. They would drag them out of the house, the innocent person yelling, "What did I do wrong?"

Those arrested on Maui were taken to Ha'iku Internment Camp. They were later sent to Sand Island Detention Center or to Camp Honoliuli on O'ahu. Still others were shipped off to war relocation camps throughout the United States. Wives of internees suffered without any income from their absent husbands. Without the help from the federal government, many wives had to work in the cane fields to provide income for the rest of the family. Expectant mothers had even harder times. Many worked while pregnant, standing on their feet all day.

Internees at Sand Island Detention Center were treated like criminals and/or prisoners of war. The internees slept through rain and wind in tents with dirt floors.

Many of the U.S. mainland internees were forced to abandon their farms, businesses, schools, and high paying jobs because of incarceration. They were thrown in internment camps in the desert or desolate places surrounded by high barbed wire fences and armed guards, including the infamous Manzanar.

Hawai'i internees, unaccustomed to very cold desert weather, especially felt the cold winds that ripped through their living quarters through cracks in the walls. Unfamiliar with mainland food, Hawai'i's Japanese internees hardly ate any of the bad food served to them. Many of the internees died of the cold, starvation, or loneliness.

Here in Hawai'i, fearing the search for contraband, Japanese communities destroyed or hid all reminders of Japan. Family heirlooms, treasures, and belongings that might be associated with Japan were either destroyed or hidden with the hope that they could be retrieved later.

Many sons and daughters of the *Issei* generation feared being arrested by associating with wives and families left behind by husbands who were arrested and sent to internment camps. Over one thousand women and children left Hawai'i between 1942 and 1943 to join their husbands and fathers who were kept behind barbed wire fences in internment camps. Most of those who went to see their spouses were totally shocked by the way they were treated. They felt that their husbands had done nothing wrong, and yet they were dealt with like criminals in a prison. With the rumors of mass evacuation of Japanese from Hawai'i to the mainland, hand luggage, trunks, blankets, and heavy winter clothing became popular items for sale in stores.

During the war, I did laundry for military men stationed here on Maui. The soldiers from a platoon of enlisted men in the battalion dropped off their clothing twice a week in individual laundry bags. I would wash, dry, starch, and iron their military uniforms and civilian clothing. I was paid well and, on occasion, I was given a little extra money for a job well done, or a special request for uniforms that needed to be cleaned in a hurry.

A lot of the Japanese housewives earned extra money by doing laundry for single Filipino men. They also married Filipinos who did not bring their wives to live in Hawai'i. Many wives of Filipinos refused to come after reading letters about poor conditions from other Filipino housewives who had been living here in Hawai'i.

Your father was released from Hawaiian Commercial and Sugar Company (HC&S) during the war. He was assigned to work for United States Engineering Department (*U.S.E.D.*) as a heavy equipment operator, at a pay of fifty cents an hour. Later, there would be a song written called *U-S-E-D*. It went:

U.S.E.D. workers everyday, fifty cents and hour, four bucks a day
U.S.E.D. workers every day, they make you whistle for your money
I went downtown to buy me a car, I gave the man the money, he

gave me the car
I step on the gas, the four tires went flat lei ana I ka sabatoge
Fort Street ewa, mauka, makai too many sighs maka pia the eye
You can have the car, that's not for me, I'll holo holo on the
H.R.T.
I took my girl on an automobile ride, the moon above was shining
so bright,
I pull down the shade, she pull down the shade, lei an I ka no
dice.
Haian ia mai ana kapuana la, my song is ended, my song is pau,
If anyone here doesn't like my song, can kiss my cheeks and roll
along.

U.S.E.D., part of the Corp of Engineers, wore black rimmed badges with an identification photograph. This was given for security measures to all Japanese civilian employees working under contract for the government. If one wore a black-rimmed badge it meant that some work areas were off - limits, such as underground tunnels and ammunition depots. Those who were assigned work at restricted areas had to be accompanied by armed guards so they could monitor movement.

In 1942, four classes of badges existed: 1) for a non-Japanese with no serious criminal record, 2) for a non-Japanese with a criminal record, 3) for those of Japanese ancestry with U.S. citizenship, 4) For *kibei* (American born Japanese) who were educated in Japan, 5) Japanese who were not allowed to do government work and were likely to be interned.

Your father was given a black-rimmed badge with the word – restricted – written on it. He, as an American, felt that Japanese had been singled out in contrast to other nationalities at work and blamed for starting the war with America. He felt worse later when he found out that people of other nationalities married to Japanese were also issued black-rimmed restrictive badges, confirming the suspicion that Japanese-Americans were definitely segregated.

From the start of the war until the near end of the war (October 24, 1945), one of the general orders issued during Marshal Law

108

was the freezing of job positions. Everyone had to continue working on the same job until Marshal Law was lifted.

Because of Pearl Harbor, Japanese Americans were berated by different nationalities by being called *Japs*. Wherever we went, in schools, buses, movie theaters, stores, and even on the streets, we, Japanese Americans, heard that slur used over and over. They accused us of starting the war because we were the same nationality as those who attacked Pearl Harbor. We were branded.

Japanese were definitely blamed for starting the war, especially when rumors spread that many Japanese-Americans could not be trusted. We were falsely charged for spying for our mother country, Japan. Yes, there were a few spies caught on O'ahu, but what was more alarming was that educated Japanese were sent to concentration camps all over the U.S. as well as here in Hawai'i.

Many of the First (*Issei*) and Second (*Nisei*) Generations will never forget the harassment they received, especially from the Portuguese. They kept on saying from the top of their voices, things such as, 'Because of you *Japs*, there is a war and we have to suffer for it.' *Haole* (white) racists also berated the Japanese by labeling us *Japs* or yellow skin pieces of ****. No other nationalities cared for or even glanced at the Japanese while the war was in progress. If any of other nationalities were seen associating with Japanese, they were reminded of the war in progress, the devastation of Pearl Harbor, and how many Americans were being killed in the South Pacific.

Most of the harassment ended abruptly when news came over the radio that the 442nd Regimental Combat Team in May of 1943, with 3,000 men, left the grounds of I'olani Palace and ended up in Europe to be with the 100th Infantry Battalion. All of them were Japanese fighting for Americans.

From a Maui News article: *The end of the war in Europe, the Japanese were the most decorated soldiers with 18,143 individual Decorations of Valor and seven Presidential Unit Citations.*

The United States Army issued a press release on the 442ⁿᵈ Regimental Combat Team. 'They had the fire, the courage, and the will to press forward that make crack infantry of the line. They would, and often did, drive until they fell from wounds or exhaustion. They were never driven a back step on many months of battle against an enemy who counter-attacked skillfully and often.' The announcement was repeated a number of times on the radio. The Japanese people finally felt like proud Americans.

The 442ⁿᵈ Regimental Combat Team and the 100ᵗʰ Infantry Battalion were fellow Americans fighting for the United States. They were willing to give up their lives for America and not for their forefathers' birthplace, Japan. Many left their families at home to fight in the war, knowing full well that they may never come home. Many families lost their sons to the war and, yet, many came home, to be still called *Japs*.

Can you imagine how they felt inside? Days after fighting the war, coming home injured, these brave men were still being labeled *Japs. One of the soldiers who fought in the war said over the radio, 'I gave my life to fight in the war, and, yet, when I returned home, you still have the nerve to call me a Jap. I don't want to hear anyone say that word again for the rest of my life. I will be offended. What if I called you ugly names instead of calling you by your true name? How would you feel? I feel hurt when you call me Jap. See, we, too, have names for you, but we don't call you that to your face. We as Japanese have more pride than that.'*

When I heard that statement, I had to clap. Finally, someone told the truth.

The war had effects on the infrastructure of the camps and its surroundings. The Pu'unene Airport, a mile beyond the pavement of Camp 6, had a three thousand foot long and five hundred wide run way for planes to land. From the beginning of the war, Pu'unene Airport was used for military aircraft, until the year 1943.

110

In 1943, civilian aircraft was allowed to use the Pu'unene Airport for landing and taking off and transporting civilian passengers from island to island. Hawaiian Airlines started civilian service in the summer of 1943 at that airport. Planes had two propeller engines and the back of the plane had small wheels. The front had bigger wheels making the plane look upward toward the sky. The plane was small, without much passenger capacity. Before 1943, civilians traveled by ship from Pier 2 in Kahului Harbor. With weather permitting, the ship took most of a night to get to the other islands.

Eventually, the main airport for the island of Maui, Pu'unene Airport, was declared unsafe by the Department of Commerce because of its location. It was not approved because the airport was less than five miles (required distance) from the peak of the West Maui Mountains.

June 2, 1942, at the ripe old age of twenty, I gave birth to my first son, James, at Pu'unene Hospital. After twenty-three days and surgery, my son died from intestines that had entered a hole in his lungs. Due to the lack of medical knowledge and training at that time, my son could not be saved.

Soon after the death of my son, I accepted a job as manager at the Pu'unene Naval Base Station because of my cooking skills, and because I got the help from a lady from Camp Four. All military personnel ate at the lunch counter.

Upon the constant insistence of my husband, I finally agreed to try to have another baby. I was successful and became pregnant with my second son, two years after my first son had died. Because I was pregnant, I had to resign from my position at the Pu'unene Naval Base Station.

You (Donald) were born on June 22, 1944. A few days after you were born, we were transferred to a makeshift hospital in Pa'ia. We were transported by plantation truck to a mill town clinic and stayed there for five days. We didn't have any family visitation because your father was working during the day and couldn't

111

leave the camp because Marshal Law was in effect during the night; it had to be one of the loneliness times of my life.

We left the hospital five days later. We were transported from Pa'ia to Camp Four by a plantation truck. We actually held a very small party in your honor. We're sorry it couldn't be big, but we had very little money at that time.

At the end of the war, the United States Engineering Department (U.S.E.D.) was dismantled. The government eliminated the heavy equipment operator position. Your father returned to HC&S. He was hired working as a laboratory assistant. That job didn't last too long because the pay was too small.

He requested to be transferred to the Field Department. With experience as a heavy equipment operator with the United States Engineering Department, he landed a job as a tractor driver for HC&S. His main job was to clear the fields for planting.

After the war was over, many reminders of the military's presence here on Maui was ever so visible. Here on Maui, concrete bunkers stood along shorelines where ammunition was once stored. Military equipment left behind was sold to civilians. There was a business in Wailuku called Apana's that sold shelves and shelves of military clothing, guns, and equipment.

Your dad was fortunate to purchase one of the Jeeps left behind, the first vehicle we ever owned. With help from his brothers and friends, the Jeep was in top shape after a major overhaul. It was a useful vehicle to have around. Your father could haul things and also go fishing with me.

For those fortunate to own cars during the war, gasoline was purchased for nineteen cents a gallon with coupons at the office operated by the military. No more than five gallons of gasoline could be purchased at one time and, because of the blackout, no one could drive his/her vehicle during the night hours.

After the war, some Japanese families turned hostile and racist toward other nationalities. Some refused to allow their sons and

112

daughters to associate with other ethnic groups. Fathers went into a rage when they heard their sons or daughters talk about other nationalities. There were severe punishments. That's how it was in Japan anyway. There you married into your own race or you didn't marry at all.

Some of the other nationalities apologized for their fathers' sins, for not being friends sooner. They felt sorry for what was inflicted on our nationality and attended church and prayed that racial relations might get much better for us. On our first meeting, other nationalities came to our house and brought peace offerings of fruits they had grown in their yard. And yet, as there are some exceptions to the rule, there were some who blamed us for the war and the sufferings they endured.

After the war, old friendships were rekindled. The friendships that were renewed were those who hadn't slurred us. They were good friends because they didn't think that we started the war. Some were honest to admit that they had sadly held back their friendships with us in case someone accused or berated them of being friends with *Japs*.

I honestly thought kindly of those who came to my house bringing peace offerings. In fact, I really and truly felt an inner peace and a gratitude for their friendship in my heart. From that day, I became very close friends with them. Of course, none of them were *haoles* (whites).

Because of limited earning power of the camp residents, a barter system (exchange of goods without money) was developed and worked beautifully in the camps. This kind of exchange had been going on for some time. Whenever someone gave us some vegetables or meat, we would respond with giving that person whatever we had to give. There was always something available. Everything was given willingly. Whenever a family had a good fortune, say, a lot of fish that they could not eat, they would share it with other neighbors, whatever nationality they were. Lots of sharing, friendliness, and *aloha* (love and compassion) were exchanged among the camp residents.

Unions were organized on Maui in 1944. In 1946, plantation workers in Pu'unene went on strike for six months. Soup kitchens (food supplied by unions) were organized. Most of the food was supplied by the union, which made it possible for workers on strike to cook food at a designated site. Groups of families within camps shared meals to show unity and support of those striking for higher wages and benefits.

Soup kitchens in Camp Four were organized with rotating schedules. Each woman had a specific time and date to cook. Many camp members helped in the preparation of meals. Although the unions gave most of the food for the soup kitchens, residents of the camp helped in gathering other foods that were not available for a complete dish. People who went fishing contributed their catch. Many of the camp people went to various farms in Kula and asked for non-sellable damaged vegetables. Those who raised pigs or chickens often supplied meat for the soup kitchens.

All in all, there was enough food for all the camp residents. In fact, some of them ate better at the soup kitchens than they did at home before the strike. People had no choice but to come and eat at the soup kitchens. They had no food at home, were on strike, and hadn't worked for months. They not only came to eat but, after they ate, some stayed to socialize with other camp members.

Individuals felt equal to everyone else because they all had been unemployed for months and had no income. Their situation created a sense of togetherness. Help was there when it was needed. No one needed to ask.

The strike situation gave many women the chance to pick up new recipes, to learn a better way to cook, or to teach those who did not know how to cook. Some women taught while some women learned. Even the experienced cooks learned better ways of cooking. These cooks were so experienced that they didn't measure by the book, and, yet, the food tasted very good. Some of those women fared so well that it encouraged them to open their own successful restaurants.

Men learned that life in their own camps were no different from other camps scattered throughout Pu'unene. Everyone struggled from time to time. Because they worked together, many camp members from one camp invited friends from other camps to share meals. In contrast to the earlier days in the camps, there were now no restrictions on where we ate, and who ate with us.

After the strike, four services were changed by HC&S out of retaliation. (1) No firewood was delivered to the residents to heat their *furo*. (2) Kerosene was no longer free. If one needed kerosene, it would be available from a vendor for a price. (3) Originally free, the cost of water was now one dollar a month. (4) Home rentals increased from twelve to fifteen dollars a month.

There were always families looking for a bigger house. Many wanted a bigger place to raise a larger family. The demand was so great that no sooner did one family move out, another would move in. Others looked for a place closer to their work. Some were disgusted with the neighborhood or wanted to live close to relatives. In other cases, a male family member would get married and move in with his parents, especially if the male was the eldest son, the one who would inherit everything that the parents had.

Some individuals did not get along with their brothers and sisters. They would move away when they got married. They looked for a smaller house with less to clean. Some were lonely and had no family or few visitors. Imagine not having your family near you because they moved to another island or to the mainland.

On April 1st of 1946, a tidal wave stirred residences of Kahului. The April Fool's Tidal Wave traveled half a mile inland. Originating in the Aleutian Islands, this catastrophe was caused by a number of earthquakes with a magnitude of 7.8 and 8.4. A hundred-foot *tsunami* (tidal wave) struck Scotch Gate in the Aleutian Islands. The worst area affected by the tidal wave was the Big Island of Hawai'i. Seven waves struck at seven in the morning along the Hilo Coast as well as three times at Laupahoehoe along the northeast coast of the Big Island. The tidal wave also caused thirty-six foot smaller waves on O'ahu and some thirty-three foot waves on Maui.

On that fateful day, one hundred fifty-nine people perished. The tidal wave took only about fifteen minutes to destroy nearly the whole town of Hilo. The waves averaged thirty feet, but a sixty-foot wave on the Big Island did the worst damage to Hilo. Residents had to remove all of the debris and rebuild that town again.

Back in Pu'unene, our main shopping was done through the peddlers who went from camp to camp. These mobile sales people usually purchased their supply of goods from a store in town. They stocked their trucks, went to the camps, and sold them from the side opening of their vehicles. Whenever they ran out of goods, they returned to the store to re-supply. Practically everything imaginable could fit into those trucks. Because of the peddlers, we didn't need to go to Kahului to shop. In most cases, these roving sellers charged the same prices for items sold at the Kahului Store. Other peddlers came, took orders, and returned the next day to deliver goods. Taken strictly on a charge basis, the bills payable at the end of the month.

There was also a Camp Five Store about two camps over from mine, close to Pu'unene School. It was owned by the sugar plantation and sold general merchandise, household items, appliances, clothing, and groceries. In front of the store was a service station that sold only one grade of gas. However, rather than shop at the Camp Five Store, most of the residents went to Kahului to shop because of the cheaper and wider variety.

Trash in camps was either burned in barrels in the backyard, in open fires, or in pits to heat the *furo*. Dumpsters provided by the sugar company were located in strategic places at each camp. Every week, filled dumpsters would be replaced with an empty one.

There were more changes at the plantation companies in the fifties. After the cane was burned, tractors would uproot the stalks from the ground, pile them high in a row at a central location for the cranes to pick them up, and load them onto waiting tournahaulers.

Beginning in 1950, tournahaulers transported huge amounts of sugar cane. Wider paved roads were constructed on strategic locations to accommodate those huge monsters that carried cane from the fields back to the sugar mills for processing. Chains were installed on the tournahaulers beds to lift the stalks for processing. It unloaded the cane quickly. They would drive up to a certain area. A crane made especially for picking up the bar lined with chain-nets attached to a rod lifted the chain-net and unloaded the cane to the ground. Another crane would pick the cane up and unload it onto a waiting conveyor belt that carried the cane into the mill for processing.

Because of the massive tires (much taller than human beings), tournahaulers were so versatile that they could go into the fields where cranes were and could move tons of it at a time. Tournahaulers would wait in line to transport the cane to the mill. In no time, fields could be cleared of the crop.

Then the process would continue over again. The fields were plowed and trenches dug to ready the planting of the sugar cane. Once it was planted, irrigation and fertilization would commence. The cane grew to full potential between eighteen and twenty-four months. The process would then start all over again. Different machinery was used for each step that completed the job much faster.

Trains and tracks became obsolete with the introduction of the tournahaulers. The only place trains and tracks were used was between the mill and the pier where raw brown sugar was transported to California for processing.

Because of technological advances, plantation workers had to suddenly learn to run these new machines or take on different jobs. Your father, because of prior experience, was hired as a tractor driver. His main job was to level the fields before trenching and planting the cane. Your father had a tough job. Dust would kick up and he inhaled all of it. His shirt, pants, and shoes would always be dirty. That made things very hard for me

117

because I had to scrub all of his clothes long and hard to get rid of dirt.

Using both my father's and my history, I tried to understand the true picture of both generations. Both generations strived to make a better world for the next to come. By knowing about the past generations, we cherish the values handed down to us, are made aware where we came from, and know the direction we are headed. Maybe some of our past practices were not right, but our intentions were honorable. We made a lot of mistakes. Along the way, though, each generation must correct these mistakes and learn from them. If we didn't learn from these errors then we haven't learned nothing."

"Do you understand everything that I've told you, Donald?" With that, she went into the house to make dinner.

Isn't it strange that she asked me the same question my grandfather did? What was going on? Was something mystical happening in front of my eyes? Was I imagining things? Is there something happening that I will someday understand? A lot of questions entered my mind that day.

SANSEI GENERATION
Part II
Chapter Four

All that I have learned from my grandfather and my mother started to fall into place. I now know that I have a background, the past, to work on. Now that I know my families' past, I can now work on my past, proceed along the present, and, most importantly, provide a solid foundation and goals for the future.

Sometimes dreams do come true if one works hard enough to attain that dream. Sometimes they don't come true because of tragic events or circumstances beyond our control. Dreams can be achieved, and dreams can be taken away. I've seen many people who had grand dreams and, yet, they evaporated because of obstacles placed in the way by others. And, to have successful dreams, someone has to help along the way: a coach, teacher, mentor, an admirable person, a minister, priest or anyone who may inspire and encourage.

Before I begin stories of my camp days, I emphasize that some of the names are made up for those who are alive at this writing. I did use real names for those who have already passed on. I'm sure some of them have talked at one time or another to descendants about their struggles and glories, but little or nothing has been written about them.

As I mentioned earlier, all that is said in this book is the truth as I perceived it. Truth prevails under all situations. I've told many people that if they lie, they should be a very smart person. They'll have to remember that lie or they'll get caught sooner or later.

Here's a brief history about me, Donald. I was born on June 22, 1944, one year before WWII ended. I lived in Camp Four until I was a high school sophomore. In fact, my family moved out the end of summer of 1960. I had lived in the camps for sixteen years. I believe this qualifies me to tell you about my camp life, its trials and tribulations. I recall many details but was assisted by people I interviewed.

I will begin with the chores I had to perform while attending Pu'unene Grammar School. I did these chores as far as I can remember back when....

My chores included making the fire to heat the water for the *furo* and feeding the chickens in the back yard. My father had a coop and plot back there. He raised some tall green weeds that I had to cut into small pieces on a board with the cane knife. I then mixed the weed with the chicken feed and gave it to the hens. I hated those chickens because everywhere I stepped in the coop, I picked up that awful poop under my feet. It smelled awful so I had to wash it off with the hose. But I couldn't get rid of that odor with plain water; I had to resort to soap.

School was about a mile or so away. We walked to and from the campus every day of the week unless there was a holiday. To get to Pu'unene School, I had to pass through Spanish B Village, pass the Tournahauler road, walk on to a paved path, and pass both the church and teachers' boarding house.

I am proud to say that my alma mater, Pu'unene School, with kindergarten to eight grade, had an enrollment of one thousand students in its prime. Two things contributed to that. First, there were many camps situated around the school. Second, for some odd reason, although the families struggled financially, they bore more children than any other town on Maui. Most camp families had an average of four children while other families had upwards of ten or more. I knew one clan who had eighteen children. I also know of a family who had the exception of only one child – me!

Those who had many children had some of them sleep at their grandparents' home or with other relatives and friends. Their grandparents adopted some children so they could be medically covered. Other couples, which had children early in life and were not married, allowed their parents to adopt their grandchildren because offspring from the unmarried were considered shameful to the Japanese.

Pu'unene School's layout consisted of a large administrative building in the middle of the schoolyard that faced the main road. In front of the building was a road that circled the flagpole. The first floor on the front of this building housed the administration office to right and the library to the left. At the back of the first floor were the sixth grade classrooms. The second floor housed the seventh and eighth grade classrooms.

This building was oddly designed. There were five entries with two staircases in the building. One entrance was in the front, one at each end of the first floor, and two with stairways on either side of the building to get to the second floor.

On the left, facing the administration building stood two other structures. The one by the road housed two classrooms for second graders. One farther inside housed four classrooms, two for third graders and two for fourth graders. Behind this building was a playing area and, beyond that, was the cafeteria. Next to the cafeteria was the girls' bathroom. Behind the administration building stood a portable with two classrooms for fifth graders.

To the right of the principal's office was a huge playing area. Near that was a long structure for first graders as well as a projection room. In back of this building was a large playground that included the track field and basketball court.

Also in the rear of the administration building was a woodwork shop and craft shop. For some students that shop meant a lot because it was there that they created many beautiful things. I remember to this day a sailboat created by a student out of one piece of lumber.

Beyond the wood and craft shop was a building for six graders. Both the fifth and sixth grade building looked like today's portable classrooms. They were built to be moved anyplace, anytime. The boys' bathroom was located parallel to the girls' bathroom, although farther away. I remember a lot of fights that occurred in those bathrooms.

121

Across the road, fronting the administrative building was a parallel ditch and small bridge that led to a library. Originally, the library was in the administration building. I assume that space was needed for more classrooms. Across the library was a building that housed the kindergarten. Next to the kindergarten was a church that, as of this writing, still exists.

The dress code for boys at Pu'unene School required pants and shirt. Shirts were often made with a material print called *palaka* (checker board design) that came in red, blue, black, or a combination of these colors. Then again, the poor like us wore hand-me-downs. Some children wore shoes, if they could afford it. Those who could not afford them wore slippers. And still, some of us went bare foot. I hated wearing shoes so I never put on a pair until my eighth grade graduation; it was a requirement for a diploma. Girls' dresses were more dignified. They wore skirts and blouses with white shoes and white socks to school. Blouses were heavily starched, while the skirts were merely ironed, their required lengths below the knees.

Pu'unene School was decorated with an assortment of trees. These large trees shaded the school and assisted the trade winds by keeping the classrooms cool. Among the trees planted were monkey pod, elephant ear, and April shower trees.

Monkey pod trees have huge umbrella like branches with smaller branches of leaves. Tiny pink blossoms turn into eight inch long black pods. These pods are filled with a sticky substance and a lot of tiny seeds and fall to the ground in the spring. By the end of summer, these pods dry up and crumble. If they fall onto the road, cars run them over, gluing them to the road until the pods dry.

Also cooling the grounds were elephant ear trees with their huge trunks and tiny branches with small leaves. Flowers develop into shiny dark-brown pods that are shaped like large ears in a semi-circle about four to six inches in diameter. Within the pods are large seeds.

Another beautiful tree is the April shower tree. This tree has

122

medium sized leaves. Its blossoms are the beauty of the tree. The colors of the blossoms can be yellow, reddish blue, purple, pink, or white. I couldn't figure out why that plant had the name April shower when the flowers bloomed almost all year round.

There was another type of tree that plantations planted along ditches in certain areas of camps. We called these trees – boat trees. I believe (not sure) these were actual species of the African Tulip Trees. First, when this not-so-beautiful tree produced orange flowers, it eventually died. The dried open pod would eventually fall from the tree to the ground. It resembled the shape of a boat. When I was young, we would float these pods down the irrigation ditches. It bobbed up and down in the irrigation ditches, and swerved front to back, comparable to a canoe floating in an ocean current.

Irrigation ditches were all over the place. They ran parallel to the main roads and through the camps. A standard irrigation ditch measured eight feet wide and about three feet deep. Most of them were situated near a camp or business, some cemented, some not. The irrigation ditches located in cane fields were dug out dirt ditches. These trenches, whether concrete or dirt, ran for miles along the camps, through them, and into the fields to water the cane. These courses were the sources of survival for the crop. Smaller ditches branched out from the main waterways.

The central sources of water for these irrigation channels were streams that brought rainfall, river water that flowed down from the mountains to the *punawai* (a large pond to hold water). There were natural springs, water from wells dug up by previous immigrants.

These wells went down a couple of hundred feet. Looking for spring water, these immigrants dug and dug until a sufficient water source was found and pumped up to supply water to the ponds that also came to carry its name. These wells are still operational today. The irrigation ditches were also used to carry water from the main source to a man-made pond, a number of them situated throughout Central Maui. These *Punawai's* supplied water to the irrigation ditches.

There was an irrigation ditch that ran parallel to the school with a bridge that crossed to Alabama Camp. It was on this bridge that some of my male classmates gathered every day after school. I remember one very hot day. Some of us decided to take a swim but gauged the level to be no more than three feet. We couldn't see the bottom because the water was murky. Because the water also ran shallow, we decided to jump feet first into the ditch.

Michael was chosen to jump in the water first. He was hesitant but we taunted him over and over, "Last one in the water is an Old Maid." We called him chicken until – suddenly - we heard a splash, then a cry from Michael. He yelled and yelled. We peered over the bridge, surprised at the abrupt jump. Michael was struggling to stay above water.

One of the boys took off his shirt, bent over the bridge, lowered the shirt down into the water, and attempted to tow the nearly submerged Michael out with the makeshift lifeline. Fortunately, Michael finally snagged part of the shirt and was pulled to the bank of the ditch, two boys grabbing each arm.

Michael got abrasions on his back from falling into the concrete ditch. There were some deep scratches and bleeding. However, what we saw was more frightening. As we lay Michael on the ground, we noticed a half broken bottle embedded in his foot that looked abnormally white. After we yanked the shard from his foot, we noticed that the huge cut was turning blue. Blood gushed from his wound. The red flow from his slashed foot was pumping out simultaneous with his heartbeat. The same shirt that had rescued Michael was tightly wrapped around the cut with a single knot.

While all of this was happening, an adult passing by with his vehicle realized that something terrible had occurred. When he saw a body lying on the ground, he stopped the car, helped carry Michael into his back seat, and lay him down. He placed a car cushion under his right leg to prevent more bleeding. He said, "The leg should be higher than the heart. Blood does not flow up hill."

124

At the hospital, a nurse cleaned the wound and discovered an additional piece of embedded glass. She had to use a long pair of tweezers to pull it out. Michael received thirty-five stitches on his foot and remained at the hospital for two days as a precautionary measure.

Michael stayed home from school for a few days. When he returned, our daredevil limped through class; he had a hard time mastering the use of crutches. He walked on his toes to stay off of his foot. One day, Michael accidentally walked directly on his whole right foot and screamed. A small pool of blood marked where he had stepped. After a few weeks, he was back to normal. Every time we talked scar stories, he'd remind us of the day he got his.

On some weekends, my dad and I would gather *kiawe* (Algaroba Tree) beans. These green beans turn yellow when ripen and fall to the ground. Whenever that happened, fishermen would say that it was *menpachi* season. A *menpachi* is a red fish, generally caught in rough water either with a reel or a straight pole at least 20 feet long. Most fishermen use a reel and pole, a floater, a light stick, and a small piece of lead that keeps the hook below the surface of the water, a curly tail fastened to it.

Kiawe trees grew all over the island, on long hillsides, along shorelines of beaches, on uninhabited land, and even in pastures where cows ate the falling beans. *Kiawe* trees are found only in dry climates and low elevations, and infested with termites. They were never used for building houses, only to burn firewood for the *furo*, cooking or making fences. It was very hard to cut and would split when dried.

The *kiawe* beans were not easy to gather. First of all, these trees had long thorns on their branches. Low hanging branches would often poke gatherers in the face or on their head. When I pick up the beans from the ground, I got painfully poked on my hand by the barbs. The sharp thorns even stabbed feet through rubber slippers. I once heard that a thorn had pierced and flattened a car tire.

I remember spending whole days picking those *kiawe* beans, the bags supplied by Haleakala Dairy. My father collected enough to fill about fifteen of those bags in one day. Since I was only nine years old, I used a bucket to gather them. When the container was full, I would carry it to an empty bag and fill it on my own. We went from one tree to the next until my father got tired; he would call it a day.

He loaded and stacked the filled bags on to the back of the Jeep and fastened them with a rope to prevent them from falling off. We would go straight to Haleakala Dairy to weigh the bags and see how much money my father would get for them. I don't remember if he got paid by the pound or by the bag. He always went into the room with the scale and counted his money. Did I get anything? NO!

Mr. Asakura supplied us with *kiawe* bean bags from the bean mill, which, of course, was owned by Hawaiian Commercial & Sugar Company (HC&S). He supplied gatherers with as many bean burlap bags as they needed, all recorded, of course. If my father planned to pick beans the following day, he would pick up more bags.

Because he was paid low wages, bean picking became a part-time job for my father. Every little bit helped. Picking *kiawe* beans was hard work, but my dad was used to hard work. He left school after finishing the sixth grade because he was the eldest. Because he was the eldest, he had two jobs. One was to provide income for him, and the other to care for his parents. He worked hard all his life and was so exhausted that he really didn't want to be interviewed by me. He only gave me tidbits.

'By the time the Japanese immigrants arrived and settled in the camp, Sam Sing Camp and *Pa-ke* Camp (combined and known to residents as only Sam Sing Camp) were already established. Sam Sing Camp was named for a well-respected Chinese leader who resided there among his fellow immigrants and owned a store and restaurant.

There was a camp across the hospital called Hospital Camp that was later renamed Camp Four. People from earlier generations called it Sam Sing Camp; even later, the camp took on a third name – Hospital Camp. After the expiration of their contracts, many of the Chinese immigrants moved away, looking for better pay and better working conditions. Many packed up and left for the mainland (the Continental United States).

The remaining Chinese had congregated into one small portion of Sam Sing camp. By my time, there were only two single men, a couple without children, and a family with two daughters.'

One of the Chinese gentlemen who lived in Sam Sing Camp had an unusual way of roasting peanuts. I considered him a genius. Into a large wok (pan used to stir-fry), he poured sifted beach sand to remove all of the junk and then added raw peanuts into the sand. He mixed them around on an open fire, avoiding touching the sides. He finally proceeded to roast the peanuts. They were all roasted perfectly and never burnt. Some of the residents came to watch him prepare the peanuts that he sold inexpensively in brown bags overflowing with the treats.

This man had a secret way of roasting the peanuts. How did he get it salted? How long did it take to cook the peanuts to its right consistency? He said that someday he would reveal the secret and that the shared secret would make someone very rich if they sold it at ball games. Believe me, I have never tasted roasted peanuts that good. The secret? Dream on…

The other single man in Sam Sing camp came from China, but he was reported to be a fugitive. He is said to have been a priest in his homeland. The other two Chinese families stuck together, minded their own business, worked in the cane fields, and avoided trouble like most.

A few Filipinos moved into Sam Sing Camp. As time went by, more and more Filipinos settled in and the Chinese population decreased.

Long ago, there were train tracks parallel to the store. One end of

127

the tracks went over a wooden bridge that ended in the cane fields. On the other side of the bridge, the track continued straight down the road, eventually curving toward the mill. The train transported workers to the field, hauled sugar cane, and carried firewood to the camp residents. Later, train cars and tracks were replaced by automobiles and paved roads.

One day, one of the tournahauler's tires broke loose, rolled into a car, and smashed it like a pancake. The four tires on the car were flattened, but, luckily, there was no one in the vehicle. If someone had been in the car, rescuers would have had to pick up body pieces. The tournahauler tire ended up down the road, about a mile away from the accident. I believe that if someone had been walking along the road, that tire would have killed that pedestrian.

HC&S decided when they got the tournahaulers, that they would burn the cane fields. They believed that burning them would be the most feasible way to get rid of the unneeded leaves. The sweetness of the cane would fill the air during burning. I recall enjoying the sweetness within the smoke.

One of my favorite pastimes, barefoot and on my bike, was to carry a knife in my shorts pocket and ride to a field claiming to have the sweetest cane. I'd cut off some chewy stalks with my handy knife. I chewed so much cane that I didn't need to go to the dentist; the fibers acted like a natural toothbrush and cleaned my teeth.

I'd break off the cane as close to the root as possible. That was always the sweetest part. Then I'd break it about two feet above the root. All sugar cane stalks have a hard section and a soft section, similar to a bamboo, to maintain its sturdiness. I'd cut off the outer layer of the cane with my pocketknife between the hard sections and the long section where it was softest. I would then run my knife in a circle around the hard section and discard it. Then I would slice the cane into carrot stick lengths. Finally, it was time to enjoy its sweetness. Because the inside of the cane is fibrous, after I sucked the cane juice out, I spit the fiber out like chewing tobacco. My friends and I spent hours and hours of

128

enjoyment chewing sugar cane in the fields, whether it had been burnt or not.

One day, after a field had been torched close to our camp. I decided to go and chew a few delicacies before anyone got there. I hopped on my bike and headed directly to the burnt field. But Charlie, my friend, had beaten me there and was chewing away when I arrived. He was about ten feet into the thicket and enjoying himself. He convinced me to come to where he was. He told me that the sugar cane there was sweeter than where I was. I decide to join Charlie.

We stood there, so intently chewing sugar cane and talking up a storm so much that Charlie and I did not hear a tractor getting closer and closer to us. Before we realized what was happening, it was too late. Charlie and I tried hard to get out of the cane field, but the sugar cane stalks tangled our feet. The way the cane grows added to our complication because as sugar cane matures, the stalks get longer and longer and, during its course of growth, they tend to crisscross every which way. Every time we tried to run, we'd get snagged and fall. We tried yelling, but the sound of the tractor swallowed up our voices. The driver could not hear us.

Everything went black. When I came to I was lying on my back on the ground, with no cane around me and no tractor in sight. As I got to my feet, my leg hurt terribly. Something was definitely wrong with my right foot. I had a hard time placing any weight on it. A terrible burning sensation raced through it as if it was on fire. When I started to walk, I had the feeling of needles piercing down my whole leg. The pain was unbearable. I managed to walk, but only a few feet.

When I looked up, I caught a glimpse of Mr. Sakamoto sitting on the bridge nearby. I yelled to get his attention. When he turned, he couldn't believe his eyes. There I stood, right in front of him, no more than ten to fifteen feet away. I was totally black with burnt cane soot from head to toe. The last thing I remembered was Mr. Sakamoto running toward me. I had again passed out from the pain.

When I came to, I was in the arms of Mr. Tengan in the back seat of a car. I know I was there because I was stretched out. I also know that we were heading to the hospital, Mr. Tengan reassuring me that we were almost there.

I kept thinking that the doctor was going to stitch me up like Michael, and then I'd be able to go home and have dinner. The only punishment I'd have to face would be my father and mother's lecture. I would also have the pleasure of staying home from school for a couple of days. Boy, was I wrong!

When I arrived at the hospital, I was taken by nurses to a room to wash the soot from my body. I sat in a basin, my feet dangling over its rim. I could see all the bruises on my legs and the front part of my body. I must have had more bruises all over my body because it really ached. The nurses were extremely careful as they washed my upper body first and then my legs. When they had finished, I was slid onto a hospital bed and wheeled in to emergency.

People lined up along the walls of the corridor to the emergency room. I passed by friends from the camp and HC&S workers. Before doctors worked on me, a supervisor from the company came in to the emergency room and asked me a few questions. He asked if I was the only one in the cane field when the accident occurred or if there were others. I immediately told him that Charlie was also with me.

Doctors went to work on my leg as soon after the supervisor left the room. I saw a cut under the foot of my right leg. It stretched from the baby toe, up to my heel, then clear across to the left side of my foot. When the doctors opened the cut, they could clearly see my bones. The slice looked as though someone had hacked me with a fillet knife, then scraped me to the bone to get as much meat as possible.

The doctor stuck his whole hand into my cut, hoping to thoroughly clean the soot that had accumulated. He must have used a lot of alcohol because I screamed in agony and passed out a few times.

130

During my recovery period, I stayed in a special room. Day after day, doctors wheeled me into the emergency room, until my cut was cleared of all the dirt and soot. I counted being wheeled into the emergency room three times. On my last visit, the doctors sewed me up and bandaged my foot.

I was finally taken into a regular room that had two beds. Who do you think was lying in other bed? It was Charlie, in all his glory. He started crying when I saw him. I didn't know why but this is what he told me later.

He said that I had told the supervisor that my friend was still in the cane field. Orders went out to search for him. They found Charlie in a pile of sugar cane with his feet up in the air. If the workers hadn't found him within a few minutes, then Charlie could have been part of the cane the crane would have picked up and loaded. My friend would have been on his way to the mill in a tournahauler.

Luckily, he had ended up with only a sprained knee and a few bruises on his body. A few days later, he was released from the hospital. Before he left, he and his parents thanked me for saving his life. That's why he cried the first time I saw him after the accident.

I was released from the hospital after spending almost three weeks there. A week after I was released from the hospital, I used a crutch to return to the second grade. I didn't know how far the school was from my house until I had to use a crutch. It was quite a feat. I was fine three weeks later. I was totally healed and was back to my usual self. I resumed riding bikes and chewing sugar cane, as if nothing had ever happened.

When I came home from school, I would do my usual chores that included setting the fire for the *furo*, making sure there was enough water in it, and feeding the chickens. I remember one particular day when I was hurrying to finish my chores. I had cut the grass from the garden and had gone into the chicken coop to chop the grass smaller. As I was walking, I stepped on a board

131

and, low and behold, a nail had poked through my feet. I turned nauseous when I saw the end of the nail sticking out at the top of my foot. I yelled a blood-curdling scream. No one heard me so I started to walk out of the chicken coop to seek help, the board still nailed under my foot and the spike sticking out at its top.

I kept yelling. I was only a few feet out of the chicken coop when my father came running from house. When he saw the bottom of the nail on the top of my foot, I thought he was going to pass out. He turned quite pale. He told himself not to panic. He helped me to stand up. He put one foot on the board and yanked my foot off the board as fast as he could. I almost passed out. When I saw the nail, I couldn't believe it. Some of my flesh, skin, and fat were still on it.

He immediately turned the board upside down and started to slap my foot under where the nail entered. He did that about four times. He told me that he had to do that to get the circulation back into my feet. He also told me that my pain would decrease during recovery. He was right. His process was one way to deal with a nail poke. I had gone through two terrible events in two months that usually take a lifetime for others to experience.

As long as I can remember, my father smoked cigarettes. He always carried a pack in his pocket. He knew that cigarette smoking was a bad thing but he could not quit. I'm sure he tried quitting once or twice before but, because of temptation, he'd go right back to smoking. About this time in his life, he just plain gave up on trying to quit. He always told me that the most satisfying time to smoke was after eating dinner, coming home from work, or on the toilet. He always reminded me that if he ever caught me smoking, I'd have to smoke a strong cigar right in front of his face. I presume he just didn't want me to start.

Of course, I never took heed to his warning, especially when he lectured me constantly about being good, doing the right things, and eating healthy foods. Every time he smoked, it seems as though he felt guilty, yet he kept on doing it.

The lectures about smoking got me wondering. What did it feel like to inhale smoke from a cigarette? Like a stupid fool, I had to try. Marlboro, non-menthol, filtered, came in a red and white, flip-top box. This is what I saw on the kitchen table or coffee table in the living room. When my father came home from work in the afternoon, he always asked me to run to the store to buy him a pack. He'd give me fifty cents to buy his cigarettes and a twenty-five cents tip to buy whatever I wanted.

At first, I would buy things like a Big Hunk candy, a bag of Maui Potato Chips, an apple or coconut turnover, or a bag of flattened cuttlefish (*ika*) prepared with soy sauce and sugar and packaged in a cellophane package. For drink, I would buy a bottle of Nickel Cola, Coke, Pepsi, Seven-Up, strawberry, or crème but Nickel Cola was cheaper than any other soda and its bottle was larger. My taste for orange soda, however, was forever halted when I drank one, only to find at the bottom of the bottle a large, dead cockroach.

I was nine years old, and fighting a temptation. I wondered what a cigarette tasted like? What was it about smoking that made my father light a cigarette with a match and inhale and exhale smoke from his nose and mouth until the cigarette barely hung to the filter. What made him smoke the cigarette until he could hardly hold it in his hands? Why was he telling me to buy more cigarettes when there were twenty in a pack and he smoked one pack a day? At times, he acted in desperation hunting for cigarettes, knowing full well that the store was closed. "Where did I leave my cigarettes? Have you seen my cigarettes?"

I kept on wondering what it tasted like. I decided that the next time he'd ask me to buy him cigarettes, I'd take that extra twenty-five cents he gave me and buy myself a pack of non-menthol Marlboro, filtered, in a red and white flip top box, just to see for myself what the feeling was like. I knew that sooner or later he would ask me to buy him a pack.

The following day it happened! My father came home from work, sat on the chair, took off his shoes and socks, and realized that he did not have any cigarettes. I eagerly awaited his command. He yelled for me, "Donald...?" Standing at the door, I

133

finished his request, "Go buy me a pack of cigarettes!" "Yeah," he responded, "and here's another twenty-five cents for you to spend. Go, now. So when I'm finished taking a bath, I can smoke a cigarette."

At this time, a Filipino family operated the store. It was no more than three houses away. This time I ran to the store faster then usual. I hopped up three steps to a platform with railings on both sides. Another step up and I was at its entrance. The store was a converted house with no partitions. It was just one big room with poles to hold up the roof. I approached an elderly Filipino lady behind the counter. She was the owner's wife, smoking a *toscani* (rolled Filipino cigar), the smell everywhere in the store. It smelled bad. I shook like a leaf, stuttering as I spoke, "I...want...two...packs...of...Marlboro Cigarettes, non-menthol...filtered...in a red...and white...pack...with a flip...top...box ...please." It felt like ten minutes passed, as if she were weighing every word. The vowel and consonants barely came out. It was more of a muffled sound.

Taking the *toscani* from her mouth, she disinterestedly uttered, "Is that all you want? Did your father give you extra money for candy?" "N...o," squeezed out my answer. "How come he wants two packs of cigarette, instead of one?" Oh, oh, did she know what I knew? Did other boys who wanted to smoke pull the same trick. "I don't know. All he told me was to buy him two packs of cigarettes...instead of one...this time." I could hardly talk. My mouth was dry.

I sighed when she said, "Okay, tell your father I said hi!" She replaced the *toscani* into her mouth, inhaled a deep puff, and blew out a cloud of smoke at me. I coughed. I quickly slipped two packs of cigarettes from the rack and two matchbooks from the box on the counter. As soon as I slammed the money down, I grabbed the two packs of cigarettes and the matchbooks and bolted as fast as I could down the stairs.

I hid one of the cigarette packs and one of the books of matches in the bushes before I headed home. I had planned a good permanent hiding place my illegal purchase ahead of time. I'd

134

pick it up later, when the coast was clear.

I gave my father the other pack of cigarettes and disappeared to my room. I felt so guilty. I tried to stay calm and collected. Every so often an anxious thought seeped into my mind. I wondered...what if the lady at the store ran into my dad today and mentioned that I bought two packs of cigarette, instead of one, and hadn't requested the usual candy.

The following day happened to be a Saturday. There was no school, but I nevertheless got up early, brushed my teeth, changed into my play clothes, and left the house. I got on my bike and headed straight to the hiding place of the contraband. After I picked up the cigarettes and the matches, I bee-lined out of town, far, far away, to a place where no one would find me. I hid in the cane fields, deep in the towering stalks. I seated myself and performed the same routine I had seen my father perform a number of times before. I held the middle of the cigarette pack between my thumb and first finger of the right hand, my left palm open. I hit the top of the pack of cigarettes in the left palm a couple of times. I came to realize that the filter was on the top of the pack; so hitting the top compressed the tobacco against the wrapper inside.

I slipped off the small cellophane, lifted the flip top box, and yanked out the foil that covered the cigarettes, grabbed a hold of one, and proceeded to place the cigarette, filter side, onto my lips. I lit the cigarette and inhaled just as my father had done so many times before. Cough...cough...cough. This time I'll inhale more. Cough...cough...cough. I started to feel funny, then dizzy. I wondered if it only happened to youngsters like me?

I had to tell a close friend of mine, Jimmy, about this. I'd let him try smoking and experience for himself what I felt that day. When the sun rose in the morning, Jimmy and I were back in the cane fields, not chewing cane this time but sitting on an embankment...smoking. He imitated exactly what I had told him. Jimmy inhaled deep and released the smoke through his nose. He told me that he felt funny and dizzy, too.

135

Jimmy and I decided to invite other kids in the neighborhood to try smoking tobacco. A few were reluctant, most tried but didn't like it, and others resisted, riddled with fear that they'd get caught. Snitches were definitely not invited to our smokers' club.

Eventually, one of the jealous boys who was not invited to participate in the fun and games, told his parents. All the intrigue ended when word got out that a bunch of ten year olds were part of a smoking ring.

On the way home from one of our smoking adventures, I asked Jimmy if he wanted to chew some sugar cane. "Sure, as long as we are as close to the bridge as possible. I need to stay near my home. I have to do something later."

Some sugar cane was sweeter in some fields and less so in others. Perhaps they were sweeter because the plantations were experimenting with different types of sugar cane and had developed a better strain, or maybe it was the soil.

We were always on the lookout for purple cane. Some sugar cane stalks were purple in color but the leaves no different. Purple cane was always sweeter and softer than regular sugar cane – and rare. I came across it only twice. It was so sweet that, when chewed, it actually made me cough.

HC&S rarely planted purple cane in the cane fields. Why didn't they? I would think that the sweeter the sugar cane, the more yield per field. Maybe the stalks of the regular cane were smaller, and more cane planted per field would yield more sugar. It also could be that the purple cane was more susceptible to diseases in contrast to regular sugar cane.

Jimmy and I rode our bikes to the destination to chew sugar cane. As we got closer to the bridge, I challenged him to a race to our destination; I heard a soothing yet penetrating voice say to me, "Who learns more – a man who speaks, or a man who listens?"

I turned my head to where the voice came from, I saw an elderly oriental man, perhaps in his sixties, standing along a picket fence.

136

He was about five feet, two inches tall with salt and pepper hair and dark skin, probably due to working outdoors every day. He was thin, slightly bent over, and had a round face. He wore khaki pants well above his ankles and a white t-shirt.

As we stared into each other's eyes from a distance, I felt that this would not be the last I'd see of this stranger. The expression written on his face confirmed my thoughts, "Yes, we will see each other many more times."

I had a strange sensation. It seems as though I had seen this man before and, yet, I hadn't. I passed through this area a number of times, but I had never noticed him.

As I rode over the bridge, I felt troubled. I had to ask Jimmy who the man was. Jimmy had also seen him by the fence, but he hadn't heard anything the old man had said to me. Jimmy answered my question, "He's a Chinese man who has lived there as far as I can remember. He hardly ever talks to any one and minds his own business. My dad thinks that he used to be a priest in China before he came to work here on the plantation. Some of my dad's friends claim that because he does not communicate with anyone, he must be a fugitive. They say that he ran away from China because the government wanted to kill all of the priests there."

That night, the Chinese man's question bothered me. I was obsessed by the look in his eyes, and the premonition that I would see him again. The question burned in my mind: "Who learns more – the person who speaks or the person who listens?" This man fascinated yet puzzled me. He's got to be a very smart man, a learned man. But why is he talking to me? How come Jimmy didn't hear the guy talking? After many hours of thought, I finally made up my mind to visit the Chinese man the next day, after all my chores.

As soon as I got home from school the following day, I changed my clothes, raced through my chores, hopped on my bike, and zipped toward the strange man's house, up the hill and near the bridge.

When I reached the gate, I swung it open. As I walked along the sidewalk, I noticed the colorful daisies and flowers. I approached the front of the house, walked up three steps to the porch, and knocked on the door.

I heard a gentle voice say, "Come in, the door is not locked." I opened the door. The first thing I noticed was that there was no furniture. *Goza* (Japanese woven straw mats) lay on the floor, wall to wall. *Zabutons* (Japanese cushions) were scattered throughout the room in an orderly fashion. The living room was simple and neat.

"Please sit," he called from the kitchen. I seated myself down on one of the zabutons, I had to ask the question. I bluntly asked, "Who are you?" He came from the kitchen and sat right across from me. He did not position himself like an ordinary person. He actually bent his knees before he sat. As he sat, he told me that he was willing to share his past with me.

"Let me explain first, that I've heard that some have spread rumors about me that are untrue, that I was a priest and a fugitive from China. That is not true. I am, like your parents, a child of immigrants. I know who my father was but, unfortunately, I did not know my mother.

My father was born in China. He immigrated to the United States of America. He arrived in America on a ship that was overcrowded and unsanitary. The people who were below deck were packed like sardines in a can. Many died of suffocation from diseases onboard due to lack of toilet facilities, and from starvation. Those who died were thrown overboard. All of the immigrants left the ship with sores that refused to heal for months. Many of them had permanent scars from these sores.

When my father arrived in the United States of America, laws prevented him and others from marrying non-Chinese women. This prevented them from voting, holding public office, and operating certain businesses. Chinese were also restricted from living in places of their choosing. Because of this, a community

138

of Chinese or Chinatown was formed. Chinatowns were mainly bachelor communities because of the high cost of bringing women from China to the U.S.,

My father married the daughter, of an early immigrant, who died of complications while giving birth. That is why I told you that I didn't know my mother. I was the one she gave birth to.

My father was an immigrant worker who worked from farm to farm throughout the western states. He took work wherever jobs were available. He harvested vegetables, fruits, and nuts from the state of Washington to California. The workers were never allowed to take home anything for personal consumption. Those who did were immediately fired.

Each day, after returning from long hours in the fields, my father made it a point to teach me what he had learned while growing up in China. I had daily teachings of Confucianism, the philosophy that all are born good and that if one follows his own right conduct and duties as a man, one can achieve perfection. Included in his lessons were the teachings of wisdom and compassion of Buddhism. I also learned of Taoism, how to live compassionately, knowingly, and how to flow with the present moment.

My father, on occasion, was asked to practice the Chinese spiritual belief of *feng-shui*, the art of placing certain items within the household at a designated location, the harmonically balance in building a home, and even the search for a suitable gravesite for prosperity.

At the age of nineteen, I left my father to seek work here on the sugar plantation, as your grandfather and father had also done. I was tired of moving from farm to farm as a migrant worker as my father had done for years.

Here, with beautiful weather, I had hoped to settle down, and not move around as I previously done. My first job was at the Honoka'a Plantation on the Big Island of Hawai'i. After a while, I was laid off due to lack of work.

Kaua'i where I found odd
I later moved to the Island of

139

jobs fixing homes for a white gentleman. I was not working full time at that time; I barely made enough money to pay my room and board. I was fortunate, however, to have known a gentle lady who gave me leftover food from another boarding house she was managing at that time.

One day, I glanced at the Kaua'i newspaper and noticed that Maui was hiring workers for the plantations. I wrote a letter to HC&S with the full intention of moving here and received one back from the company stating that I had been accepted. I quit my job and moved to Maui. Although I was accepted, I did not work for a few weeks.

I arrived here thirty years ago with little or no money in my pockets; I had no choice but to make do with what I had. I soon ran out of cash after purchasing needed items at the Camp Four Store. Since I was a new person here, I was not allowed credit from the store. I even tried borrowing from my countrymen but to no avail. I begged for vegetables from the assigned plots of residents. Since I was an unknown, I was denied over and over again.

Because I could not buy food until I got my first paycheck, I resorted to chewing sugar cane to stay alive. I hung a fresh piece of sugar cane under the rafters outside of my house. When it dried, I would replace it with a fresh piece, a tradition I've kept to this day. Every time I face struggles in my life, I look at the sugar cane to remind myself of my bleakest hour when I had nothing.

After being on the job for a while, I decided to settle here in Sam Sing Camp, since my countrymen were living here. Because I was planning to settle here, I decided that I'd write a letter to the woman I knew in Kaua'i to convince her to move here to Maui to live with me.

I made every effort to locate then relocate this gentle woman with a chance of marrying her, if she would accept my hand. I led a lonely life and wanted to share mine with a person like her; I dreamt of living with this kind woman for the rest of my life. I believed that she was the person I had been seeking for all my life. As the philosopher says, 'In absence-love grows.'

140

One day, I received a sad letter from a drinking friend of mine from Kaua'i. I found out through his letter that the gentle woman had died in an accident in the boarding house she was managing. At that time, kerosene was stored under the kitchen in barrels. A fire broke out in one of the bedrooms close to the kitchen. No sooner had the kitchen caught fire, and then the kerosene barrel blew up. She was the only one in the kitchen at that time.

When I first read the letter, it felt like it was a nightmare. A day later, it really sunk in. 'I should have' – kept running through my mind. I should have asked her to marry me before I left Kaua'i. Why did I wait so long? I cried myself to sleep that night.

This was the second time I cried in my life. The first time was when I said good-bye to my father on the docks of San Pedro, California. Deep in my heart I knew that I would never see him again.

When I began researching and talking to other Chinese counterparts about life in the camps, I found out that in 1852 the Chinese were the first major group of immigrants to arrive, so they were well established before the Japanese imported labor began arriving in Hawai'i. As soon as their contracts expired, a number of them quickly left the plantations in Hawai'i for better jobs and more money on the Continental United States. The Chinese settled in all of the forty-eight states. Some even went prospecting for gold, the less fortunate building the U.S. railway system. When I arrived in Pu'unene, Sam Sing Camp or *Pa-ke* Camp was thriving because of the influx of Chinese to the camps. The Chinese population, after some time, dwindled to only four households in what eventually became known as Camp Four.

I have just given you my history. I am not a priest but I do have some knowledge of those religions I previously mentioned. I could be a priest, but it's what you have in your heart that is most important than being called a priest. Priest is only a title given to a person who thinks and believes that he can change the world by preaching to his world, a church.

You have come here not to know my history but to find answers. I will ask you questions from time to time and, if you do not know the answers, I will reveal them. Now to the question I asked you yesterday: Who learns more, a person who speaks or the person who listens?

A man who talks says things that he or she has learned, nothing more. People who have learned much might say a lot of things that may be helpful to another person. Remember that what one has learned is spoken in words, whether good or bad. Remember, also, one observes reactions while talking. The man who listens learns the most. You have to listen carefully to comprehend what the other person is saying. In other words, you have to listen carefully to provide information to your brain. Have you noticed that I did not say anything about hearing? Hearing is listening to sounds. Listening is comprehending sounds and sending it to the brain. I hope that you have been listening to me and not only hearing me.

Before you leave, think about this? Why are we here on this earth? Better yet, for what reason have we been put on this earth?"

Again, I was left with a question that I knew was going to bother me until I returned to see the Chinese man again. I still didn't know his name nor did I know how old he was. I obviously learned that he was not a priest from China, although he could be one.

That night as I lay in bed, I realized that his parents shared the same predicament with my grandfather and mother. They endured a lot of suffering, but never gave up. Yet, my immigrant grandparents were focused. They knew what they wanted or was there, perhaps, no choice in the matter? Did they truly believe in their minds that it was either/or? Were they really afraid of the decision they made in venturing out to lands they have never seen, read, or heard little about?

It was strange. I felt as if the things that happened in the past few weeks were meant to be. I've never felt this spooky feeling before.

A couple of years later, I heard that, Matsuo Kawamoto, passed away. He was the fisherman that made and sold durable boats. It was a big blow to my uncle who was fortunate to possess one of those boats. Sadly, he never again talked about Matsuo, his fishing partner. I could see the loss in his eyes and by the different way he acted. He went fishing alone and eventually gambled his money away shooting craps. Don't get me wrong. Sometimes he would win a lot of money but, more often than not, he lost a lot.

One morning while I was sleeping, I heard my father yelling at me to come out of the house and see what my uncle had caught. With all the excitement my father was generating, I had to see the special catch for myself.

I ran out the front door. I couldn't believe my eyes. I saw two of the biggest fish I had every seen lying on the grass. My uncle cleaned the boat while my father stood proudly over the giant fish. I was amazed how big they were. The type of fish is the *wahoo* (called *ono* in Hawaiian – defined as good tasting). You can eat the *ono* by drying it, frying it, or, what I consider the best way, cooking it over charcoal. Because it has a lot of bones, the eater must be careful.

After cleaning and cutting up the mammoth fish, my uncle and father gave chunks from one of the fish away to family, friends and the poor. My father dried the rest. As soon as it had dried, he cooked some of it over charcoal. We devoured it for dinner. He kept the rest for future meals, sometimes using portions of it to make soup.

The wahoo has an elongated body with a pointed head. It has a dark blue-grey, upper body and a lighter color on the lower half highlighted by purple-grey stripes. *Ono* can weigh up to seventy pounds and grow to five feet in length. It lives in deep blue waters and tends to travel long distances to find food.

My uncle truly loved his fishing. He knew where to go to find certain types of fish in deep waters. He knew exactly where they were by using all possible man-made and natural landmarks. He also knew the seasons for certain species. He hung around other fishermen and learned a lot from them.

Once while fishing, my uncle had a bad accident. A large hook got embedded in the palm of his hand. After returning home from fishing, he cleaned his boat, gave my father the fish he had caught, and then finally decided to go to the hospital and remove the hook from his hand. When he returned from the hospital, he told us that the doctor had to cut into his palm to get the hook out. If he had pulled the barb from his hand, the pain could worsen, or cause further damage. He endured ten stitches in his hand, was bandaged with gauze, and taped over. He didn't go fishing for a few weeks after that. He was embarrassed so he kept the accident a secret.

There were times when I wanted to share a secret with another person but, since I was an only child in the family, I sought out my friends. As children, we found a place where we could go and just talk without adults. I relished such a place. Remember the bathhouses among the homes? The hideaway was between roofs of the joined buildings, the only one in the camp to my knowledge. There in the middle of the two adjoining gables was a valley. A mango tree had grown adjacent to the bathhouse, and it was so big that its branches leaned over that roof, creating a canopy for the gang's retreat. It was there under the shade of the spreading mango tree that we all congregated. We used a stepladder to get on the roof. This ladder was home made by one of the residents; everyone used it because the general rule was: anything left outside was community property.

At times we took our lunch and had a party up on the roof. We shared our food and talked story. This is where we sought refuge for hours on end. There we learned each other's secrets, shared our likes and dislikes, predicted and reviewed the happenings for the day like homework, sports, fights, and every little thing that that came to our minds. One thing we did not talk about was a girl.

Most of the time, it was boys only day on the roof, but, at times, we allowed girls to join in. It was one fun place for all the kids in the neighborhood. Our parents knew exactly where we were by

144

the loud shouts and laughs. Sometimes, we'd laugh so loud that we could be heard houses away. I do believe that some of the parents actually listened in on our conversations.

The only thing that would stop us from going on the roof was rain. Some days, it would rain hard, sometimes for a whole week. We'd wait a couple of days to resume our gathering. As soon as the word went out that we were meeting at a certain time, all of us would make our lunches and head straight for the roof, our safe haven. 'Bring your lunch' was the order for the day.

One day, I was the first one there. I climbed the ladder with lunch in hand and started to walk across the roof. Because of the steep angle, I walked with my left foot higher than my right. When it rained for a length of time, the wooden shingles on the roof tended to get slippery.

I'd walk a few steps and I would skid. I should have turned back. Instead, I decided to continue. All of a sudden, my right foot separated from my left, putting me in an awkward position. My legs were split like a football center. Luckily, I fell forward, flat on my stomach, aware that I'd soon be skidding toward the edge of the roof. This is when I decided to swing my left foot toward my right foot. If I was going to skid, I planned to skid feet first. As I started to slide, I tried to grab anything I could hold on to on my way down, but there was nothing to grasp. With desperation, the only thing I could do was to rake my fingers on the singles. I had no fingernails (I had bitten them during nervous situations). I guess my weight and the dry clothes prevented me from falling off the roof. I ended up with half of my body dangling over the edge. I froze, too scared to move.

I was shaking like a cane stalk in the wind. There was a concrete sidewalk directly below. If I had let go, I wondered what position I would end up in on the sidewalk. How badly could I get hurt? A whole lot of questions raced through my mind. I definitely had no intentions of letting go. I immediately yelled for help. It seemed like an eternity before someone came to rescue me. Guess who was my savior? It was Charlie with stepladder in tow. Talk about paying back a life for a life. After that incident, I vowed that I would never climb that roof again. If friends wanted to talk, my feet would have to be flat on the ground.

As days, months, and years went by, I became more and more scared of heights. Whenever I went to high places, even if there was a railing, I'd have this feeling of imbalance; I felt I was going to fall over. Even thinking about heights makes my palms get sweaty. I refuse to go on any amusement rides that pertain to heights. I totally hate Ferris Wheels.

For most camp kids, the bicycle was the only means of transportation. We'd venture along miles and miles along plantation roads looking for fun. Whenever kids needed or wanted something, we knew exactly where to go. If we needed to get brown sugar for our parents' cooking, we knew which train car in the mill yard had the sweetener. They scraped handfuls of the brown crystals into a brown paper sack that we brought from home. If we wanted sugar cane to chew we knew the exact fields to satisfy our needs. If we wanted to raise tropical fish, we knew which *punawai* had the most fish.

The many ponds and ditches throughout the camp were perfect breeding grounds for mosquitoes. HC&S workers complained about their many mosquito bites while working in the cane fields. A few were allergic to them. By scratching, a large welt would appear, and the more they scratched the area the more it became infected. To combat this problem, the plantation imported platys, mosquito fish, swordtails and *talapia* to eat the mosquito larvae thriving in stagnant water. When the ditches were not flowing, the ponds got stagnant. The plantation imported all types of tropical fish to the ditches and *punawai*. The fish entered the ditches and when the watercourse eventually dried up, the fish would die. Nothing was wasted; the dead fish became good fertilizer.

The punawai was sort of like a holding pond for water to irrigate the sugar cane fields. It had been dug up, about three-fourths the diameter of a football field. There was a measuring stick inside of the pond to determine its depth.

Many of our adventures took place at the Taketa Punawai. It must have been about five to six miles away. Taketa Punawai was named after the custodian of the reservoir. He lived in a house by the man-made pond, but moved to a bigger one after he got married. The home was already gone by the time we visited the Punawai. No trace was left where the home stood.

The pond's main source of water came from either mountain via streams, or pumped out from under ground wells. The source of Taketa Punawai was a flowing stream on the *mauka* (mountain) side. Taketa Punawai had a concrete ditch for water to flow to the sugar cane fields. This cement causeway was eight feet wide and four feet deep with a valve to control the flow of water. There was a ditch used for overflow water about a hundred yards away. When there was too much water from heavy rains, this ditch could release excess water and prevent bank over-flow. The banks were constructed of dirt piled high. Should any of them break because of heavy rain, the resulting erosion would totally destroy the *punawai*. In addition, the flow of water would destroy cane fields near the reservoir, the mud from its bottom completely covering a field. The cost to rebuild one of these *punawai* was enormous and took about three weeks to reconstruct.

The overflow ditch was the place we rode our bicycles. There were three common mango trees that grew along the ditch, although there was nothing common about them. It was the name of a strain of mango that everybody liked.

In this overflow ditch, there were tropical fish called platys. Because they came in a multitude of colors, they caught our eye. Many of the fish we caught had at least three to four colors or the rainbow on their bodies.

With a scoop net and a bucket, we'd catch a surplus to take home. There were three problems to this. First, we had to travel five to six miles from home by bike, the bucket hanging on the bicycle's handle bar. We tried to be careful not to spill any water out of the container as we rode up and down bumpy dirt roads. Second, the hot sun did not help the cause. The temperature of

147

the water warmed with the heating of the metal buckets, causing some fish to die. Last, we had no pump to feed oxygen in the water for the fish. By the time we got home, most of them were floating face up.

My childhood friends and I were so greedy for tropical fish that we'd over-catch them. The survival rate dropped. In the end, it was not worth traveling the six miles to and from the pond. However, eventually we'd return to relive our joyous past.

After returning from Taketa Punawai, we'd often go to the back of the house and eat mangos in season. We'd eat the half ripe mangos with *shoyu* and Hawaiian chili peppers. We'd eat not only one but three or four mangos. Sometimes we'd get stomachaches later that night from eating too many fruits and chili peppers. Then again, it's like wiping out the tropical fish supply; we over - did everything.

We had two mango trees in our back yard. One was known as *Pake* mango. The down side of this mango is that, when it gets ripe, the strain gets stringy and sticks between the teeth. There was another nameless mango tree that hung over the garage. This mango was round and when it was ripe it would fall onto the garage roof. I never tasted the mango, nor did members of my family. My father must have tried it long ago and declared it the forbidden fruit of our yard.

Here are some hints to enjoy a half-ripe mango: remove and throw away the thick skin when peeling it or cutting it with the knife. With the knife, cut the flesh from the seed, located in the middle of the fruit. Cut the flesh into bite size pieces and place in a bowl. Pour a mixture of soy sauce, sugar, salt, black pepper, and three or four Hawaiian chili peppers over the mango pieces. Marinate for a few minutes. Then, eat as much as you can! This is the recipe for a classic stomachache.

I was a young kid, with little or no knowledge of the happenings of the world. I found myself gullible to the stories older people told me. They easily whipped me into fright frenzies a number of times.

148

One night, my mom and my dad decided to visit a family about five houses away, so I tagged along. This family's off springs were two boys and a girl named Sumiye, who was much older than I. Sumiye's parents conversed with mine in the living room while Sumiye and I talked in her bedroom. She liked drawing faces while I watched. I have to say that those representations looked real, although I never met anyone who matched the sketches. She must have had a couple hundred of them drawn on scratch paper. What was really amazing was that no two faces looked alike. She drew beautiful, ugly, smiling, and sad faces that she copied from magazines, newspapers, and from her imagination. She drew blacks, whites, Asians, and faces of other nationalities. It was something to pass the time away; something she liked doing. I had never seen anyone draw faces as well as she.

At times, when she got tired of drawing faces, she would ask me if I wanted to hear a scary story. I always pathetically answered yes. Here's one she told me: "A long time ago there lived four sisters with their parents in a plantation house. Being they were a close-knit family, they did all activities together. The parents shared everything with their two sets of twins. They were more than a year apart and knew each other's schoolmates.

These twins were so identical that people had a hard time telling them apart. Confused friends called out one of their names to see who would answer. Of course, that didn't work most of the time because the twins would mischievously fib as to who was who. When they got older and started dating, they even confused their boyfriends.

One day, their mother fell and died instantly of a massive heart attack. The family told friends and relatives that her ghost had visited them the same night before she died. Everyone thought that they were crazy.

Within a month after the mother died, the father was driving home after visiting friends. The family car collided into an pole. The youngest set of twins hit the front windshield and died

149

instantly from massive head wounds. Days later, the remaining family members told relatives and friends that the ghosts of the mother and the twin daughters had visited them during the night of the funeral. Again, people thought they were insane.

Not long after that, the second set of twins died in separate incidents. One died while swimming. She dove into a concrete irrigation ditch and hit her head on the concrete bottom. The second died mysteriously in her sleep.

The father, the one and only survivor, repeatedly told friends and relatives the same story. His departed family had visited him during the night of the funeral. Again, no one believed him.

A year and a half later, while drinking with his friends into the wee hours of the morning, the father suddenly became ill. He stood up, fell face forward onto the concrete floor, and died of a massive heart attack.

After the funeral, a strange thing happened. During the night, strange noises were heard along the camp road. All of the neighbors ran out to see what was happening. Dogs were barking. And there, in plain sight, the whole camp witnessed the complete family walking together along the road. Many friends and relatives who doubted the previous apparitions were now convinced."

I didn't realize that my parents had gone home before Sumiye concluded her story. She decided to walk me home in the dark. As we got closer to my house, I decided to get even with her for scaring me with spooky stories. "Look! Behind!" I yelled suddenly. Her imagination saw something. I thought her head was going to twist off when she looked back toward me. Her face turned pale. She bolted as fast as a scared cat toward her home, never looking back. I also had a bad nightmare that night.

I couldn't sleep for a period of time in my life, not because of scary stories. I started to believe that I was at a crossroads in my life. Everything seemed in chaos. I had to visit the Chinese man again to ask him more questions and, this time, ask him his name.

150

It was about time that I went to talk story with him. I hadn't seen him for a long time.

I woke up early in the morning and performed my routine. I brushed my teeth, washed my face, changed my clothes, ate breakfast, grabbed my bike and headed straight for the house near the bridge.

When I reached the gate, I opened and closed it behind me. As usual, I walked up the three steps to the door and knocked to announce my presence.

'Come on in,' came the reply from inside. As soon as I saw him, he asked me, 'You haven't been here for a long time, and you haven't forgotten the question, right?' 'I remember the question you asked me. It was: Why were we put on this earth?'

He answered, "We came to this earth to learn. Whether good or bad, we are here to learn. We should learn as much as possible: by reading, by traveling, by being aware of the different customs of different lands, by trying old and new things, or by learning by trial or error. I have to learn by talking less and listening more.

In return, we need to teach the good things we have learned. We need to remember the right things and teach those who do not know. We teach others so that they may pass on knowledge, both past and the present, to the next generation so that they might be able to carry on and become better than the previous generation. See, in this way, they, in turn, can teach future generations what you taught them. Always teach right and not wrong. If you are uncertain of something – find out. That is your job. Teaching means knowledge learned.

Everything you have experienced or felt within, seen, read, touched, internally or externally, whether good or bad, until the day you die, is why you are here.

I am not saying here that schoolteachers are the best teachers. In fact, I think some may be the worst. Here is the reasoning. Many of the teachers who have gone to college believe in their minds that what they have learned is fixed in stone. Some believe that

151

they know practically everything on the subject they were taught. Because of this, many teachers have closed minds. There is a limit of what you can learn from them. You've seen it in the schools. At the end of the year, you ask, what have I learned? Only what the teacher knows and tells, no more.

Each individual is placed on this earth for a reason. He or she is the only person who can accomplish this task that needs to be done on this earth. In time, he or she will discover what the task is. It may take all but a few seconds, or a day, a week, a month, a year, maybe a few years or, sadly, a lifetime. When we fulfill our destiny, we leave this world through death. If we have accomplished what we have been sent to do, then our job is done."

Before leaving, I asked the Chinese man his name, instead of calling him Chinese man every time. He told me that his name was Choi. He never gave me his first name. So, I decided to call him Mr. Choi in total respect.

As soon as I went home that day, I enlightened my father as to who the Chinese man was, and why I wanted to go and see him for answers. I was quite surprised when my father did not discourage me from seeing Mr. Choi. In fact, he told me that because of his lack of knowledge on the subject of religion and the world, that whenever I wanted to go and see Mr. Choi, it was alright with him, as long as I first completed my chores.

Back to the life of kids, one day Jimmy was sitting outside my house, waiting for me, a bag of marbles in his hand. As soon as I saw the bag of marbles, I realized that I had promised him a game and had totally forgotten about it. With all the happenings, the game was the farthest thing from my mind. I remember what my father once told me. 'When you promise somebody something, you'd better go through with it or don't promise anything.'

Marbles came in candy stripes, swirling colors of red and white, white and blue, milkies, translucence, white glass, little solids, small glass, solid colors (like those used in Chinese Checkers), and waters (clear glass). I liked the bum-boozers best, the largest of all the marbles.

The best way to shoot a marble (I was taught) is to place all of your knuckles on the ground and insert the marble inside the first finger between the tip and nail of the thumb. The marble is shot by the thumb going forward quickly, the shooting with knees bent on the ground for balance.

On the ground, Jimmy drew a big circle, about six feet in diameter, with a small circle, about six inches in diameter, in the middle. The outer circle was the boundary used to shoot marbles into the inner circle. Any marble that ended outside the inner circle was fair game. These marbles would be easier to shoot at because it would be closer to the outer circle. Players are permitted to raise the shooter's hand by using the left hand as a bridge or brace for the right hand. If the player is left handed, the opposite occurs. Players may move about the outer circle to position themselves for a better shot.

The object of the game is to get the marbles out of the bigger circle. The shooter kept each one that was shot out of the bigger circle. The idea is to end up with more marbles than the bet called for. Obviously, the person who ended up with the most marbles is declared the winner.

Before any game like marbles, there is a game for choosing sides called *jun-ken-po*, also known to many as paper-scissors-stone. This was one of many children's games that arbitrarily decided things. The object of this one-handed game is to guess what the other person's intent is. One participant beats the other by out-thinking him or her. A clenched fist stands for stone, two pointed fingers for scissors, and an open hand for paper. Since scissors cannot cut stone, stone is the winner. Scissors can cut through paper, so scissors is the winner. Since paper can wrap around stone, paper beats stone. If two people came up with the same hand gesture, it's declared a tie. The process then starts again until someone has something different. The law of elimination prevails.

After about an hour or so of marbles, we'd both get tired of the big circle game. Someone would then suggest playing four holes. To play four holes, players need a place where the dirt is hard and flat. The game configuration is shaped like a baseball field. The holes are aligned like bases, each base separated by a distance of five hand spans.

The idea of the game was to try and put the master marble in each hole from first base to home plate. But there is a catch to the game. A shooter can use a hand span to blast the opponent's marble elsewhere away from the hole. This makes it harder for opponent to get the marble into the hole. Once the marble is shot into a hole, the player can continue to advance, again with the use of a hand span. Normally there is a bet before the game. Generally, the bet around the camps was five marbles. The losing player had to forfeit the five marbles to the opponent.

After hours of marbles, Jimmy and I often sat on the porch and discussed plans for the next day. During one of these porch-planning sessions we agreed to go to The Pump the next day, early before the crowd got there.

The next day, Jimmy and I rode our bikes to The Pump, about two miles from Camp Four. The Pump was a two hundred and fifty-foot deep hole dug by immigrants. I was told that when they were looking for water, the immigrants of the sugar plantation surprisingly tapped into an artesian spring. On one occasion I was allowed to go down the elevator with Mr. Yasui, the caretaker, and actually see the pool at the bottom of the elevator shaft. The temperature dropped at least twenty-five degrees as we descended. The elevator shaft was narrow with concrete walls on the sides to prevent erosion or cave in. I thought that when we reached bottom that the pool would be small, but was I wrong.

At the bottom of the shaft was a small lake. He told me that swimming was inadvisable because the temperature of the water was about thirty degrees colder than the surface water. He informed me that the sugar company would never run out of water from this well. I believed him because I always saw water running from it along the Ha'iku ditch. I also noticed small red shrimp swimming in the underground pond. He told me that, at times, the shrimp would multiply and tint the water red. When he first saw the red water, Mr. Yasui thought that colored dirt had leaked from the wall

There were two big pipes at The Pump that always had water spouting from them. The water would empty into a long wide concrete ditch, the water depth about two-and-a-half feet most of the time. The water traveled about twenty-five feet and emptied into a six-foot concrete irrigation ditch. The Ha'iku Ditch had a vertical cast-iron pipe submerged about a foot from the bottom. That pipe carried water to another section of the cane field about a half-mile above The Pump. Its holding area was about twenty by twenty feet wide and about eight feet deep and was used to irrigate the cane fields. Once in a while we'd swim in that square milky dirty pond. Downstream water in the Ha'iku Ditch would level to about three feet. There was always water, sometimes dirty, that ran from the opposite side of the ditch that was used by the irrigation man to water the nearby cane fields.

Jimmy and I swam close to where the water exited from the two big pipes. I say close because I heard that when the water pump stopped, the output was reversed. It was not likely that we'd be sucked in, but we did keep our distance. Those two pipes were about two feet above the level of swimmers. It was a small, yet strong, waterfall that was always cold whether summer, winter, rainy season, morning, or afternoon.

Jimmy and I liked the area where the water poured out. We would slouch down and, with the current, get carried away to the entry of the Ha'iku Ditch. It was named that because the water flowed to Ha'iku.

On occasions, before we went to The Pump, we would ride our bikes to Walker Hill, a place named like many others, after a prominent *haole* (caucasian) who was a sugar plantation boss. At the top of Walker Hill were the boss' large home and a tennis court. No one from the camps seemed surprised that a white person lived there.

Plantation trucks that irrigated the fields used the road that led to

Walker Hill and beyond. The road also led to residents who lived at a higher elevation and by camp people who lived above Pu'unene.

There is no way to accurately describe the horrible condition of the road. One of our favorite pastimes was to race down Walker Hill while avoiding the holes. Because of the steep incline, Walker Hill was the perfect place to catch a thrilling ride on our bikes. The downhill racecourse covered about a third of a mile. Fragments of rocks also riddled Walker Hill road. Water seeped into the cracks in the road, creating a gap between the road and the ground. The constant weight of vehicles caused the weakened part of the road to create holes in the blacktop. Consequently, rocks of various sizes were strewn all over the route. Kids on bikes would race down single file. Because of the numerous potholes, a rider was bound to hit one of those craters, fly over his handlebars, and end up on the ground, usually with his bike on top of him. Riders had scratches and salmons. A salmon was a big patch of skin that had been scraped away; what remained looked like the orange/red fish flesh.

Walker Hill had two lanes, so when we rode down it, two bikes raced in one lane and two in the other. How committed or how chicken were the riders to make it across the finish line? Whenever a car ascended or descended Walker Hill, two of the riders would eventually have to bail off the road. Danger awaited beyond both shoulders of the route.

On the left side of the road, large monkey pod trees grew with low hanging branches partly concealed by high growing grass. In addition, stones of every imaginable size were scattered in the tall undergrowth. Beyond that, there was a soft dirt road and, farther beyond, the ditch that ran along the cane field.

The right shoulder happened to be a better place to crash. There was only a patch of trees and a concrete ditch, three feet wide and a foot and a half deep. When the cane fields were irrigated, water flowed from the Ha'iku Ditch. If a rider happened to ride his bike into the ditch by accident, he probably would be swept away by the swift down hill current and receive, without question, injuries to his body from the concrete bottom. One could even possibly drown if he got tangled up in his bike.

On this unforgettable day, when Jimmy and I got to the top of Walker Hill, Peter and Gerald were already there. There was always a challenge and a bet before we did anything daring. We were always trying to prove ourselves as to who was the best or the bravest. I swore that one day we'd kill ourselves testing our true grit. Today it was a race down the hill.

All four of us lined up. Two were in one lane, two in the other. We stood, posed on our pedals. Someone shouted, 'Go!' Off we went, pumping as hard as we could to zoom down the course as fast as possible.

Suddenly, a desperate cry came from one of the downhill racers, 'Watch out! There's a car behind us!' It wasn't me; I didn't see the car. Peter had enough room to squeeze into the lane that Jimmy and I occupied. Gerald, however, was less fortunate and resorted to a hard left, sailing full speed off the road and into the tall grass and its rocks. He flew so fast that he didn't see the overhanging branches. He cleared the embankment, crossed the dirt road, cleared the dirt ditch, and ended up a good ten feet deep in the cane field, his bike on top of him.

When we finally reached Gerald, we found him in a daze. There was a big lump on his forehead and bloody marks all over his body, his shirt torn. His faithful bike, luckily, was spared with only a flat tire. Needless to say, he pushed it all the way home.

That was a natural occurrence with us. Our general philosophy of bravery was that it was all okay as long as one could still walk away after such an accident. Scratches and salmons would disappear in a couple of weeks.

When Gerald went home, his mother swabbed mercurochrome on his red badges of courage. Mercurochrome was the general remedy for all open wounds. The first thing out of the medicine cabinet was the stinging reddish-orange liquid that stained our clothes.

157

It was great fun riding our bikes down Walker Hill but it was not funny when we had to push our bikes up to its crest in the scorching sun. As the sun rose higher in the sky, it got harder to push our bikes to the top.

Not too long after Gerald's accident, the same four daredevils decided to race down Walker Hill on our bikes again. As usual, our bet was about who was the fastest.

Off we went! We streamed down the hill like four knuckleheads; the only sound of whirling tires and the cranking pedals. All was fine; perhaps a world record would be broken that day. Suddenly, Gerald's tire hit one of the crushed rocks on the road. He flipped over the handlebar, tumbling while trying to hang on to his bike. The bike itself finally came to a stop, but Gerald, unfortunately sailed five feet past it.

The hospital was down the road. Gerald was in such bad shape that we had to carry him there. We took turns piggy-backing him until we got to the emergency room. He had scrapes all over his arms and legs, and even on his head. He looked so bad, blood all over his body.

We visited Gerald at the hospital the next day. We couldn't help but laugh when we saw him. This guy was accident-prone. There were black and blue bruises all over his body. The doctor told Gerald that he was a lucky guy. Adults tend to automatically tighten up when they're falling and end up with more serious injuries. Kids tend to let things roll, without thinking and, as a result, are less prone to injury than an adult. If Gerald had tightened up, the doctor definitely believe that his patient would have had broken bones. He spent a few days in the hospital and was released.

As soon as we left the confines of the clinic, the three of us fell onto our backs on the hospital lawn, laughing, holding our hurting stomachs. There we retold, from every angle, Gerald's solo flight through the air and his donut-roll down the hill.

Often, after racing down Walker Hill, we'd park our bikes to swim at The Pump, the happening place. Some swimming ability was a prerequisite. A few newcomers had almost drowned there. Remember the vertical pipe that ran underwater in the Ha'iku Ditch? Someone once got stuck between the pipe and the bottom of the ditch. If a rescuer hadn't jumped into the ditch to pull him out, the victim would have died that day.

What I haven't mentioned yet was that there were lots of crayfish in the Ha'iku Ditch. Many of us made homemade spear guns to poke them. A story circulated that a guy was once spearing crayfish between the pipe and the bottom. Because the flow of the water behind him was too powerful, it took him awhile to swim backwards and break from the current. My luck was much better. I brought home about twenty-five crayfish one day. It was our dinner that night, believe it or not.

Everyone knew about The Pump. It was probably a place where some of our parents had learned to swim in their younger days. Everybody who wanted to learn to swim, sooner or later would end up at The Pump. It was such a popular place to go, so popular that, especially in the summer, it was sometimes too over-crowded.

One day, on the way back from The Pump, another friend, Jerry, asked me if I wanted to see something very unusual. He said that all I needed was my bike and a flashlight. Being the adventurous type and willing to try anything for the first time, though afraid of getting hurt, I reluctantly said yes.

Jerry told me this had to be seen at night and only at night, and that the following evening might be ideal because there won't be any moon out in the sky, making it a very dark night. If we didn't go the next night, we'd have to experience this unusual thing on another date.

As soon as I got home, I asked my father if I could go somewhere tomorrow night. I told him that Jerry had something to show me. He readily agreed and gave me one of his flashlights.

159

Jerry has always been a clown and a go-for-it-all type of adventurous guy. He was neither afraid of the dark nor of anyone. If a person looked funny to him, he'd tell it to the guy's face and often end up in a fight, that he always won. However, he was also well liked because, as a friend, he would defend you to the end. He helped me out in a fight no matter how big or how tall the opponent was. He never took anything for granted. Actually, he was crazy!

The following day, after doing my chores and eating dinner, I listened to my favorite fifties music as I waited for Jerry. It must have been about seven o'clock when he showed up. The sun had set about an hour ago and it was dark and windless. It had been blowing all day, but suddenly the trades had stopped at about six-thirty.

With flashlight in hand, we rode our bikes along the dirt cane field road. Even with the flashlight, I failed see a rock ahead of me. I flew over the handle bar of my bike, tumbled on the hard dirt road, and end up on the embankment. I had dirt all over my clothes and body, and there was nowhere to wash up. I hurt badly, but I was still curious about Jerry's mystery. He and I laughed as we recalled Gerald's similar past incident off Walker Hill. Although Jerry hadn't been there when it happened, he had been told about Gerald's misfortune. He was familiar with our accident-prone friend, so, like everyone else, he too laughed until his stomach hurt.

About a mile into the cane field, Jerry whispered, "Stop the bike! Leave it here! We'll walk! Don't make any noise." We tread softly for another thirty yards. Suddenly, I heard sounds. They were oohs and aahs coming from a short distance directly in front of us.

"Crawl," Jerry whispered, "toward the oohs and the aahs. I'll wait here for you." I crept on hands and knees. It was so pitch dark that I couldn't see past my nose. There was no moon or stars in the sky. Closer and closer I wriggled my body to the sounds of pleasure or pain, perhaps too close. Because of the high weeds, I didn't realize that there was an irrigation ditch with quiet flowing water that ran parallel to me. I made another lurch forward, but it was too late, I toppled into the irrigation ditch rolling smack into a guy standing above me, stark naked. I happened to know because I tried to grab whatever I could to stand. Unfortunately, I grabbed the wrong part of his body! I pulled so hard that he screamed. I turned on the flashlight. The guy looked like a chicken that had just been plucked. The nude stranger yelled cuss words at me. I immediately knew from his voice who he was. I instinctively turned the lights on his partner, a woman totally naked. She was also a camp familiar.

I was so scared that I climbed the embankment and I ran as fast as I could down the cane field road. Luckily, the flashlight prevented me from hitting an obstacle in the dark. I had an afterthought, as I ran, that the guy in his birthday suit was chasing the light and was on my tail. I decided to turn off the flashlight so he couldn't see me. Of course, without it on, I wouldn't be able to see anything either. The prediction was fulfilled. I did not see a massive overhanging cane stalk. The large stem hit me directly on my forehead. I fell backwards onto my head. Both the welt on the forehead and headache started to develop as I lay knocked out.

Jerry ran up to me as I lay on the ground. He laughingly harassed me as I came to. I spilled out half-dazed that I had fallen on a naked guy. 'What a night!' Jerry replied. 'First, you fall off your bike, then you fall on a buck-naked guy, and now you're flat on your back. We better go home before you end up in the hospital. Wait till your father sees you in this condition.'

Sure enough, when I got home, I glanced in the mirror for the first time. I looked like I had been at war. A long red bar ran across my forehead. I had cuts and scratches, and on the back of my head I felt a *kon-to-bu* (huge lump- Hawaiian Pidgin). And again, I don't know what hurt more, the injury or the mercurochrome.

Jerry and I went into the room to have a talk about the night. He told me that they were having sex. This was my first experience of witnessing the act! Jerry explained that it was like making a

161

cake, but I told him that I never heard my mother go ooh and aah when she baked.

So, I got my first lesson about the birds and the bees. After having a good talk with my father, I learned that older people hide and do it. I also realized at that moment that there had been sex all around me but, as a young kid, I never paid much attention to it. I'd hear oohs and aahs and sometimes slight screams as the bed squeaked in rhythm. Sometimes it sounded as though the bed was going to fall through the floor. At other times, I heard softer squeaks. I thought, "Why are my parents moving beds around late at night, especially when everyone was asleep?" I found it amazing that they could move furniture around without lights. I had heard these familiar noises while passing plantation homes late at night, I finally realized after my encounter in the cane field as to what was really happening in those camp bedrooms after lights out.

This was not my first revelation that things are not what they seem to be. My grandfather on my father's side died of a heart attack after visiting friends. His demise came sooner because he had drunk too much alcohol for a long time. My grandmother was left with three sons. My father was the oldest and lived right across the way from her. Her second son, the fisherman, lived a number of years with her before moving to the mainland. The third son joined the army and later on took advantage of the G.I. Bill and went on to college.

I remember one particular day as I passed by my grandmother's house. I heard someone yelling from it. I raced onto the porch and I saw, through the screen door, my uncle slapping my grandmother. He kept pleading, "We're having a hard time with money and you are sending some to Japan." I saw my grandmother bleeding from the mouth as my uncle continued to slap her. I witnessed him hit her three times. I do not know how many times he had done this before. However, I did know that if I told my father about this, that he would have probably thrown my uncle out of the house. And, knowing my father's temper, he might have even tried to kill him.

After the two brothers left, my grandmother lived alone. At this point, my father was in control of his own paycheck to buy food for the family. Once a day, my father would take food over to her for her dinner. She never visited us. Sometimes she'd cook her own food on the kerosene stove. She'd often season a pork slab with salt and pepper and fry it. She would also cook her own *gohan*. She loved that combination because that was all she ate. I presume that since she lived by herself, she decided that *gohan* was easy and fast to prepare.

The smell of kerosene from kitchens that I passed by daily throughout my growing years is imbedded in my mind. To this day, I can still pick up the distinctive odor of kerosene.

Another distinctive smell is in my memory. There were days when I came home from school, and, as I lit the fire to heat the *furo*, I noticed my grandmother sitting on the stairs that led to the kitchen, across from me, combing her long gray hair, hair that had not been cut for several years. She'd gather all the hair and place it in a gallon can close to her. She'd later burn it. The burnt hair was quite smelly.

I asked her once why she did that? She responded by saying, "Hair is the only thing that does not turn to dust; everything else does, including human beings." I found out years later about the durability of hair when we moved my brother's body to a new cemetery. When he was unearthed, I saw his bones as well as small hairs that had fallen from the skull. Those hairs looked as though it had been yesterday when the body was buried.

Grandmother would often ask me to go to the store and buy her Kitch'n Cook'd potato chips and a bottle of Coke. She liked that combination so much that it became her standard order. She'd also give me a little extra money to purchase whatever I wanted.

Money I received from *obasan* (grandmother) was spent on baseball cards. There were five cards of different baseball players along with a slab of pink bubble gum in a colorful wrapper. The gum was the same size as the cards but a little bit thicker. I can still remember an occasion when I was eight when I tried to see

163

how many whole pieces of chewing gum I could put in my mouth and chew. My record was five, the result – a very sore mouth for a couple of days.

Eventually my collection of baseball cards amounted to a couple hundred. My baseball cards were stashed away in shoe or cigar boxes. My friends and I would trade away duplicates for cards that we didn't have. At times we would trade a lot of cards for one that was very popular. That's how Whitey Ford ended up in my collection.

Another use for duplicate baseball cards was to create sound effects. We'd take the cards, bend them at the long end, and, with clothespins, attach them to the spokes of our bicycles. When the wheels rotated, they made the sound of a sick motorcycle. The cards would wear out eventually and other faces of unpopular ball players replaced the worn cards.

It was about time to re-visit Mr. Choi. I didn't want much time to elapse before I'd see him again. I had this feeling that it was the right time. As I made the turn toward Mr. Choi's house, I heard a commotion going on in front of the store. I decided to go and investigate. Camp Four at that time was considered the gambling camp of Pu'unene, so I wasn't too surprised to see three men being handcuffed, caught in back of the store for gambling. This was not the first time nor would it be the last time this would happen. Suddenly, one of the guys bolted loose from the cops. He ran like a mongoose, so scared of being arrested that his adrenaline allowed him to jump and clear a ten-foot ditch. The cops laughed at his frantic antics and let him go.

As usual, Mr. Choi had been waiting for me. He was sitting on the top step of the porch as I approached. Before I said anything, he invited me inside. As I sat, I asked him to tell me more about life. I wanted him to tell me more about my surroundings, specifically about nature.

He said, "Have respect for things that you can handle and things that you cannot handle. Have respect for fishes, sea creatures, animals, insects, trees and all that is alive and growing.

Remember that all things that I have mentioned are living things. Also have respect for the wind, rain, and clouds and anything that surrounds you. The beauty of nature belongs here as much as you do. Do not take away from nature what belongs to it. As humans, do not take away what belongs to humans. When you destroy nature, you are destroying yourself. Without nature you cannot survive, but nature without you can survive. It is the people who live on this earth, without thinking, who mess up the earth. Who was here first, you or nature? You? I don't think so!

Here is a perfect example of nature. Have you noticed that the same trees bear the same fruit year after year and at about the same time of the year? Due to the weather conditions, the yield varies from year to year. Although, a few fruit are small, have you noticed that the fruits are generally the same size? Doesn't that tell you something?" Nature is perfect in its truest sense.

He stood, walked to the kitchen, and returned with a glass of water, and sat with his legs crossed. "What I have here in my hands is a glass of water as you can see. Water is what I want to talk about now.

Water that has been here millions of years; it's still here today, neither increasing nor decreasing. We always have the same amount of water on this earth. Water goes through an endless cycle through evaporation from the sea and the rivers. Three fourths of the earth is water. As the sun shines, water is evaporated, forming clouds. These clouds, in return, drop the water back on to land by either snow or rain and reduce the temperature of the earth.

Rainfall soaks into the ground, waters the plants, and creates fresh water springs that run deep underground. Run-off from rain and snow supplies the earth with fresh drinking water through waterfalls, lakes, ponds, rivers, and fresh water springs that eventually enter the ocean. Here, the cycle begins again. Using the water for their own use, humans and animals pass it on, and pollute a large portion (seventy-five percent) of the world's water supply."

165

With that, he stopped and told me that he didn't have much more to say at this time. So, I said my good-bye and left.

Because of the lack of money, camp families had to find ways of saving money. One of the many ways to save money was to resort to nature's bounty. With the ingenuity and with the help of local Hawaiians, the Japanese community cultivated a variety of seaweeds for consumption.

Knowledge of where certain seaweeds grew was important. These seaweeds grew at specific shorelines around the island. My father knew these locations and often dove for it. He also went to areas where the water was shallow, places where a gatherer could walk on the coral or stones to pick seaweed when the tide was low.

It was essential to know that certain seaweed needs calm waters (*Yin*) and others rougher waters (*Yang*). Seaweed needs lots of oxygenation. Throughout the year, certain areas of the island generated more surge than others. Whenever this condition is reversed, lots of seaweed ends up on the shoreline of rough beaches.

The favorite seaweed among Orientals was and still is *ogo*. The *ogo* that grows on the reefs, rocks, or sand has an array of colors. Most of the time, it is red or light brown, sometimes green. Because other seaweed tangles within the *ogo* branches, it is a pain to clean. We'd sit for a good hour cleaning it. The prized seaweed is used to make *namasu* (pickled *ogo*), mainly as a side dish.

Another *limu* (Hawaiian for seaweed) collected by my father was called crow's feet (*waiwai'ole*). It is a spongy green colored seaweed that looks like bird claws, soft and able to retain a lot of salt water. It is eaten raw or used as a side dish with onions, vinegar, sugar, and tomatoes. The seaweed grows like a carpet on the ocean floor. When the surge of large waves crashes onto the coast, branches break off, and eventually end up scattered in abundance along the shorelines.

166

Another way we, the poor, took advantage of nature's help was by gathering bamboo shoots when in season, generally between February and the early part of May. These *takenoko* (bamboo shoots) could be found in rainy areas like along the roadside on the way to Hana. Because it was time consuming and hard work, many were reluctant to trample through the bamboo forest to get the delicacies.

To get them we often left home early in the morning and took the winding roads beyond the sleepy town of Ha'iku. Our adventure led us to one of three bamboo forests. Every so often, along the side of the road, we'd see a ditch out in the open, then obscured by tunnels. Waterfalls and rivers fed into this ditch that was dug by immigrants at the turn of the century. It supplied to this day a constant flow of drinking water to the residents and nourishment for the cane fields of Central Maui.

As a precautionary measure, the following clothing was necessary for gathering bamboo shoots: a long sleeve t-shirt, denim pants, a hat (to prevent cuts from bamboo leaves), shoes (protection from stepping on cut stub bamboo), and Vicks Vapor Rub to rub all over places that remained uncovered to prevent mosquito bites. I hope this is something new to you.

The bamboo shoots grew next to a mature plant. To pick the bamboo shoots, I had to grab the top and bend it over. With bag in hand, I would pick as many as I could, sit at a certain area, then clean the layers of leaves from the bamboo shoots to a certain point and cutting off the top leaves. After placing all the shoots in bags gently, we would head back to the vehicle with the filled bags swung over my shoulders.

That was not the hardest job. When we got home, we used a peeler and cleaned the outer layer and cut them in half. We cooked them to a boil, soaked them in cold water, and bagged the bamboo shoots to share with our neighbors. We had to change the water every day for about three days to get rid of the bitterness. I was the guinea pig that ate the bamboo shoots when we first got it; it did taste bitter.

Making our way home from gathering excursions, we'd look for wild fruits growing along the roadside. With Keanae's constant rainfall, these fruits, mostly seasonal, prospered.

One fruit we constantly searched for was the guava. The guava is an evergreen tree and a native of tropical South America. This tree has long green leaves with white blossoms and produces green round fruits that ripen to a yellow colored skin. The thick-skinned fruit has compartments of seeds in the center. Guava can be eaten fresh, made into jams and jellies, or blended to make juice. A lot of sugar must be used to make the juice sweet. We were always happy to share the guava with other families to make jams or jellies.

Kids would look for the Y branches of the guava tree to make slingshots. The branches were sought after for the weapon because of its hardness. The branch was stripped of its bark and left to dry for a week or so. A pouch made of leather was centered with rubber bands attached to the pouch and the guava branch. It was a slingshot almost impossible to break.

Another fruit that was sought after was the rose apple (*ohi'a loke* – Hawaiian). A native of India and Malaysia, the rose apple is also known as the Fruit of Immortality. Rose apples have large pom-pom blossoms located at the end of the branch. They develop into a fruit that is round, yellow, and very sweet, with a distinctive taste and odor. The rose apple is attacked by insects and becomes inedible where it was stung.

Another fruit that was located where we went to get bamboo shoots was a fruit that was not in season at the same time with the bamboo shoots. One would have to get this fruit at another time of the year, generally around the month of August. The mountain apple (*'ohi'a 'ai* – Hawaiian), a relative to the rose apple, is also the native of Malaysia. Tiny pinkish-red blossoms pop out all along the trunk and along the branches of the tree and eventually develop into fruits. The pulp of the fruit is similar to an apple, yet softer. The flesh is white and the skin is reddish. Because of its delicate skin, this fruit bruises easily, so care is needed when handling it. Because the tree was known to be sacred, temple

168

idols were carved from its wood. Since then, a variety with white skin instead of red has been developed. These apples have a distinctive sweet flavor, but don't taste like apples.

One of the many freely available foods was the breadfruit. Brought to Hawai'i by the early Polynesians from Tahiti, the breadfruit (actually a starch) was used as a staple source of food, its trunk for the construction of canoes. Each fruit can weigh up to an average of two pounds. As a food item, the breadfruit can be boiled, baked, fried, or, after its skin removed and boiled, pounded into *poi*. Like *taro*, Polynesians ate the starch in place of potatoes or rice.

Another item for the picking was the jackfruit. Its tree produces a fruit that weighs up to seventy pounds. It is quite long, always green; and one of the largest fruits known to man. The fruit grows along the trunk of the tree. I never found out how the picker knew when the fruit was ripe. Boiled, baked, or fried, the fruit tasted delicious when cooked with butter. The large white seeds tasted like chestnuts to me. They could be roasted and eaten. I have never seen anyone eat it raw.

In the late nineteenth century, Japanese immigrants smuggled seeds of other fruits like the loquat in their pockets into Hawai'i. These seeds were planted in the uplands of Maui, and produced an orange fruit with large seeds in the center. Growing in bunches, these fruits ripened in early spring, were sometimes sweet, sometimes sour, depending on the type of soil they were planted in and how much water was given to the tree. Loquats were eaten from the tree with the skin removed. Sometimes the seeds were removed and the fruit became part of a salad. Sweet loquats were a special treat and offered or exchanged for other commodities with the people of the low lands.

As I grew up, I realized that everything taken from nature should never be wasted. My father once said, "Respect nature for what it is. Do not hoard nature's gifts. Take only what you need or are willing to share. Be thankful for a chance in your lifetime to reap the harvest of nature. Not many are so blessed." My father taught me a good lesson on this subject.

My father had another lesson of wisdom. "Do not enter the water when the seas are rough with high waves or milky waters. There will always be another day when the water will be calm and clear." I'll never forget a similar heeding an old Hawaiian man told me a number of years ago. He said, "Take only enough from the sea and you will be blessed with another day. Take too much and you will be part of the sea." I never thought that my father had the same philosophy. I guess that it's part of the code of those who really love the sea.

My father was born on August 11, 1919. He went as far as the sixth grade before he was forced to go to work. Being the oldest son, he had to work to help support the family. This was tradition in Japan that was continued in Hawai'i. His parents thought that it was more important for him to work instead of finishing school. The only thing he was capable of was working at the sugar plantation. This is not to say that he didn't know other things besides company work.

I can honestly say from living with him, that he would have been capable of doing well in school if he had continued. In fact, he could have become a learned man. He caught on so fast that it seems as though he needed only a one time-explanation. He was one of a kind. My youngest uncle once told me that my father's mind was being wasted. He knew long ago that my father was unique but circumstances prevented him from continuing school. I'm not bragging about my father. Many others also told me that.

A good example of my father's skills was that he was a good skin diver. He often caught so many fish that he and I had a hard time carrying them in rice bags to the car. His knowledge took him to a specific place for certain species. He was one person one could rely on to catch fish. He was that good. He never disappointed any one. He was a guy who didn't only try; he actually did it! He caught so many *uhu* (parrot fish) that he would share the surplus with his neighbors.

My father reminded me of the Polynesians who were the first to settle in Hawai'i. I learned in school and books that they

170

explored, crisscrossing within the vast triangle of Hawaiian Islands, New Zealand and Easter Island prior to A.D. 1500. After 2000 B.C., Polynesians, including the Maori of New Zealand, explored the rest of the South Pacific. They eventually settled in all the major islands by A.D. 1000.

Their main diet included taro, yams, sweet potato, coconuts, breadfruit, and bananas. All of these foods came from Southeast Asia except the sweet potato that came from New Guinea.

Aroids (taro-like plants) were an agricultural creation of the Polynesians. The Cook, Hawaiian and Society Islands cultivated these plants that grew and thrived in pond-like fields.

They brought along domesticated animals from Southeast Asia such as pigs, dogs, and chickens. Although their main diet consisted of fish from the ocean, many of the previously mentioned animals were consumed in large amounts at big gatherings.

Polynesians explored all the islands of the huge triangle, although most were not actually settled. The Hawaiian Islands, four thousand kilometers away, was one of their favorite destinations. They arrived: men, women, children, domesticated animals and seeds for planting. The two main reasons given for the migration was either the overpopulation in the Marquesas or Tahiti, or forced departures, as in defeat in war. Whatever the cause, they came in double-hulled canoes, eighty feet long, with a platform. These canoes, identical to the modern catamaran, were big enough to carry a house.

What was interesting and amazing is that Polynesians returned to their native land many times thereafter. Their return to Polynesia allowed them to get more seeds, plant cuttings, animals, and people. After the Polynesians arrived here, the term Hawai`i was given to the archipelago, perhaps after its discoverer, Hawai`i-loa.

Polynesians used the moon, stars, and wind currents to travel to Hawai`i. They used only a few homemade navigational instruments, but were well-versed sailors of the sea.

Here in the new land, they found indigenous plants and birds. They made use of native plants in their daily lives both as food and medicine. As time passed, seeds, other than those brought by settlers, drifted on debris along ocean currents. Birds traveling on wind currents left berry and flower seeds in their droppings. Many of the plants originally brought by the Polynesians are here today, but many have disappeared because of overcrowding, alien species, and the mismanagement of the wilderness by people.

Climate and seasons changed very little within most of Hawai`i. This allows plants and animals to prosper. The winds that blow from the Northeast, known commonly as the trade winds, cool the humid conditions and draw rain clouds that pass over the islands in a regular pattern, keeping the slopes along the mountains and valleys fertile and green.

Storms that come from the west or south with a lot of rain during and after the winter months also generate Kona winds, because it seemed that it came from a town on the south side of the Big Island of Hawai'i. Whenever there are Kona Winds, today called variables, there are bound to be warm winds and rain in the islands.

With the influx of more and more Polynesians to Hawai'i, rules were needed and enforced by the chiefs (*ali'i*). There were three classes of people: the chiefs, the working people, and the outcasts. Everyone knew what was expected of him or her, and their place in society. *Ali'i* (chiefs of royal blood) were responsible caregivers of lots of land. Some of the *ali'is were* of higher ranking so the lower class chiefs served the *ali'i* of higher stature. Respected by the people, *ali'i* led a better life as leaders of the Hawaiian people.

Hawaiians believed that family *(ohana)* was important, so important that a *haku* (master) was appointed leader of *ohana* to settle problems between family members. His job was to make sure that the unit stayed together.

172

Hawaiians believed that big strong individuals were the best. Because they had strong bodies and white teeth, Hawaiians rarely got sick. Because they were isolated far away from civilization and life-threatening diseases, Hawaiians never contacted any disease until much later. With their keen knowledge of agriculture, these Hawaiians raised and ate nutritious food. Hawaiians were very clean people. Their villages were neat and the residents bathed daily. They purposely lived near streams and got pure and clean drinking water from up stream.

Lower class Hawaiians were the outcasts that were looked down upon. Some historians theorize that they might have been the first settlers of these islands, outcasts of their native land.

Some Hawaiians were born with special skills or power. These few were trained to become *kahuna* (priest). There were good and bad *kahuna*. There were *some* who knew other families' histories, those who wished death on certain individuals, and others who performed healing. These priests specialized in all needs in their daily lives.

Hawaiians believed that the gods created everything, including the creation of Hawai'i a long time ago. They also believed that the islands were children of the gods, born to Wakea and Papa.

Those who owned lands close to the ocean cared for shoreline and reefs. Open water was considered anybody's fishing ground. Along the shoreline, *wana* (sea urchin), *opihi* (limpets), and *limu* (seaweed) were gathered for food or for medicinal purposes.

Early Hawaiians studied, understood, and respected the ever changing sea and its many resources. With over 600 different species of fish available in Hawaiian waters, the natives never took more than they needed. Once in a while, they gathered surplus from the oceans and bargained with upcountry farmers, who grew the best vegetables on the island. They bargained their crops for personal consumption or as offerings to the gods.

To prevent humans from over fishing, times of *kapu* (forbidden practices) were strictly enforced. During spawning season, certain fish were deemed *kapu,* and the laws were regulated by strict penalties. Violating *kapu* meant instant death for offenders. A coconut branch placed on the shoreline indicated that fishing was restricted in that particular area. Ancient Hawaiians never took fishes, spawning with eggs or babies.

These *kanaka maoli* (Hawaiians) constructed fishponds in order to preserve a fish population. The caretakers of fishponds allowed the fish to mature. They harvested them only when needed. Rocks used to build the fishponds were carried down from the mountainside by hand and formed a semi-circle. Day after day, Hawaiians ventured up mountains for large stones until the fishponds were completed.

Ponds with shallow depths of eight fathoms (Six feet is equal one fathom.) were called *kaukala.* Those with depths of twenty to forty fathoms were called *pohakialoa.* Fishermen, with full knowledge of the sea and its inshore and outer reefs and its crevices were able to locate a certain species of fish that lived in different conditions and depths.

Fishermen also needed special knowledge of which fish was reserved to be eaten only by royalty. No other class of people within the Hawaiian community was allowed to eat the fish of royalty. Those who did received severe punishment.

Because of the lack of any special equipment, most Hawaiian fishermen of old caught fish by hand. They stuck their hands under rocks, coral heads, and crevices, felt, then yanked the sea creatures from their hiding places. Some Hawaiian fishermen were so good that they occasionally caught fish with their hands while swimming in the open ocean.

Women also fished, but from the fresh water ponds and rivers. They used a weaved basket to catch *opai* (fresh water shrimp). *O'opu* (gobies) were also caught by hand or traps. *Hihi wai* (freshwater shell fish) were gathered and cooked in soups, open fires, or eaten raw. I once heard that if someone was going to gather *hihi wai* and told someone about it, the gatherer will not be able to find anyone that day.

174

Because of the separation of terrain, fishermen who lived along the shoreline and farmers who lived along the uplands were obligated to barter with each other. Farmers grew trees and vines needed by fisherman. Among them were *koa* trees needed to make canoes and *alona* plants necessary for fishing lines. These people of the uplands dictated and controlled the supply of fishing equipment. The fishermen, on the other hand, had control of gathering bounty from the ocean. Farmers did some part time fishing while fishermen did some part-time farming, both dependent on each other.

Many plants brought by Polynesians and plants that were already here needed dry climate and low lands to flourish. Taro and breadfruit didn't need to be grown in the highlands, but in any place with sufficient rainfall.

The coconut tree (*niu*) was one plant that flourished in the lowlands. It is believed that the coconut itself floated along currents and drifted here to Hawai'i where it washed ashore and flourished. The Polynesian immigrants in Hawai'i planted coconut trees that grew inland.

Fishermen who believed in the gods received good luck with their catches. With help of fishing gods, mainly *ku`ula* (stone altar near the fishing area) and *amakua*, (protector in nature) they were productive. In thankful return, fishermen made offerings of fish to the *amakua*. These family protectors came in many forms such as a shark or barracuda that helped fishermen chase fish into waiting nets.

Ancient Hawaiians acknowledged many gods that influenced their daily life. A fishing shrine called *koa* was located along shorelines to worship Ku`ula Kai, the god of fish and fishermen, his wife, Hinapu Kai`a, and son, Ai`i. When fishermen left to fish, stones were added to the *koa*. Returning from catches, fishermen placed offerings on local altars dedicated to the gods, Kuaha or Lele.

On their long voyages to Hawai'i, the Polynesian travelers picked

175

up knowledge of various fishing methods. The use of hooks carved in their previous homelands is evident by the discovery of hooks by archeologists throughout Hawaiian history. Fishhooks made of dog and pig bones prove that those animals were brought over by the first travelers. Because the hook is one of the most important items needed for fishing, different materials were later substituted in the formation of hooks. The natives later used turtle shells, dogteeth, and bird, and pig bones. Hooks made from human *iwi* (bones) were extracted from great fishermen.

Because of the variety of the mouth sizes of fish, different sizes of hooks were needed. The Polynesian version of hooks was carved with barb-less and knobbed shanks. Eventually, the hooks were made with barbs to keep the bait in place and the fish firmly hooked. Tools used to shape fishhooks were mainly coral and lava rocks.

Ancient Hawaiians visited their fishing grounds secretly. A fisherman well versed with his equipment and fishing grounds was reluctant to reveal his private place. Most of these undisclosed fishing grounds were handed down through generations and kept within the family. Because the fishing places were inherited, smart fishermen practiced conservation and did not over-fish on personal grounds.

Branches of the hau tree were cut and bones of dogs or pigs were used to make goggles to fit the eyes. String from sennet was used to join the goggles together. Eventually, in modern times, clear glass bottles were used to make lenses that fit both sides of the goggles. Swimmers and divers used *limu* or spit to prevent the glasses from fogging, so they could see the ocean beneath the surface clearly.

With the eventual added advantage of the spear gun, Hawaiians became more proficient divers. Different spear guns were used for different prey. The weapons made it easy to spear fish in open waters or those confined within coral heads or crevices. Spears were also used to catch fish in schools in the shallows of shorelines.

Another form of spear was made solely for catching octopus (*he'e* - Hawaiian), *tako* (Japanese). People of Hawai'i erroneously call an octopus a squid. This is wrong because a squid is actually a calamari. But, since everyone called it squid, squid became its name. Squid can be found in cracks, crevices, coral heads, pipes, along the side of coral heads, between two coral heads, between reefs and sand, and more often swimming on reefs. Others sometimes are totally disguised. The best way to find squid is to look for dug out holes. More than likely it's their home. One of the reasons they might not be in the hole is because they are feeding elsewhere or someone else has previously speared the squid. *He'e* is a master of disguise. He blends with the background and changes into many different colors. Unless one is trained to spot squid, he will not find success. *He'e* can be difficult to locate. One can swim past a *he'e* and never realize it. The record catch of a *he'e* as of this writing in the state is seventeen pounds. I've heard of fishermen fishing the deep waters have caught bigger ones. None can be taken under a pound according to state law.

Another variety of octopus sharing the Hawaiian waters is commonly known as night squid (*puloa*). Appearing after dark, this squid is easier to locate by its reddish color with white dots throughout the body. It is said that a three-pound *puloa* is capable of escaping through a dime size hole in the bag. Not only is it capable of escaping, the *puloa* bites when grabbed or handled. It was avoided during torch fishing (*lama lama*) because Hawaiians believed it was bad luck to eat the night squid.

The best time to fish is early in the morning or late afternoons, with overcast skies being the ideal condition. Fish tend to feed during those times. When it is overcast, fish tend to believe that it is dawn or dusk. Fishermen contend that high or low tides make a difference and prefer incoming to outgoing tides.

Today, bait used on fishing excursions includes imported medium shrimp, live *opai* (Hawaiian glass shrimp) caught along the shoreline in *limu* and in rocky and sand areas. *Ohiki* crab is found along sandy beaches, *'a'ama* (black crab) running along the rocks, and sea worms in waters close to a muddy, pebbly

177

shoreline, dug at in about two to three feet of water in certain places. Squid and calamari can be used for catching *'oio* (bone fish), *ulua* over ten pounds and *papio* (both blue trevally) less than ten pounds. Different fishermen use different types of bait, including baits that are seasonal along with artificial lures bought at a store. Baits mentioned above are not only for one type of fish, but for different species as well.

With the advent of new fishing gear, such as throw nets, surround nets, fins, snorkel gear, knapsack torches or lanterns (used for *lama lama*), fish traps, crab nets, and high powered spear guns, fish have little chance for survival to maturity. Without proper management of fishing, slowly and surely the supply of fish will be depleted from the ocean.

The State Department of Land & Natural Resources was formed to regulate the taking of fish and marine life. They deemed it necessary to create non-fishing seasons for some species, just as the ancient Hawaiians did. During certain months of the year, especially during the summer, specific species during spawning weren't allowed be caught.

With the Pacific Ocean completely surrounding all of the Hawaiian Islands, the likelihood of loving the water and its warm temperatures is more than likely. Likewise, learning to swim was, and still is, an essential part of growing up. And yet, there are a few who have not learned how to swim. There are always a few who simply detest waking up early in the morning to do anything, much less fish. It's sad that many water activities are available and, yet, some people did not take advantage of it.

Fishing was a pastime for many people in the camps; children learned the art while growing up. At one time or another, most locals have had the chance to go fishing with their parents or friends. Many acquired the adventure of fishing and, yet, there are some that refuse to go near the water because of a bad experience or a total dislike for the sport of fishing.

I was initially one of those who hated waking up at 4:00 a.m. to go fishing. But my parents, nevertheless, woke me up. By 5:00

a.m., my father, mother, uncle and I often headed in a topless military jeep for Makena, along Maui's south coast. Even Kihei, with its sunny beaches along the way to Makena, could still be cold, chilled by the winds that ripped down the side of ten thousand foot Haleakala. There were days when the cold actually numbed our hands and feet and sent shivers throughout our bodies. The warmest clothing didn't help at all; the cold winds seemed to penetrate the heavy covering.

We would pass Kihei and proceeded toward Makena on an old bumpy road that wound through lava fields with protruding rough rocks. The innumerable holes in the road made it very hard on our *'okole* (bottoms). Every so often, the bumps caused us to rise airborne off our cushion-less seats. We bounced up and down hurting our butts until we reached our destination.

The only residents of Makena my father knew at the time of our fishing adventures was a family named Kodak who owned a house at the end of the road. They were descendants of the famous Kodak camera family, and they had spent lots of money to have water pipes, electricity, and a sewage system installed in this isolated area with no infrastructure.

At the very end of the road, one can see what is known as the King's Highway. The road was constructed with lava rocks and yet is completely flat. It stretches about eight feet across with foot high walls on both sides that wind for miles along the south coast. This highway is truly a marvel and engineer's fascination. Conceived over a hundred years ago, some of the road still remains intact. Hawaiian kings and their subjects used the road exclusively up to the 18th Century. Some people claim that *menehune* (short Hawaiians with red eyes) can be seen walking the King's Highway late at night.

Sometimes, we'd reach the beach before the sun came up. We had to be careful when we walked the path of the lava rocks in the dark. If we were not careful, the sharp volcanic shards could leave nasty gashes on the side of our legs, making it a miserable day of fishing. These wounds took weeks to heal.

179

As soon as the sun rose over Haleakala, we carried our fishing poles, the container of fishing supplies, spears, spear guns, fins, goggles, lunch, and military canteens filled with fresh water along the path to our favorite fishing grounds. By the way, no trees grew in the lava flows. In other words, there was no shade to protect us from the direct sun.

When we reached the shoreline, my father would first scout the area. His main concern was hunting for *tako* that might be searching for food or, as my father called it, sun bathing. When lucky, he might catch one or two. These were not small *tako*. They averaged between two to four pounds.

My father's favorite prey was the *uhu* (parrotfish). He would carry a few spears with his spear gun when he entered the water. He waited patiently behind a rock and, as soon as a parrotfish came near, my father speared it. He left the speared *uhu* alone on the sea floor, attached another spear to his gun, and waited for another to approach. My father knew that when he left the speared *uhu* on the ocean floor, another would come along to see what was happening. *Uhu* are quite inquisitive, which was to my father's advantage. He would spear up to three before gathering the catch from the ocean floor and bring it to the surface. This was a task considering my father's trophies were about two to four pounds and much larger at times. There were two types of *uhu*, blue and brown and both tasted the same when steamed.

Another favorite fish my father liked to spear was the *Kole*. As mentioned before, knowledge of breeding grounds of certain fish was the key to success. *Kole* (yellow eye tang) is no exception to the rule. Although considerably smaller in size, *kole* hid in large numbers near large coral heads. *Kole* spearing was no different than *uhu* spearing. Again, my father would spear a few before gathering the speared *kole*. When fried, the color of the oil turned yellow, but, nevertheless, this fish was very good to eat.

Kole, which normally grew full grown to about six to eight inches in length, was considered fish for royalty in old Hawai'i. If one gave this fish away as a gift, which was rare, it was considered worthy of friendship between giver and receiver. It is thought in

180

old Hawaiian times that *kole* buried at each corner of the house brought good luck to the household.

For my mother and her brother, these fishing trips meant fishing for *mamo* (sergeant major). A twelve to fifteen foot light fiberglass straight pole made in Japan was used. It had a four pound test line, a floater above (painted with red nail polish), with a small piece of lead between the small straight shank hook with a small piece of bought shrimp hooked on. When the floater sank, that was the clue that fish had taken the bait; one had to have fast reflexes to lift the pole up quickly. If there was a fish on the line, the pole would be pulled downward. Often, *palu* (tomato sardines in a can, mixed with bread) was thrown in the water or smeared on the bait for an attractive scent. Mother and brother would generally catch about twenty *mamo* in a day.

Most times, when I was young, I went along for the ride with my father on these fishing adventures. I generally swam along the shallow shoreline and looked for small fish. Once in a great while, I would spear a *tako*.

Like any other disinterested kid, I complained about how hot it was, ate lunch first, and drank practically all of the water from the military metal canteens. My father always carried extra water for me. One of my jobs was to go back to the jeep to refill the canteens with cold water from the canvas bag that hung on the side of jeep.

We would leave the fishing grounds as soon as the Hawai'i winds started to blow. They were called that because they were generated from the Big Island of Hawai'i. We could see the strong winds approaching across the channel and white caps (miniature waves) breaking on the surface of the water, making it hard to fish or dive. Depending on the time of the year, these winds blew as early as 10:00 in the morning or early afternoon. We usually packed up and left when these conditions arose.

And who was that bag boy? He was the one with the dirty job of carrying the sack of slimy fish to the jeep. I smelt like fish all the way home.

There were only few available coolers before the sixties as far as I know. Fish that were caught was left in rice bags in ponds that had no eels until it was time to leave. The ponds had cool water brought in by the tide, a holding place so the fish wouldn't spoil.

Fish was only one item of exchange in the camp barter system that really worked. When my father returned home from fishing, he would share some of his catch that he speared with the neighbors. When the neighbors had an ample supply of other goods, they, in turn, would share it with my father. It was always a give and take situation. For the unfortunate who could not give in return, their misfortune was felt. It was not because they had nothing to give but they were not industrious to go out to gather something and share it. Consequently, because of their selfishness, they were isolated and had a hard time struggling for food.

This is what made the camps unique: practically everyone shared their good fortune. These were beautiful gestures that helped everyone's skimpy incomes. The family that shared always had enough to eat.

My father tried many times to make it a point to give fish or *limu* to those families who were extremely poor. Some of the impoverished told my father that they could not return his kindness and, yet, they were inconsiderate and wanted more. For those who were honest, my father really went out of his way to help and just plain ignored those who wanted more.

The principle reminded me to visit Mr. Choi again.

"Mr. Choi, I heard my father the other day mentioning the respect he had for the ocean, and it kind of reminded me of you and early Hawaiians. You all spoke in the same way, about similar things."

"Well then, where should I start?" asked the Chinese man. After a short pause, he began.

"Every adult knows who they really are by the way they talk,

182

their inner feelings, their actions and reactions, and their ability to judge and reason.

As a person, you will eventually know all of these feelings. Good or bad, is determined by you and you alone, by the way you perceive the way life should be. That will be your action and/or reaction to the world. Your inner feeling will determine whether you have peace of mind or a mind constantly in turmoil. What has been taught and said to you, what you accept or reject, is your decision.

You'll have a lot of respect for some and equal disrespect for others. Those you disrespect will teach you nothing. They will only criticize you. Those whom you respect may teach you everything. It relates to your ability to accept or reject both good and bad. When and if you have the ability to screen good from bad, then, and only then, you will have the knowledge of wisdom. Only spiritually attuned people would understand what I have told you.

Separate those who think they know but know not and those who consciously constantly know. The latter are the ones you must seek out. Everyone in their lifetime comes across those who have wisdom. Although they are few, recognizing them is not difficult if you know what you were looking for. Many who possess this wisdom will not live long enough to teach you all they know. There is so much to learn in one lifetime." With that, he ended.

Even after enjoying myself during the day, I had to do my chores and make sure that there was enough water in the *furo*, that the wood was burning, and that the chickens were fed. When I fed the chickens, I'd cut what I called chicken weeds that were only good for them. I'd cut them about two inches from the ground, and took a few bunches to feed the chickens. Then I'd cut all the greens with the cane knife into little pieces, mix it with regular chicken feed, and gave it to the animals. Chickens loved the feed and weed combination. There was nothing left in the bowl by the time I left the coop. Before leaving, I'd give the fowl some fresh water; the water was always dirty because they stepped in it.

When the chickens were full-grown and plump, my father would grab about five of them, tie each of their legs together with string, and carry them to a grassy area. He would remove the string from its legs, move a cutting block into position, cut off the chicken heads with a cane knife, and let them go. Without their heads, the chickens would run like crazy in pain about ten yards and eventually fall over. What a mess! Blood was all over the grassy area. We'd have to hose down the murder scene with cold water as quickly as possible to prevent the blood from drying and drawing flies.

About this time, water would be boiling in big pots on an open fire. The chicken was grabbed by their legs and dipped in the scalding water for a few seconds. The extremely hot water made it easy to pluck its feathers. After the feathers were plucked, my father would hold a chicken one by one over an open flame to burn off the little pinfeathers. The smell was identical to hair that my grandmother burned in a gallon can.

After he washed off the burnt little pinfeathers, my father would proceed in cutting open the chicken to get rid of the innards. He would save the liver and the gizzards, later to be fried with the chicken. A couple of the chickens were given away to neighbors. After he gave away the chickens, it was time to eat lunch.

There was a place in Alabama Camp, along Pu'unene Avenue, that prepared an unbelievable *saimin*. Hamada Saimin Shop was the one and only place that served the delicious noodle soup. I would assume that everyone who enjoyed it on Maui had sooner or later eaten Hamada's specialty. The place was packed for lunch, for that is the only meal they served. The *saimin* noodles were made from scratch, the ingredients an unrevealed secret family recipe. The additives were a combination of the *dashi* (soup base) with the noodles in the bowl, with a final touch of green onions and thin slices of roast pork or roast beef on the top. There it came in large and small servings. The best time to eat the delicacy was on rainy or cold days. Oh, don't forget the important utensils: chopsticks and the large mouth plastic Chinese spoon.

The external wooden building of Hamada Saimin was exactly like the Camp Four Store. The interior partitions were located differently. To the right were three booths that sat four people comfortably on two benches and a table. To the left was a showcase filled with pastry and, next to that, a glass cabinet filled with candy. Adjacent was a small table where the bill was paid. There was a short separation from the wall and the entry to the kitchen where the *saimin* was prepared. Straight ahead was a room with no doors and big table in the middle that could hold several families. Along the table on both sides were benches for people to sit. It was not uncommon for two families to share the room.

Hamada Saimin generated so much income selling their secret ingredient *saimin* that they decided to sell the store, retire, and return back to their homeland after many years of hard work. The Hamada family sold the shop to Sam Sato who had a business in Camp Three.

Sam Sato decided to purchase Hamada Saimin and move to Pu'unene because most of the residents at that time were moving out of Camp Three in search of larger and better homes. The residents were being forced out of their homes by the sugar plantation to use the land to plant more sugar cane.

Sam Sato must have learned the secret ingredients of the Hamadas because he did not skip a beat and continued with an equally successful restaurant. After the Hamada's left Hawai'i, the *saimin* remained just as tasty as the original owner's.

One day when I got home from downing that delicious prized soup, I got on my bike and went to see Mr. Choi. Entering the yard, I called for Mr. Choi. There was no answer. In his yard, daisies bordered the sidewalk leading to the porch. There was a wooden fence completely around the perimeter of the yard. In one small corner of it, Mr. Choi grew vegetables. Although the vegetable plot looked small, the space was used to its fullest. There were enough vegetables to feed one person. The vegetables grew in stages. Some were young, others half grown, and still others mature and ready to be picked. There were no weeds in the garden. The grass was cut low, well maintained, and never grew outside of its borders. All in all, the yard was simple and neat.

Walking on the sidewalk leading from the porch to the bathroom, I opened the door to find that there was a small *furo* to the right. A back wall had a door that led to the toilet. There was no shower, only a pipe that extended over the *furo*. It was a cold water pipe. There was no sink either. I would assume that Mr. Choi did his laundry while he was taking a bath.

I knocked at the front door. No one answered. Turning the knob, I found the door unlocked, which was not unusual. In those days, no one locked their house doors or the car doors. Sometimes you could actually spot the key in the ignition of the car.

I entered the house, hoping Mr. Choi wouldn't mind my looking around. I called again. I got no answer, so I decided to explore the house. The bedrooms, kitchen, and the parlor were identical to our house, but there was no furniture. If a wooden square table and a bench were considered furniture, then there was furniture. Nothing was out of place throughout the entire house. There were no doors for the pantry. Canned goods were neatly stacked, and all the dishes were arranged according to shelf sizes.

In one of the bedrooms, there was no bed, nightstand, or dresser. In one corner of the room was a bookcase nailed to the wall with no books. Instead, clothes were neatly folded and stacked on the shelves. A straw mat was on the floor with a *futon* (Japanese comforter) in what seemed Mr. Choi's bedroom. Another patched quilted comforter was folded and on the *futon* that was obviously used as a blanket. There was a wooden block with a *zabuton* (cushion) wrapped completely around it. This was his pillow.

The second bedroom had absolutely nothing in it. The floor and the windowsills were totally clean. There wasn't a speck of dust when I ran my hands across the windowsills to check!

Not a single book could be found in the house. All the knowledge and wisdom Mr. Choi acquired was kept in his head. I had not seen any paper, pencil, or pens anywhere. No pictures hung on the walls.

"Have you been here long?" came a voice from the living room. "Is that you, Mr. Choi?" I was startled and asked the question as a defense mechanism. I didn't hear him enter the house nor did I hear the door slam.

"Mr. Choi, why is it that you don't have many things in your house? I've gone to homes that had so many things that they didn't know where to put everything. Your house seems a little spooky because it is so empty."

"Less you have …less you worry about. More you have…more you worry about. Same thing. Is it not easier to clean a house if there were fewer things to move about? Is it not easier to find things? Is it not easier to take care of things? Simplicity is the best life to live. Why worry when you don't have to?"

"Then, why do people have different ideas about life? Some need more and more, while others need only just a little…like you." I must have seemed naïve, innocent, yet puzzled.

"Those who have a lot…need more. Those who have a little make do with what they have. Calm down and relax when you go through life. Why worry, when it's not necessary. Maybe, you'll be able to see life in a different perspective as I have.

Many people are the hurry-up type while others are the laid-back type. Many will hurry through life as long as things are going well and under control. These are the ones that seem to stress out.

Then there are people who seem as though they're in no such hurry; never take risks or get excited; they go with the flow, roll with the waves. Be like a bamboo blowing in the wind. Bamboo does not resist the wind, it bends with it, and whatever way the wind wishes the bamboo to bend. Its center is hollow and nearly impossible to break, and more so when it dries. In China, bamboo is tied together as scaffolding. That is how strong bamboo is.

I am not saying that one should not take risks in a lifetime.

187

Taking risks helps you to also learn. When you fail to take a risk because of lack of confidence and past disappointments, anguish sets in. You feel that the world is against you. If after all this, you have not learned from taking risks, then you will have the same disappointments and anguish all over again. Smart people continuously take a risk, not because they enjoy disappointments and anguish, but because they want to become tremendously successful. It's not wrong to be wrong sometimes. Determined individuals see over the hill. Over the hill is where success can be found.

Some people will not find out about themselves soon or ever. Throughout a lifetime, most will not be able to find their inner self. It is the reflection of how one analyzes their thinking that makes them sees how it affects their life on this planet. Sadly, many will not find inner peace.

For many of those who have found their inner peace, no matter what the situation might be of the outside world, good or bad, these individuals have accepted the situation and always look toward the better side of life. They are at peace with themselves. They are one with themselves. They have found the true meaning of life. They are spiritual. What's ironic is that no one can take that away from them.

Listen to the people who give you advice. If their advice is the same as your thinking, go for it. If it is not, then use your inner feelings and look deep inside of yourself. Only you are going to have the answers for such a situation and you will be right.

For every action, there is an equal or opposite reaction. Our mind works in mysterious ways. When we listen to our inner voice, everything seems to work out. Learned people call this – a voice from heaven. So many successes come from this inner voice. Everyone hears this inner voice sooner or later in life, but few follow that inner voice.

Let me explain what this inner voice is. Have you ever thought of doing something when, all of a sudden, something inside you said, 'No? You did it any way and it turned out wrong? Then you'd say to yourself. I shouldn't have done it! That something inside you is your inner voice. Wouldn't it be great if you always had that inner voice? Spiritual people do. They have it all the time and use that power to help other people. They do not use that inner voice for evil purposes. If they did, they would lose their inner voice, as much as you would, if you didn't listen to it.

Donald, next time I see you, tell me the one word that would determine your future. Do what young kids do – play! Playing helps cope with the everyday problems one encounters. Enjoyment helps to forget all the bad things."

I awoke the next morning to a very familiar smell. I had experienced the aroma many times before. It was the sweet smell of smoke from the burning of sugar cane fields nearby. Without the slightest whisper of wind, it lingered in the camp. I looked out the window to see the thick white smoke; it created an eerie feeling as if a demon was about to lunge out from the heavy fog-like smoke. I had read books and seen pictures of the thick London fog. Two to three inch-long black ribbons, curly carbon leaves of the sugar cane leaf dropped like black rain. Ashes from the burnt leaves rising in the sky, are transported aloft, and, depending on the condition of the wind, return either far or near. It was actually a nuisance because these black bands needed to be washed off everything. After the fields were set ablaze, clothing left hanging on the lines outside overnight usually had to be cleaned again. In most cases, the trade winds would eventually blow the black humbug toward Kihei.

Remembering about cane smoke, I remember when I was eleven years old and already a second year smoker. I hadn't forgotten my father's warning that if he ever catches me, I'd have to smoke a cigar in front of him. I had smoked a couple of cigars, just to practice for the inevitable day when I got caught. Sometimes when I couldn't get cigarettes, I would ask a neighbor for the fern stems that dried up on the plant. I would cut the roots and the leaves off and would light the fern stem. There was a small hole in the stem that I sucked to keep it lit. I liked smoking the fern stem. I often carried a few in my pockets. Every so often, someone would ask me what the fern stems were for. I would tell

189

them that it was for breathing underwater, a kind of organic snorkel. The only thing I did not show them was the matchbook in my pocket. My gullible friends bought that explanation.

Because the sugar cane fields completely surrounded the camps, without the trade winds, the smoke would build up so thick that it caused a stinging sensation to the eyes that, when rubbed too much, causing the eyes to swell. This was totally unavoidable.

Once the fields were cleared, the areas became dust bowls. With the advent of trade winds blowing fifteen to thirty miles an hour, small whirlwinds kicked up making dust storms or dirt devils inevitable. What was worst was that the tractors also kicked up the fine dust during the leveling of the fields. This dust was so fine that it easily infiltrated house window screens. Even with the windows completely shut; the fine dust penetrated cracks and crevices – and there were a few *puka,* (holes) in those old homes.

The dust was easily inhaled and was so bad that it affected people living in the camps. Fine dust caused eye irritations. We couldn't see what it was doing to our lungs, but we could see the color of our mucus change from clear to brown after we blew our noses. What about the fertilizer used in the cane fields to kill the weeds and to make the cane grow faster and bigger? I'm sure it was in the dust. My father always said that one day we were going to get sick from the dust.

After the sugar cane is harvested, the field is leveled, trenches and ditches dug, sugar cane is planted and it was watered often. The settling of the ground and the sprouting of the sugar cane would take about a month. Within eighteen months to two years, this process would continue again. No matter what happened, the camps endured.

I remember that my father cleaned the roof whenever there was harvesting nearby. He would take a hosepipe, climb onto the roof of the house, and hose down the wooden shingles. The nasty powder found its way on and under the shingles. On rainy days, this fine dust would get wet and sit damp for a couple of days; it softened and weakened the shingles, thereby creating leaks.

I think the world could have learned from my life in the camps. We were so close that I truly believe that most cared for one another. The greatest healing force in this world is love. Without love, nothing can survive. Mr. Choi once told me, "Everyone is loved by someone, no matter how good or bad that person is."

'Ohana, treating each other as part of their own family, included various ethnic families who lived in camps. Helping each other in time of need and celebrating in times of joy was the general protocol of the camps. Generally, there wasn't a party that another race did not attend. In many cases, there were multiple ethnicities involved. They were not there because they were forced. They were there because they were invited and wanted to be there. They had as much fun as anyone else. We were all there and we were one. That's the way it was and that's the way it should be. The sad reality, however, is that not all races felt that way.

After raising chickens for the longest time, one day, my father decided to raise ducks in the same chicken coop. It became another one of my chores to feed the ducks bread and water or left over rice with water. At one end of the coop, my dad made a wading pool for the ducks. The man-made concrete pond was no bigger than a bathtub but shallower. On rare occasions, my father and I would take a scoop net and go to the ditch to catch *medaka* (mosquito fish) and feed them to the ducks. They went crazy, quacked noisily, and climbed over each other to get to the *medaka*, all of them consumed in a few minutes.

I believe it was about time that I went to see Mr. Choi again. Since it was summer, I decided to visit him in the morning. Immediately upon arrival, I leaned my bike against the fence and opened the gate; I went straight to the entrance and called his name. He was home this time, so I climbed the three steps onto the porch and entered the house.

As soon as I sat down on the *zabuton*, he immediately asked me if I remembered the question he last asked. I said, "Yes. You asked me if I knew one word that would decide my future.

191

Frankly, I do not know the answer."

He proceeded. "One word that would determine your future is choices. Sooner or later in your life, you will have make choices. The choices you make may be right or wrong. If you make the right choices, your life will be easy. Every right choice you make will make you a better person as time goes by. Remember, in one of my talks, I mentioned that you must hear your inner voice. Your inner voice is coming from God. That inner voice is given to everyone. The problem is that not everyone listens to that inner voice. Those who do, make the right choices.

Now let me talk to you about those who don't listen to their inner voice and make the wrong choices. That person who makes wrong decisions will suffer for the rest of his life. Getting to be old takes a long time. But when you become old, you realize that time has gone by so fast. There is an old saying that you can work hard now and have an easy life later or get an easy life now and suffer when you get older. Make your choice.

There is something I haven't told you. As I said, all people are given inner voices. To hear this inner voice you must concentrate, meditate, and believe. Three inches below the belly button is the main force of all people. To the spiritual, this is known as *ki*. This area is mentioned in many martial arts from the Far East. This is your focal point when you meditate. If you believe, meditate and listen; you will hear that inner voice I am talking about.

There are times when the inner voice tells you without meditation. Have you had a situation where you had to decide something and this inner voice told you not to do it or to do it? Everyone has that feeling that something inside of him or her was trying to say something and you did not listen and made the wrong decision.

When you hear people tell you that I should have done this instead of that, that person has made the wrong choice. You will hear others say that because they made the right decision, everything turned out right. That person made the right choice.

You make a choice with the help of the inner voice.

Maybe I've repeated this but think about it! Have you ever dreamed where there were people that you knew in the dream and yet, when you woke from your dream, you didn't know them in your real life? What about dreaming about a place that you have never seen before? Years down the road, you'll see that place you dreamt about. You know the place as if you've been here before and, yet, you never have. Further more, you know what is beyond that corner because you had seen it in your dreams. Was it in your dreams or was it a subconscious reality from your past life? Don't you feel at those times that you've been reincarnated?

On this earth, we see good people and bad people. It is said that everyone is born equal. That may not be true and, yet, that might be true. If it is true, then every one of us is tested in a lifetime to see who becomes bad, good or in between. If it is not true, then that means everyone is not born equally. Some are smarter than others and some are better than the others. Some are more spiritual than others while some are not spiritual at all.

I believe that it is not true that we are born equally. I believe that we are programmed to become whoever the Supreme Being (what humans call God), decides who we will be. In all of us humans there are differences. We are all different in some way or the other. It's the way we think, the way we dress, the way we talk and walk, and the way we perceive life.

In your lifetime, some things will sound logical, others illogical. You will determine what is to be retained. What you let go seems immaterial to you. There is no doubt that you will continue to learn throughout your entire time in this life on earth. No person on this earth knows everything, therefore, learning continues.

Questions will be imbedded deep within you, questions that only you can answer. These questions must be answered before you can move on in your life. If not, inner peace would be very hard to be attained. Some things will be troublesome and others easy. What might be troubling to you might be easy to others. What might be troubling to others might be easy for you.

193

We are free to live our lives and free to go as we please. Religious people have tried to show the easy and simple way, the way we have found to be very, very satisfying." With that, Mr. Choi ended and I left.

My grandfather hoped to return Japan someday, so he gave his children Japanese names so that they could easily fit in when they returned to their motherland. Later, many of the Japanese names were changed to English to fit in with the local people. Many of the men with Japanese names were assigned nicknames by their friends and replaced their original names.

I assume that this was a turning point when the Nisei generation felt as though Japan was another country and that the United States was their home. My father and mother never talked about returning to live in Japan. They talked about visiting it merely to see their parents' villages, but that was all. Their parents talked so much about the old country that inquisitiveness was the only reason to visit Japan.

My father was a tractor driver responsible for the leveling of the fields before trenches were dug to plant the seedlings. He'd work three shifts in rotation. One week he'd work from 6:00 a.m. to 2:00 p.m. The following shift was from 2:00 p.m. until 10:00 p.m. Then, on the third week, he'd work the graveyard shift from 10:00 p.m. to 6:00 a.m. He'd always returned home filthy, covered with dirt from head to shoes. After a *furo* bath, he was transformed into a totally different man in contrast to the dirty laborer from *hana hana* (work).

During one of my father's graveyard shifts, he actually worked near a grave (*haka*). One night, my father and another Filipino worker set out to level the fields, each on their own tractor. Suddenly at 1:30 in the morning, both of the tractor lights went out. They both started to feel very cold. They also felt as though someone or something was watching them. Out of the blue, Pedro, the other man, started screaming and running toward my father. In back of Pedro was a ball of fire with a tail. The fiery

194

object followed Pedro until he was close to my father. The ball of fire then sharply veered straight for the sky and disappeared from sight. Seconds later, the tractor lights went on and the cold feeling disappeared. Everything returned to normal except for my father's co-worker who refused to continue. He was so frightened that he was still shaking to the end of his shift. During the meal break and after Pedro had calmed down, my father asked him if he knew what was chasing him. He claimed ignorance. After a long pause, my father claimed that he knew what it was; Pedro had been chased by a *hei no-tama* (fire ball).

Many people believe that during the decaying process of buried human bodies, gasses from the decay seep through the ground and, when it reaches the surface, these gases mix with the hydrogen and oxygen of fresh air. The result was a fireball. Pedro asked my father why the fireball was following him. My father told him that he was haunted by it because Pedro was *kolohe* (rascal) or plain *pilau* (dirty/nasty).

There are stories of *kahuna* (priest) sending fireballs at each other during the night. People testify such occurrences as quite normal among the Hawaiian people of old. I also heard of one *kahuna* who made it rain over only one house, while the houses of others remained completely dry.

I once witnessed a fireball, but from a distance. I'm sure most people never witness seeing such phenomena in their lifetime. I do know they exist, but how they fly across the night sky is still somewhat mysterious to me.

There were incidents at Pu'unene Hospital that seemed to verify the theory of souls leaving the human body after death. Years ago, a watchman was hired to guard the hospital grounds on horseback. At times, this watchman swore that he saw a figure leaving the hospital – through the walls of the building! The watchman believed that it had to do with recent deaths there. He claimed that when a male, female, or child passed away, a figure of the deceased passed through the walls of the hospital. Seeing ghosts is another unexplainable subject. Some have seen them; some have not. I have never seen one yet, but was told that when

195

a dog howls long and loud at night, it must have seen a ghost.

There are also stories of night marchers or Hawaiian zombies. If by mistake, a person builds a house on the path of the night marchers, strange things happen. People have heard the sound of *pahu* (drums) and seen the flicker of the torches. Unexplained knocks on the walls of houses indicate that night marchers are proceeding through the area. I once was told that if a local does not buy a certain house, no one else should buy it, or if there was an unexplained urgency to sell the house, then something must be wrong. It's spooked!

Another unexplainable incident includes youngsters who talk to some one not visible to the naked eye. Some of these kids are led out of the house by an invisible being – probably from the spiritual world.

I have heard of many stories of supernatural sightings and happenings that occurred in the camp. If a newcomer experienced some of the above-mentioned phenomena, they might seriously consider moving back to the mainland.

After all of this, it was time to visit Mr. Choi.

He started off with a question, "Do you know what a salmon is? You are like the salmon. When you need to know the philosophy of life, where do you go? You come directly to me."

Salmon is a saltwater fish that swims in fresh water to a designated river when it is time to spawn. Adult salmon struggle to swim up stream, sometimes dying along the way, to the place they were born. The salmon is focused in reaching its destination.

At a predetermined time, salmon swim upstream in a predestined river, understanding the dangers that lurk within it. Hungry eagles, bears, and humans are among the many dangers of the river. Salmon, upon arriving at the predestined pond where they were born, carry out the tradition of females laying their eggs by the millions so that the males can fertilize them. As soon as the adult male and female salmon dies, then the eggs hatch.

196

The newborn salmon remains in the area until a certain time, then travels down the river, as generations did before. Despite perils along the way to the ocean, those who survive continue to grow within the confines of the vast ocean.

Do as the salmon does. Whatever you do in life – focus. Know where you came from and where you are going. Those who focus on one part of their life tend to be successful in other ventures as well. The will must be there to succeed. Where there is a will, there is a way." Again, he stopped talking and went into another room.

I returned to Mr. Choi's house the following day. I had a funny feeling that he had more to say. That feeling is like two minds blending. One mind says this and the other says the same thing. It's something that cannot be fully explained.

The next day, Mr. Choi began, "Let me tell you another story. A sparrow had been standing alongside an embankment with its wings covering its legs for a long time. Standing alone, obviously hurt, the sparrow never made a noise. A child saw the sparrow, picked it up gently, and took the sparrow home. When he arrived home, the child puts the sparrow in a cardboard box with a bowl of fresh water and a bowl of cooked rice. With gentleness, the child stroked the sparrow on its head.

Later, the child went riding on his bike in search of a dead sparrow. Within an hour, he found one. He returned home with the dead sparrow and sought the help of his dad. When the father asked the son why he had the dead bird, the son pointed to the broken leg of the sparrow in the box. He asked the father to fix the leg of the sick sparrow like the leg of the dead bird. The child suddenly became aware of the difference of a normal leg, although the sparrow was dead, and yet, he also saw the broken leg of the sparrow that was alive. He hoped that the father would use the example of the unbroken dead sparrow's leg to mend the broken leg of the live sparrow. The father realized that it was the son's attempt to use the leg of the dead sparrow to heal the leg of the live one. He proceeded to mend the broken leg of the

197

sparrow. Within a month, the sparrow's leg had been totally healed with the feeding and care of the child.

On the night before the sparrow was to be released, the child was saddened that he would have to release the bird. The child was so attached to the pet that he couldn't see it being released the next day.

By the time the morning arrived, the child realized that the bird was not meant to be held captive but released to the wild to be free, to fly, and to live its own life as a sparrow. When the child released the bird, it looked back directly into the eyes of the child. It circled, flew to the nearest tree for one glance back, and then flew away.

Every day, the bird returned to the same tree to see the child playing in the yard. To never forget the child's kindness, the bird returned to the same tree time after time. The sparrow actually made sounds to let the child know that it was in the tree watching at him play. This went on for quite a while. Finally, one day when the child was playing in the yard, he realized that he did not hear the sound of the sparrow. The bird never showed up. The child became aware that the bird would no longer come to see the child play.

The child, knowing that the injured sparrow needed help, had sought the help of his father with the use of a dead bird. By helping the sparrow, the child got attached to it. However, upon realizing that the bird needed its freedom, the child not only released the bird, but also released his own attachment to the bird.

This is how everyone should be in life. Everyone should be like a child who is willing to help and seek the advice of others. He makes a decision to take care of the situation but lets go. Life must go on. The sparrow needed help, remembered the help, and returned in gratitude. As in life, without understanding, compassion, and focus on the job to be done, there would not be much to living."

One day when I arrived home, I could hear my parents discussing the topic of one nationality marrying another because one of my relatives was planning to marry an Okinawan. I was really interested in my parent's discussion because I wondered how Japanese and Okinawans were different; they all looked alike to me. Aren't they also Japanese?

Okinawans came from a branch of islands off the coast of Japan. They did whatever they could to survive. They raised pigs for a living. Because they picked up the left over vegetables or discarded food to feed the pigs, they were considered dirty and smelly like the slop and the feces they worked in. Okinawans or Uchinanchu were badly treated by the nationalist Japanese. This prejudice was carried on in the Hawaiian Islands.

In fact, when I recently visited Okinawa I found out the following: Okinawans faced American mistreatment as well, attacked by barbarous American soldiers during WWII. They not only harmed and killed them, but also raped their young schoolgirls. There is a natural monument, a very deep and wide hole in the ground in Okinawa that documents the young schoolgirls, between thirteen and eighteen, who committed suicide by throwing themselves into that very deep hole rather than be raped by American G.I.s. My understanding is that so many bodies were piled up that blood seeped to the surface.

I was so ashamed to see that. For a while, I was not proud to be an American. How could a soldier rape an innocent child? Is this what war is? Does anyone have the right to do whatever he or she wants to do on foreign soil including raping innocent young children? I was totally humiliated because of what those Americans did. Think how many innocent lives were ruined. I shouldn't be the one to judge them, but I hope the guilty parties suffered for their sinful act.

Okinawans tend to have larger eyes, more hair on their bodies, and a darker complexion than the Naichi (Japanese from Japan). Naichi singled them out by referring to their physical features. Many of the Uchinanchus, to avoid ridicule, tried to act like main island Japanese. Many, consequently, changed their names to match Naichi sounding names.

No Naichi was allowed to marry an Uchinanchu. It was also forbidden for any of them to ever look, let alone, appear with an Uchinanchu in public. Until the end of the World War II, physical and occupational distinctions were exploited between the Naichi and Okinawans. Even later, after education, a few determined hardheaded Naichi refused to accept Okinawans. However, with time, most Naichi accepted them into their families.

In earlier times, Okinawan women tattooed the back of their hands to signify wealth. At the age of forty-nine, tattoos were darkened further if the woman continued to have wealth. If the mark faded and never darkened at the age of forty-nine, then the woman was considered no longer wealthy. If this were the case, the husband would return the woman upon her death to the parents for burial.

When some Okinawan women came to Hawai'i with a tattoo on the back of their hands, they would conceal it during any photograph session because of shame. In Hawai'i, some eventually didn't bother to darken their tattoos at forty-nine; they had no interest in keeping the Okinawan tradition.

Whenever an Okinawan woman reached the age of forty-nine, the tattoo session was followed by a festive occasion with a lot of food called *ogoshiso*. I have seen a few women with tattoos on their knuckles of their hands. I was once invited to one of the *ogoshiso* parties, but I did not witness any tattoo sessions, although I did celebrate with the family. The party was made in a *kochinto* manner (just so). Families at that time believed that the tradition should be followed and that Okinawans should be proud of their heritage and there was nothing to be ashamed of. They believed in the family unit and the propagation of wealth.

I have known many Okinawans in my life and have the fondest respect for them. None have tried to hurt me in any way while I grew up in the camps, and none of them showed me the slightest indication of intolerance or hostility. They were and still are very

200

good people.

As I grew up, I began to see changes to the kind of hate that had existed between Okinawans and Naichi. By that time I attended school, all nationalities were on friendlier terms. They knew of the hard times they all had endured and were now actually helping each other to survive and make their community a great place to live. The time of healing had arrived when both realized that it was time to correct the wrong.

However, there was always an exception to the rule. Those who kept their ways of hate never changed. They kept their hate behind closed doors and, every once in a while a glimmer of that hate would surface. Two days before I left the camp, I lost my first love because of racial hate. The girl's mother said that I could not marry her daughter. To this day, I hear her words echo exactly as she said it to me. After that, I was devastated. I gave up. That was an example of how hate can dampen one's life. It surely did mine.

Japan has been characterized as a culture of shame more than a culture of guilt. Both shame and guilt are part of the Japanese make-up. To the Japanese, Westerners lack human feelings, are harsh, and self-righteous. *Amae* (to look to others for affection) is an attitude that begins with loving dependence on one's mother, then acceptance and approval by a group. Friends are rarely made but, when made, Japanese hold on to them closer than usual. Japanese clearly work best as a group or team.

In Japan, the earliest people acquired and mastered skills that seemed effortless. With the use of self-control and self-discipline, a skill is acquired through the act of will. Japanese strive on inner strength. One of the most outstanding characteristics of the Japanese people is diligence or *kimbensei*. The old and basic part of the Japanese personality is ambition and drive.

An old Confucian adage says "A women should in youth obey her father, in maturity, her husband and in old age, her son." This was practiced among the Japanese. A sexual double standard is still common in Japan where the woman is restrictive and the man is free to do what he pleases.

It is also said that the Japanese have the tendency of taking American products and making them better then the original. The Japanese strive in making things better suited for modern life.

The Japanese were never short in celebrating various occasions. The biggest of all celebrations was New Year's (*shogatsu*). Because many Asian people were farmers and fishermen, they showed respect for a rich harvest and a bounty of fish by visiting a Shinto Shrine to pay respects to the natural universe and one's god.

For many Buddhists, a dried squid is placed under two large *mochi*, one on the other, topped by a citrus fruit on the family altar or *hotoke sama*, On the side of the altar, raw rice is placed. It is wrapped in waxed paper for a bountiful harvest. Dried seaweed (*konbu*) is also offered on *washi* paper for cleanliness and purity, and a can of beer or soda is left for the dead to drink. On the day of the year's end, the above items are placed throughout the house and in cars along with wishes for good luck during the following year

Green *soba* (Japanese noodles) is served on New Year's for a harmonious continuation from one year to the next with hope of good luck and much happiness to the family.

On New Year's Eve, families take flowers to the grave, clean gravestones, place fresh flowers in the vases, and offer *mochi* or tangerines with a can of soda or beer, the preferred beverage of the dead. Hopefully, by the turn of the New Year, all debts will be paid, if possible. If one has a good dream on New Year's Eve, then good luck will be upon that dreamer for the rest of the year.

Buddhist Temples at the stroke of midnight ring temple bells that symbolize the ringing out of one hundred and eight vices that inhabit our bodies. A service follows and at the end of the service *sake* is served, a toast for good luck for the up coming year.

Omamori (amulets) replace those of the previous year at the Maui

Jinsha Temple during the New Year's festivities. *Onamori* represent one's health, general welfare, and guarantees of a safe journey. The *omamori* is placed in men's wallets and women's purses. A service is also held at the stroke of midnight.

Food served early in the morning on New Year's Day includes *ozoni* soup (generally Japanese vegetables and chicken). *Mochi* is added to the bowls of soup for good luck. Boiled eggs are also eaten for fullness and strength for the New Year.

During lunch, *sekihan* (rice cooked with red beans), white rice, s*hoyu* pork, *sushi* (both cone and rolled), spareribs, fried chicken, macaroni and/or potato salad, *nishime*, ham or turkey, *sashimi* (when available), and pickled, fried, and boiled vegetables. For desert, *yokan* (red beans gelatin*), kanten* (clear or milky gelatin), jello, cake, or cookies are enjoyed. To quench a thirst, one drank *sake* (rice wine), beer, or soda. Relatives and friends of other camps were also invited either for lunch or dinner.

In the camps, the men would go from house to house as a gesture of good will from lunch until, about eight or nine at night on New Year's Day. Some who drank beer or whiskey did not make it back home until eight or nine in the evening. Generally, something different was offered at each house. The main idea was for the men to have a drink together for good luck in the New Year.

Wives stayed at home and prepared food for the guests who would drop by during the day and evening. During the year, wives learned different dishes. New Year's was the time to show off their new recipes.

At the end of the year, pig farmers shared their slaughter with the people who left their five-gallon slop cans to be picked up. A slab of pork was shared and eaten at the New Year's celebration.

Boy's Day was another important celebration of the *Issei*. The Feast of the Horse Day (*Tango No-Gekku*) is held on the fifth day of the fifth month, a time that symbolizes the masculinity and strength of the newborn son of the family. It is celebrated in the first year for the first-born son.

Carp streamers (*koi nobili*) made of cloth or paper, believed to have originated in China, was flown in the Hawaiian trade winds for Boys' Day with *fuki nagasi* (colored streamers) accentuating the waves of a river. These were attached to the top of a bamboo pole that symbolized the circle of life.

Celebration of Boy's Day promoted the continuation of the name and traditions of family that rested with the oldest son. Prayers were uttered for the oldest son to grow strong and healthy and prevent evil things from happening.

Magnificent dolls dressed in clothing for battle and riding a horse were enclosed in a glass box with wooden frames and given to the oldest son as a gesture of good luck. The tradition continues to this day.

Girl's Day was celebrated in the same matter but, instead of horses, girls were given dolls encased in glass and wooden box frames. The celebration featured a variety of ethnic foods that included rice, *sashimi* (raw fish), *shoyu* pork, *sushi*, spare ribs, macaroni and/or potato salad, *nishime,* ham or turkey, and dessert. Drinks included beer or soda. There was more than ample food to feed everyone on Girl's Day camp celebrations.

With the good, comes the bad. My grandmother on my mother's side had passed away five years earlier. I don't know what she died of, but I do remember that on her funeral day an exceptional amount rain poured down from the sky. Certain people believe that if it rains a lot, then that person is going to heaven. I believe that God was crying for her.

There are three exceptional people that influenced my life. First, there was Mrs. Kawamoto. When we were invited to her house, she always made sure that we ate first. Sometimes we'd visit with her for a couple of hours before her dinner. When dinnertime rolled around, and it was time for us to go, she'd insist that we stay for supper. Again, she always made sure that we ate first. I believe that she did this because her family was poor. She always made sure there was enough food for visitors. She never ate dinner when we did because there was not enough food. She even sacrificed her husband's prepared lunch for the following day. She never spoke a bad word nor did she ever get angry with anyone. In fact, her whole family was always sweet and kind to my father, mother, and me. They never sent us home even if we came uninvited.

The second influence in my life was my grandmother who died on July 26, 1954. Her eyes reflected one of the kindest persons to ever walk this earth. I remember once when my cousin and I were wrestling on one of the beds in her house. We were acting childish, yelling at the top of our voices. She came in and spanked both of us. Later on, I saw her crying. I asked her, 'What's the matter?' She told me. ' I had to spank both of you because you were making too much noise. I'm so sorry for what I've done.' Even when she scolded, she was soft spoken and gentle.

The third inspiration has to be my father. He was a man of very strong convictions. He was a man who when he said no, meant no. When he said yes, he would back me up one hundred per cent. Even though he lacked schooling, he never gave up on challenges. I know he never lied. His only vice is that he swore a little. All in all, he did his job, never called in sick, and never complained. He was forty-seven years old when he died. He found out too late that he had stomach cancer. The doctor and my family never told him to spare him the anxiety. As his health deteriorated in the hospital, he confided in me that God must want him in heaven because he felt his job was done here on this earth. I do believe that.

One night, my father asked me to check on my grandmother (*obaban*) who lived across from our house. My mother and father had gone to visit my grandfather who was living in the next camp. *Obaban* had not been feeling well all day, so I was told to check on her in case she might need some assistance.

I totally forgot about her. When my father came home, he went directly to see how my grandmother was doing. Evidently, my

205

grandmother had passed away sometime in the night. When I found out, I ran to the house to see her. She was lying on her side in a fetal position. I was aware of death, but I had never known how serious it was until the person who was very close to me passed away. I came to realize that I would never hear her voice, let alone see her again. My grandmother, Mizu Yamasaki died on November 21, 1959.

After a while, I realized that my grandmother, who was living across from us, would never be with us again. I'd never again see her smile. I'll never again see her sitting on the porch combing her hair and burning it in a gallon can. I'd never again smell pork frying on her kerosene stove. I'll never forget the Coke she drank and the Kitch'n Cook'd Potato Chips she so enjoyed.

Soon after her funeral, my father gave all of her clothes away. Clothing of a dead person bestowed good fortune to its receiver. What couldn't be given away was set ablaze. The remaining things of the deceased were turned to ash, that later became dust.

Something definitely had been wrong with grandmother's health. I spotted her on several occasions walking around the house at a quick pace during the day. She repeated it three times, oblivious of events happening around her. I asked my father, but he would not give me an answer. I believe that she had some kind of seizure that began to affect her actions.

For a week or so, I had been troubled about the death of my grandmother. I felt guilty. I thought that I had been the one responsible for her death because I hadn't checked on her the night she died. I hadn't followed my father's instructions. Two particular things bothered me. First, that she might have had some last words to say to someone, and I wasn't there. Second, she might have had a final request.

I had to see Mr. Choi.

"Don't be troubled by feeling guilty for what happened," he counseled. "In all probability, it was meant for her to die in a quiet way. Remember, that was the night that she was supposed to die. One thing you cannot stop is death. The day you were born is the day you start to die. Every day that passes brings you closer to death. Death is inevitable; you cannot stop it.

Many Japanese believe that when a person dies, his or her spirit is turned into an insect, animal, or non-human form, a re-incarnation. It's an assumption that if an unnoticed creature is evident in a home, then it is a re-incarnated soul. For example, it could be a giant black moth that suddenly appears in the house after a death in the family. The creature lingers there until the burial of the deceased.

It is also believed that, on occasion, if a deceased person were treated badly by a living person, the spirit of the departed would appear before the living abuser at night. It is further believed that when a dead person appears in a dream, only the upper part of the body can be seen in a dream."

I believe this because after my dad died, when I dream of him, I see him sitting at the table with his leg up on the chair. He used to do this when he was alive, while eating at the kitchen table. But I never saw his feet. It was always covered by his arm.

Mr. Choi continued, "I'd like to ask you a question? When you dream, do you dream in color or in black and white? If you dream in color, could it be your imagination saying that this is the color it should be?

Let me continue what I have been saying. What you have experienced is grief. Why do people grieve? There are three things that happen to a grieving individual. First, there is the initial shock that a loved one is dead. Second, there is anger combined with grief for what happened. Third, there is acceptance of the death. We finally believe that it did happen and there was nothing anyone's earthly powers could do to prevent the inevitable death.

Here is a word you will hear again in your lifetime as long as you read and study eastern religions. The word is reincarnation. As I have said earlier, reincarnation means to be reborn again as another person or thing. The word thing for the Japanese means an insect, animal, or any creature alive, except a human. Some religions believe in reincarnation and others don't. I believe that we will be reborn as other human beings or creatures of another universe.

Life is easier to live for those who believe in reincarnation. They know that they will be born again. Then, there are those who believe that when we die, there is nothing. You simply do not exist; there is no heaven or hell. What we experience in life is our heaven and hell, good or bad; therefore, one should cherish the good in this lifetime.

If you could draw a straight line as far as you could draw it and farther beyond our universe, how far would that straight line go? We have a word in our English language called eternity. What is eternity? Is it as far as the eye can see? Is it beyond or is it past that? If we are in a universe, don't you think that it's logical that there are other universes? How many do you think there are? Two hundred, two thousand, two million, or maybe two trillion, no one knows for sure.

I believe that you were once taught about the meaning of the word infinity. That word goes beyond imagination. Could it be that we will be reincarnated into a different universe? Consider the possibilities of many universes.

In Tenrikyo, a religion based on *toku* (merit), good receives merits and bad receives demerits. Based on reincarnation, the deceased are re-born within the same family and they keep on returning until they become good. Before you enter this earth, a body was lent to you. It will be yours until you are dead and buried and leave this earth.

Buddha believed that one must follow the Noble Eightfold Path: right seeing, right mindedness, right speaking, right doing, right living, right endeavors, right remembering, and right concentration to reach Nirvana.

Because of this, I have come to the conclusion that we are

reincarnated many times, until the Superior Being deems us good.

We are programmed to become whomever the Superior Being decides who we will be. In all of us humans there are differences. We are all different in some way or another. The way we think, the way we dress, the way we walk, the way we talk, and the ways we perceive life are all different. In one's lifetime some things sound logical while others sound illogical. You will determine what is to be retained. What you let go is immaterial. There is no doubt that you will learn through your entire life on this earth. No person on this planet knows everything. Thereby, learning continues.

Questions will be imbedded deep within you, questions that only you can answer. There will be unanswered questions. These questions must eventually be answered before you move on in your life. If not, you will not achieve inner peace. You may be affected by troubles that may not affect others. What might be troubling to others may be easy for you. We are free to live and do as we please. Spiritual leaders have tried to show us the easy and simple way, a way we find to be satisfying.

Taoists have believed for centuries that the word *Tao* (*Dao*) is translated as: way, road, method, technique or principle. The *Tao-Te-Ching,* credited to Lao Tzu, states that Tao is all existence created by dynamic opposition. Taoists believe in meditation, wisdom achieved by close observation of things or phenomena in the world surrounding us. Taoism is not a religion.

What matters is not the situation, but the way we perceive it, what we believe, what we create. This is the power of the self-fulfilling prophecy. If a tree falls in the forest and no one hears it, does it still make a sound? Yes, you'll say. It makes the sound of one hand clapping. This is Zen Buddhism.

It is not what we look like or what we do, but who we are that brings meaning and purpose. A wise man once said that a person who has nothing to die for hasn't a life worth living..

As time passes, you'll wonder where time has gone. You'll have your doubts about planting a tree because you might not live long enough to see its fruits. Unable to run the miles you did as a youngster, you'll walk instead. Even walking makes you tired and you'll have to rest along the way. You'll also notice that you're walking slower and slower each day, and you cannot do all the things you did as before.

Friends that you were acquainted with have left this earth. Now the younger generation is calling you forgetful and old just as you called your parents not too long ago. Those around you will ask you why you forget so often. Your reply should be I never forget, I just don't remember.

Another metaphor of life is the common seed of a fruit. You watch the plant grow with nurturing and watering. You observe how the flower is formed, how it blooms, how it forms a fruit on the tree, and how it ripens. The fruit falls to the ground where it rots. The seed, however, does not rot. It emerges from the ground as a new plant. All this resulted from a small seed that was embedded in the fruit.

So it is with you. The seed represents part of your parents. The plant growing is you growing. You are the one watered and nurtured; you acquire wisdom and knowledge as you, grow in life. The flower is you when you're a young man. The fruit represents your accomplishments in life as the fruit ripens. The seed is part of your newborn child. This is called coming full circle.

Although you are one, you are many. You are part of a family; a part of the lives of many other people, and they are a part of your life. In other words, you are part of their lives as much as they are part of your life. And yet, you are one with your own direction as they are part of their own direction. Is this not so?"

Mr. Choi's voice was calm, collected, and simple. He left me with the feeling that I had a lot to learn. He was well rounded in knowledge and wisdom. He was never mysterious, in control of his life and, most importantly, had found inner peace.

As I lay in bed that night, I realized that I had studied aging in school but had now become actually aware of people around me aging. At a young age, I was already thinking of old age and death. I read in books about one's life expectancy. The average life span of people around the world varies because of the consumption of certain foods and different life styles. I came to realize that sickness and death was all around me. I noticed that long time camp acquaintances had suddenly disappeared, never to be seen again.

As youngsters, we were told that a neighbor, relative or a friend had died, and yet we didn't understand it in the true sense of the word. We heard that there was a funeral and that the whole family cried, but, within a couple of days, everything was practically back to normal.

What really scared me were adults, including my parents, telling me that if I acted naughty, the ghost of the dead person would personally come to get me. I was so afraid of sticking my leg out of the covers at night. The ghost might yank me out from under the covers. A cold shiver would race through my body when I'd wake up at the middle of the night with my legs sticking out from the blanket. I'd quickly check my legs if they were still there. After all, I needed them to play baseball.

Like many camp residents, I loved baseball so much that, even as a ten year old, I pretended playing the game. I used a stick for a bat, rounded at the end for grip to prevent splinters. I threw a pebble in the air and hit the pebble, with good contact, into the cane fields. If I hit it in the cane fields, I pretended that it was a home run. Anything shorter was an out.

At that time, there was no such game as a T-Ball. When a player went up to the plate to hit, no one pitched. Instead a baseball was placed on a round base welded to a pipe. The top had a hose that would slide onto the top of the pipe. A pitcher would pretend to pitch, and the batter would hit the ball as far as he could.

I was so into baseball that I decided to try out for the Pu'unene

211

Indians Little League team. It was an honor to be chosen to be an Indian. Many who played for the Indians continued playing baseball on high school teams and, later, on AJA teams (American Japanese Association).

I attended most of the practices as a ten year old because the baseball field was close to my house. Two weeks before the season started, we'd all line up for the team selection. The first ones selected were usually returnees and automatically chosen for the season. The rest would fill the team positions for the season. If a kid wasn't called, it was a long bike ride home.

The following year, I was again on the practice field trying to make the baseball team. First, the coach had me try for second base but I was too tall to bend down to catch the ball. Of course, when I tried to stop the ball with my chest and my face, it didn't impress the coaches. I complained that the glove was too small. I was determined to be on the team so I attended all of the tryout practices. Finally, it was time for the selection of the team. I waited nervously to hear my name. Would I…? No? Well, maybe the next position… The coach tucked the roster in his pocket. I wasn't chosen again. It was a big disappointment. However, the coach called me and another unpicked player to the side to tell us that we were selected to play for another team. We were going to play for the Kihei Braves.

Mr. Clarence Oka, the baseball coach of the Braves, after working at the sugar mill, would pick us up in the camp, take us to Kihei for practice, return us back to Pu'unene, then drive himself back to Kihei where he lived. That was quite a sacrifice. He did this for the whole season, for at least three months.

It was required that we wear a protective cup under our pants during practice. My cup was too big and, when I sweated, it created a rash around my legs. After a while, it became very irritating. I decided finally that I wouldn't wear one, hoping that the ball would not hit me in the groin. I had seen guys get hit with the ball in the family jewels and curl over in pain.

The baseball stadium was located in the Kahului Fairgrounds. A specially constructed Little League Field with bleachers was at the far corner of the grounds. Games were held on weekday and Saturday afternoons. One Saturday, when we were losing by a substantial amount, I was placed in the game as a left fielder. I was told to throw the ball to the second baseman should any hits come my way. I prayed that nothing would be hit to me. My prayer was answered...

At the bottom of the sixth inning, with two outs, and a man on first, I was up to bat. I walked to the plate, shaking all over from fright. My palms were sweaty; I was almost unable to hold on to the bat. I took my stance and looked straight at the pitcher. The ball flew across the plate. Strike one! I hadn't even seen the ball. Strike two! I did see that one, and it was perfect, but I was frozen. Here came the third pitch. I hit it, but it ended up in the in field. I ran as fast as I could, to no avail. That was the first and last time I ever played in the Little League.

I had to see Mr. Choi.

"I've been going to Pu'unene Hongwanji Church. Are all the churches the same?" I asked him.

He said, "All of the churches are basically different and yet, they are the same. Some believe in the Living Soul that once roamed this earth and others believe in God. Some have altars in their homes, called *Hoto Ke Sama*.

Then there are people who don't go to church and believe, like your grandparents and parents. There are those who go to church and think they believe. It is hard to believe in someone or some thing you have not seen or heard, and yet, people do believe they exist. Some examples are: Jesus, Buddha, Confucius, Lao Tzu, Dali Lama (generations before), Mohammed, and others.

Think about this. Is it not true that air does not leave this earth? If this is so, think about this. Isn't it true that we are breathing the same air that Jesus, Buddha, Lao Tzu, Confucius, Dali Lama, Mohammed, and others breathed?

213

It is said that God created heaven, earth, and men. If this is so, then you are the creation of God. Since we are the creation of God, then, when we see each other, we should see God in each other. If this is so, then we should treat each other with kindness, as we would treat God and believe.

In this world, because there are so many people and so many different religions, it is basically very difficult to speak of one religion. There are so many different points of view or religious beliefs.

As long as one religion teaches you be a good person, isn't that religion okay? If one religion claims that it is better than another religion, then is that religion not good? One religion proclaiming that it is better then another religion is basically defying all other religions. Remember, all religions are good that teaches you to be a good person.

Remember before when I talked about choices, it is the person's right to chose. Everyone is given a choice to choose what he believes in. Make your own choice and don't let anyone else make up your mind for you. Kindness and love blossoms when you believe in a religion. In that kindness and love, a human develops, capable of helping make the world a better place to live in. Remember this saying, 'A cup that is full, cannot be added to – a cup that is empty can hold a lot.' Also remember, you should not only believe but practice religion twenty-four hours a day.

There are people who go to church to believe and pray. There are also those who go to church with nice clothes, hoping that people would recognize them with pretty clothes. There are also those who go to church and think they believe. There are those who go to church and within a few hours are gambling their hearts out, swearing, and fighting with their spouses and families. Why go to church?"

At the same time I got a dog, my uncle decided to relocate to the mainland for better pay and opportunities so my parents decided to move into my uncle's house that was located across the way. My father built a large hot house (building to raise plants) and

214

relocated all the orchids and anthuriums that lined the front of our previous house.

A couple of months after this last talk with Mr. Choi, a friend gave my father a puppy, and my father gave it to me to be my pet. The puppy was part cocker spaniel and part dachshund, better known in Hawai'i as a *poi* dog (mixed breed), Spotty was black with large white spots. From when he was a baby, we used a loud ticking clock to quiet the dog. A loud ticking clock was supposed to sound like the mother's heart beating, but it did not help. The dog cried for three nights straight.

I was allowed to take uncle's bedroom. I had my own private entrance and a door that went to the living room. The dog was smart enough to know that I was sleeping in that one particular room. Every night he would set himself outside my door and cry. I got sick and tired hearing that dog wail, and upset that he might wake up the neighbor, so I eventually let the dog in. The dog jumped on the bed and crawled under the covers every night. However, every morning the bed would be soaked wet from dog urine. One day, I got so mad from the odor of the urine, I retrieved a large towel for a dog, placed it on the floor, and commanded him to sleep on it. At first, he didn't like the towel and tried to climb on the bed, but, eventually, he surrendered to it.

About a year later, I was returning home from playing with my friends, I had a sinking feeling that something was wrong. My father was holding Spotty in his arms. He said that Spotty ran across the road and had no chance. A vehicle hit him. He died instantly.

It took some time for me to get over Spotty's death. I missed him sleeping on the towel at nights. I wouldn't see him wag his tail in excitement when he saw me. He would no longer be greeting me when I came home, nor jump on me when I sat down to pet him. I lost a dear friend the day my father and I buried Spotty.

After Spotty's death, I re-concentrated my efforts on baseball. While I practiced baseball, I was excused from picking up the mail. When I didn't play baseball any more, I started to pick it up again. The post office was situated about two-mile bike ride from the school.

Prior to the 60's, local post offices never used keys. Instead each box had a three number combination lock. At times, this combination lock would freeze and be difficult to turn, so an employee of the post office sprayed it with an oil based product to make it work better, for a while. I always forgot the combination to the lock, but because I went to the post office so many times and they all knew me, they would help by opening the lock from inside the post office. One of the clerks, Mr. Rafino Racoma, lived in the same camp as I did. More often than not, we did not have mail because my parents rarely wrote to anyone. In fact, I don't believe that there were any stamps or envelopes in our house.

Overnight, my mind changed from baseball to football. I was determined to learn the game of football. It was not difficult for a twelve-year-old tall guy to switch sports that fast. I learned how to play touch football and flag football at school. I learned the game as quick as a duck takes to swimming. If I had the chance, I would have played the game either morning or afternoons till the sun went down – as the elderly Japanese ladies called it – *futoball*. We played it in the hospital grounds.

There was a long building, which housed the dispensary ward and adult patient ward at the hospital. Next to this large building was a grassy area equivalent to three fourths of a football field, about seventy yards long and about forty yards wide. Thankfully, the grass was always mowed and watered whenever we played there. We found out later that the patients were the ones who pushed the grounds keeper to beautify the lawn.

At first, the staff was not too keen about us playing there. We were told that we could get hurt if we did not play with the proper uniforms. They must have realized later that this lawn was the most appropriate place to play. It was near a hospital, should any one of us get hurt. Further more, I think that we helped with the recovery of the hospital patients; they made up the audience that

216

watched the games. The hospitalized spectators peered and cheered through the windows at us kids. Chanting could be heard over the noise that the players generated when playing football.

There were rules to our game:
1. No more than twenty kids on the field at once.
2. No fights allowed. (There were none)
3. No pads of any kind. (Nobody could afford them)
4. If you got hurt, it was your fault, no one else's.

Teams were split in half (ten on each side). The captains chose who would be on each team, from good to *junk*. Now, if you were considered *junk*, you never touched the ball, even though you were in the game. You'd better hit someone. That was about it. Those who did touch the ball were crazy. There was no padding or protection whatsoever, not even shoes. We played barefoot. T-shirt, pants or shorts was the uniform. Tackle was the name of the game and full contact the fun of the game. Since the hospital was right there, anything went. I don't believe that anyone who touched the football finished the game without some kind of injury.

The nurses and doctors of Pu'unene Hospital must have been onlookers because whenever someone was injured, they always rushed out to treat the player, whether it be a cut or a broken arm. If we could survive this type of football, we could survive anything. There were no fights before, during, or after the game. No one had the energy. Everyone knew each other and who not to pick a fight with.

Because I was injured from a cut on my foot in the second grade, I couldn't run fast, but because I was tall, my main job was to make sure that no one got to the quarterback. I was also a receiver because I was tall. The quarterback would throw the ball high and I would catch it. The only problem to jumping high was that I was always undercut. I'd fall on my shoulders, on my back, or even on my face. I fell on my shoulder once and thought that it had come off. It dangled, the skin barely holding my arm together. The doctor popped it back. I was in so much pain that I had to see a doctor. I was given some pills for the pain.

217

On some days, as we rode home on our bikes, we'd talk football: about outstanding plays, about who got hurt worst, about the funniest incident, and about the extent of the injuries. Once, when I got home after the game, my father thought I had gotten into a fight. I had cuts and bruises all over my body. The following day, I could hardly walk, let alone sit up in bed. Actually, we were stupid to play under such conditions. I think that if we had known better, we would have discontinued that part of our lives. All in all, it was fun, but painful fun. Each time we played, less and less players appeared, causing it to be abolished sooner than we thought.

After such incidents in my life, I'd always go and see Mr. Choi for friendly advice that also included spiritual advice. When I hit thirteen, I didn't visit him. With a busy school schedule, hanging with friends, and my chores, I seemed to have very little time to spare. I had a lot of homework to do.

For example, I learned in school that the islands of Maui, Moloka'i, and Lana`i made up what is known as the Maui Group. Groups of islands were separated by the Ka'iwi Channel (commonly known as Moloka'i Channel). Alenuihaha Channel separated the Big Island of Hawai'i from the Maui Group. It was once believed that all of the islands of the Maui Group were connected as one island called Maui-Nui. When the ocean subsided during the last glacial period, the islands separated to what is commonly known today as Maui County.

The island of Maui can best be described as an island with a head and a body. The tail end of the body is Hana, while the top of the head is Lahaina. There are two ways to get to Lahaina. The unpaved road on the right side of Mount Eke along the Kahakuloa Coastline is one way. Another more traveled road is around Mount Pu`u Kukui with its five miles of a paved narrow two lane winding road along the ocean cliffs known to Maui residents as *The Pali*. We ventured mostly on the Pali Road because it was the fastest route from the camps. At times, though rarely, we'd return along the more winding, narrow Kahakuloa side of the head.

Once the capital of the Hawaiian Islands, Lahaina now has a population in the thousands. It changed from a thriving whaling port to a very laid back town, then to a tourist attraction as it is today. In 1831, missionaries founded the oldest American school west of the Rockies. That school, Lahainaluna High School, is situated on the hillside of the West Maui Mountains and overlooks the harbor.

When my father drove us to Lahaina for business or pleasure, we played our counting game. We drove past an abundant row of coconut trees along the highway. I think he personally drove fast so that I would have a hard time counting. After fifty, I gave up. On our return, my father would go slower when we neared the same coconut trees, so I could count exactly how many there were. I believe that I counted about 75 to 90 coconut trees in a row. To be exact, one would have to count them by actually walking along the row of coconut trees.

There were reasons why we ventured so far as Lahaina. One of our many visits took us to homes that were growing a special variety of eggplant. This eggplant did not grow more that two and a half to three inches long. They were purple and used for pickling. Many people tried to raise it in different parts of Maui but to no avail. Either the plant had a hard time growing, never produced enough offspring, or grew to a regular size eggplant even when weather conditions were the same. My mother always bought a few pounds from a person she later became friends with. Sometimes that lady did not have enough to supply my mother. She would contact another person who also raised the same type of eggplant. The other seller would charge my mother the same price as her friend.

For lunch, we would go to Liberty Restaurant on Front Street. The Chinese restaurant was famous for its *chow fun* (fried noodles). What made the chow fun special were the noodles. The noodles were thick, square (half of an inch on four sides), and about three to four inches long. It was cooked with ground pork, green onions, *mung* bean sprouts (*moyashi*), and seasonings in a large wok over a gas stove. The chow fun, sold in regular and

219

large sizes, was constantly stirred with a large wooden spatula, served in pink veined meat paper, and folded to look like an ice cream cone. We ordered some to go and ate our noodles with *shoyu* (soy sauce) under the big banyan tree in Lahaina town. Most times my father ordered extra so we could have it for dinner.

The famous big banyan tree was planted in the middle of town, close to the pier. It is an evergreen from India, sacred to the Hindus. Arial roots grow earthward from the horizontal branches to support the tree so as to cover a large area. It is known for its shade and, yet, its prolific roots can become troublesome if the land area is limited. When we were kids, the tree was already huge. How old is that tree today? Give or take, about a hundred years old.

After lunch, my father would go down to the pier and wait for the fishermen to return with their catch of the day. My father would buy a bucket of fish called *opelu* (mackerel family). This would be the last thing my father would buy before returning home so that the timing and ice would keep the fish fresh until we got home. When he returned home, my father would clean the *opelu*. Instead of only frying this fish, my father dried some of them with teriyaki sauce for a few days. He would freeze some while others were cooked on an open fire for dinner.

My parents got into the *kaguma* (fibers of tree fern) business while living in the front house. They sold the *kaguma* in burlap bags to orchid and anthurium growers. The growers would use the fern trunk fibers to stuff their plants in a cement pot. Fibers of the *kaguma* held moisture in, while allowing air to seep through and grow. My parents imported tree ferns from the Big Island of Hawai'i, where they are abundant in forests where lava once flowed. In these rain forests, tree ferns could grow upwards of ten feet. When the shipment arrived, numerous bags were stored in our garage. As soon as it was delivered, another shipment would arrive. My parents ordered conservatively, never blindly.

Cement pots for planting were home made with steel forms. The combination of cement and sand had to have the correct consistency. The idea was not to make the cement too watery or too dry. If the right consistency was used, those cement pots could survive for years. My father also made his own pots. My parents used the *kaguma* for their own plants. They had hundreds of orchid and anthurium plants in the hot house in the back yard. Varieties of anthuriums consisted of *Ozaki Pink, Ozaki Red, Obake* and miniatures.

Hawai'i has the ideal climate for raising orchids and anthuriums, It fortunately had the constant blowing trade winds, a temperature that seldom dipped lower that sixty degrees or no higher than ninety-five, and occasional humidity in the eighty percent range. The most preferred orchids among growers were the *dendrobium* for flower arrangements and *lei*s, the *cattleya* for proms and wedding corsages, and the purple *vanda* for *lei*s.

The hot house was a framed building with laths about an inch apart. They ran completely around the frame and on the roof. There were even laths on the door. These thin strips of wood were used to allow indirect sunshine on the plants. The hot house was full of orchid plants that had to be watered when there was no rain and sprayed with chemicals every month. It was a very expensive hobby. Raising orchids was my parent's hobby.

As I got older and began high school, my friends thinned out; they made new friends from different schools. Sand lot football has long been a thing of the past. Many of the original players either now played high school football or were more interested in girls. It occupied most of their time.

In fact, I wanted to play high school football, but my mom refused to sign the release form. I was a veteran of sand lot football, so why not play football with pads. I thought it would be pretty hard to get hurt. She told me that if I played football, she would not go to watch the games. I was so angry that I told her that I didn't care if she didn't go. I wanted to play football so badly that I occasionally took my bike and a football and headed for the cane fields. There, unseen, I'd imagine that someone was throwing me a pass and would run about fifty yards with the football in my hand. When I played pretend football, I would also

221

take a break, sit on the bank, and smoke my cigarettes.

High school boys played real football at a familiar place, The Maui County Fairgrounds. It was located in Kahului where the Little League games were played. The fairgrounds consisted of a cluster of buildings for the following displays: orchids, new products, agriculture, commercial, homemaking items, Hawaiian products, and animals. There was also a boxing arena, an entertainment stage, and the office for the Maui County Fair Association. Along the main road were booths run by non-profit organizations, selling food items and drinks. Within the complex, there was The Joy Zone for E.K. Fernandez rides and games.

Within the fairground complex was a stadium. Throughout the years, the stadium was used for horse racing, stock car racing, and football games. Lights were later added for night games.

There were three entrances to the stadium. There was one on each side of the grandstand and one in the middle. Under the grandstand were locker rooms for both football teams. There was a referee room and bathrooms on opposite sides, one for the ladies and one for the gentlemen.

The grandstand had a capacity seating of about three to four hundred spectators. When it was filled, the grandstand sometimes would sway. Although it did not fall apart, the grandstand had the capability of taking spectators down with it. Bleachers were located on both ends of the field, as well as on the opposite side. During the Maui County Fair weekend, there was a Sunday afternoon rivalry football game that always pitted Maui High School against Lahainaluna High School. Because of the popularity of the contest, reserved tickets were sold ahead of time, and because it was the last day of the fair with no admission charge, the game was always filled to capacity.

I had to see Mr. Choi. I hadn't seen him for ten months.

When I approached his doorstep, I knocked on the door. No one answered. I knocked harder. Maybe Mr. Choi was sleeping. What I didn't realize was that not only was the screen door shut but the main door as well. I sensed something was wrong. I asked the neighbor but they didn't know where he went.

So I left, determined to be back tomorrow. Well, days passed and with other plans, I had forgotten about Mr. Choi. One night I decided to definitely see him the following morning. When the sun came up, I rode my bike to the most familiar place besides my home; I had become familiar with it throughout my life. It was the house next to the bridge.

I had to see Mr. Choi. As soon as I walked up the stairs of the house, Mr. Choi came out of the door and gave me a big hug. This is the first time he had done that. I hugged him hard in return. I thought I might have hugged him too hard. If so, he did not complain.

"I'm so glad to see you," he said, tears rolling down his face. He then led me into his house where he sat on the floor.

"I'm also glad to see you after being away for ten months," I replied, holding back my tears. I brought him up to date about what had been happening to me. I also told him that I came to visit him a few days ago but there was no answer. I even asked the neighbor and he didn't know anything.

"I was in the hospital for a couple of days. Before I got released, the doctor told me that he couldn't detect anything. I honestly believe there is something wrong but I don't know what."

He diverted his issue back to philosophy. "Well, let's see. Suppose you had a choice of starting your life again, would you do it? Of course, you would have to be born again.

Everything in your life you possess right now is your whole life. If you decide to change and redo your life, this present moment would be erased. It is up to you and you alone that have the power to make that final decision.

To continue, often those who care for you the most are the ones who are a burden to you. Their expectations are placed on you to

223

be better. They want you to become something they want, minus their own flaws, of course.

However, they are mistaken. All too often, others push their beliefs upon you. Little do they know that they are, in fact, hurting you more than they are helping you. All they see is now.

If you have feelings of obligation, constraint, or even self-admiration, then you are not doing what you are supposed to. If you feel that you are not accomplishing something in life, then you are not doing the things you were born to do. This is the time to change your life.

Here is my suggestion: Be like a child who is free from worry. A child can change from crying to laughter within a few moments. The wonderful thing is that it is pure. See how a child forgets anger and turns its emotion to pure smiles in front of your eyes. Watch a child laugh; that is pure happiness. It is not made up; it comes from the heart.

Many of us have forgotten how a child acts. If this is so, then seek out a child and study his or her emotions. Learn from the child. Do you know that an adult learns from a child more than a child learns from an adult? Adults think they know more than a child. Is this not so?

In all that I've said, as sure as the sun is shining on a cloudy day, so is it that there are moon and stars on cloudy night. So should your thinking be. Believe in your thinking. Rely on what you have learned. If in doubt, go back and learn it again but, this time, learn it well. It is with knowledge and wisdom that we can remember the past and learn from it. It is with knowledge and wisdom that we can live in the present. It is with knowledge and wisdom that we can prepare for the future. These two virtues are the keys to push further on to the future. The right knowledge and wisdom are the keys to the right progress.

What you have learned from me is what I have learned from my father and those around us. Remember the first time I saw you? You were nine years old. I had watched you before that day. I realized that you were one who was always searching for answers. I was not wrong then, and I am not wrong now. I have selected the right person. Even if what I have told you is not taught to others, promise me that you will at least try to do as you have been taught, and as I've been taught by my father.

This will probably be the last time we will be talking like this. I understand that within a couple of weeks or so, you will be moving to another place. I wish you a lot of luck in your new venture. I do hope that your life will be as fulfilling as my life has been sharing my thoughts with you. You are the one that made me believe that I was put on this earth to learn what my father taught me and I, in return, have taught you. I now feel that my life is complete."

As I left Mr. Choi's home, I felt emptiness in my heart. Could it be that something was wrong with him physically and that he was not telling me about it? Could it also be the last time that I'd get to see him? I hoped not, but I had this sinking feeling that it was.

The sugar plantation built a baseball park where I practiced the game. Along with the baseball fields, there was also a tennis court and a swimming pool. The tennis court was built strictly for the *haole*. Only they could afford the rackets and balls. The tennis court was totally fenced with green nylon sheets with a gate that was always locked. I don't know who had the key.

The swimming pool was quite big for the residents. Occasionally, we were allowed to swim there. However there was always too much chlorine in the water. After a while, we couldn't see very well, thanks to the chemical that burned our eyes. Swim meets were held there. I recall one meet when a Japanese boy, much older than I, entered. He swam in every long distance event. He was the best Japanese swimmer. At times, I would see him at The Pump swimming against the current. He was conditioned because he did it for hours on end. I understand that after high school, he entered a mainland college on a swimming scholarship.

He won every event that he participated that first day I saw him.

225

When the Asian community found out that he was swimming, they came in droves to cheer him on. No swim meet was ever held in that sugar plantation pools after that.

There was also a long building along Pu'unene Avenue. That building was called called the *Haole* Community Club House and used exclusively by *haole*. *Haole*s held dances on Friday and Saturday nights.

There was another pool that was closer to the post office built exclusively for white people. How did I know? I asked the Portuguese grounds keeper one day why the pool was fenced and locked. He told me that, that pool was strictly for white families. I asked him if I could swim in it. He said that if he let me in, he would be fired.

I was so hurt by what had been said. This was my first personal experience in racial discrimination. I didn't know the words for it back then. But, I knew the feelings of racial discrimination, of hate among other nationalities throughout the camps. I heard it in conversations between them, but I never thought until that day at the pool that they were really serious about the hate from and for *haole*. That day was a racial milestone for me.

I felt the hate that separated one nationality from all the others. I felt like asking them if their Jesus was better than my Buddha or their religion was better than mine. Why didn't they just have the guts to say that their race was superior to any other in the world? I thought racism was a stupid attitude to have.

I got so mad that I went to the post office rubbish can to see if someone had thrown a newspaper in the trash. Sure enough, there were two whole pages. I went to the back of the building and defecated on the newspaper. I folded it a number of times and I went straight to the pool fence. I threw the wrapped up paper in my hand as far as I could into the pool. Buddha must have been on my side because the brown bomb landed smack in the middle of it. As I watched the paper get soaked, I saw brown emerging from it. The grounds keeper spotted me. I was now in trouble. But something odd happened. He seemed to turn away. He never said or did anything about my retaliation. I assumed that he knew how I felt about this racial discrimination. I was never reported, although they had to drain the water, scrub the pool, and refill it with water. I'm sure that the Portuguese man was laughing inside even while he cleaned it.

Don't get me wrong. I didn't think all *haole* were bad. All nationalities have good and bad people, including the Japanese. Fortunately, the good are in the majority.

Now came the part of my life when things started to change. All of a sudden, there were hairs on me where there had been none before. My voice sounded lower. Friends and family laughed at me like I was something strange.

Over night, I started to notice girls in a different way. I didn't consider them one of the boys anymore. They didn't play their silly games like they did before. Now, they talked to each other in little bunches and giggled a lot. They looked different. There were cute ones, average ones, and some not-so-good-looking ones. Their complexion and bodies had improved. They weren't little girls any longer. They looked different and acted different. They had become young adults.

I started to notice one girl in particular. It's probably because she didn't have the usual black hair that Japanese have. She had streaks of brown hair within her black hair. She had brown eyes, skinny, and two years younger than me. Because she was my neighbor, I saw quite a bit of her. Everyone was friendly to each other in the camps, and she was no exception to the rule. We conversed a lot during our years as neighbors. Imagine! We lived next to each other during all of our growing years, then, all of a sudden, I saw her differently than the neighbor I had grown up alongside.

As we matured, we talked about anything and everything, except liking each other. I believe that if she had expressed feeling for me, I believe that our lives would have been different. In those days, Japanese girls held feelings to themselves. I had feelings how she felt but those affections were never exchanged. I wished they had.

I had never had a brother or a sister so I really didn't know what love was. I was never shown any affection from my mother. She never hugged me nor was ever a kind word spoken to me. In fact, she was against everything I said. My father, on the other hand, always listened to me. Sometimes we didn't agree with each other, but we shared common ground. We understood each other and that was fine with him and me.

What I forgot to mention was that there were no professional dentists in the camps. This was not fine with me. There were some who acted like they were professionals. Whenever anyone had a loose tooth, there was always a volunteer amateur dentist available at no charge. What also came with no charge was pain and suffering for the beholder of the tooth. The dentist was the father of each kid that lived in the camps. One end of the string was tied to the loose tooth. The other end looped to the doorknob, any doorknob. To take the tooth out, the untrained dentist slammed the door, fast. Sometimes the string would slide off the tooth, and then the process would start all over again. If the extracted tooth hurt like hell, ice was applied to control the bleeding or swelling. Sometimes it hurt the victim worse to see his/her tooth dangling bloodily from the string.

We placed the extracted tooth under our pillow at night and hoped that the tooth fairy would visit, take the tooth, and leave some cash by the following morning. At times, the tooth fairy forgot to leave money! Other times, the tooth fairy forgot to take the tooth! I came to believe that tooth fairy had memory lapses and was – human. I eventually identified the impostor.

There was a financial practice in the camps called *tanamoshi*. It was basically a lending or borrowing system among friends. About five families or larger contributed an equal amount of money in a pot, with someone designated to hold the money. This was like a bank for the camp residents. The idea was that if someone wanted to borrow money, all the investors would come together for a meeting. They decided on the amount investors wanted to borrow. The investors generally approved it because

228

paid interest was required. There was a certain time allotted for the borrower to pay the loan back.

Those who invested in the *tanamoshi* used the money wisely. For example, *tana moshi* could be used to pay for a child's higher education. It was the best practice because everyone got paid back eventually. One could continue to participate in the tanamoshi or terminate it after they paid up. Those who did not borrow money had a huge advantage; they made money from the interest. The total amount of interest was divided in equal portions among those who did not borrow money.

An uncontrollable gambler could have used that money to play a card game called *hanafuda*. These cards that were brought over from Japan were very small, and had forty-eight in a deck. These cards were very hard to deal; the originals made of wood. If someone knew how to deal fast, that was a clue that shuffler had mastered the game very well. This game had four matching cards in twelve different suites. All cards are very colorful with pictures of birds, foliage, and flowers. To learn it best was to learn the game first hand from a person familiar with *hanafuda*. It is a very complicated game and becomes more complicated with the addition of *yaku (three specific card combination)*. If I kept explaining this game further, you'd eventually put your hands up and give up. This past time is still played today. Remember, I wrote earlier that there were gambling on the ships and a lot of passengers lost a lot of money. *Hanafuda* was another way to lose one's rent money.

In 1948, the sugar plantation and the subsidiary of the sugar company, Kahului Development Company worked together in drawing plans for a sub-division in Kahului to house sugar plantation workers and their families living in camps scattered throughout the cane fields of Pu'unene. By 1950, these homes were available for sale at a moderate price. The new homes had three bedrooms, a bath with flush toilets, a small living room, a kitchen, and single vehicle carport. Many of the first lots were huge, ten to thirteen thousand square feet.

Schools, parks, and playgrounds were included in the town plans for the new residences at Kahului. In later years, Kahului Development Company sold individual lots instead of house and lot packages.

As time went by, the sugar company pressured camp residents to relocate, purchase lots, and build or purchase homes in Kahului. Eventually, the camp dwellers were forced out of their wooden homes in Pu'unene. Many held out as long as they could to avoid the possibility of moving to Kahului. They moved from one closing camp to another. The reality of relocating to Kahului was a trauma to many because some had large families and lived paycheck to paycheck with no savings. Many of the women were housewives who faced entering a work force for the first time. Most families had never taken out loans, much less entered a bank; now they were required to pay mortgages. Old plantation houses in good condition were allowed to be re-located. The poorer families chose and bought abandoned camp homes instead of their own to be moved to Kahului from the sugar plantation for $1,000.00, that included the hook up of electricity and plumbing. Moving the house to the new location cost $1,200.00. A single car garage and a washroom were later added to the house.

The size of the lots varied from 7,000 to 11,000 square feet. Prices rose from one increment to a new increment. The first increment was cheaper to purchase than the rest of the others. As with the naming of the camps by numbers, the same applied to the increments that ran from one to twelve.

When my father announced that we were planning to move to the sixth increment by the end of summer, the thought of it totally overwhelmed me. My parents had bought a property in the sixth increment and my father was making a home there. My father acted like a sub-contractor and hired skilled workers to do masonry, carpentry, electrical, and plumbing. In order to save money, he personally helped the contractors as much as he could. I went there to help but I was more of a hindrance than help. In fact, I got hit by one of the 2x4s on my back when the carpenters were moving long planks. After that, I never went to the site at the request of my father. The only time I did help was when he needed to dump broken wall tiles or useless boards. My father did keep a few pieces of extra lumber that he might possibly need in the future.

On March 12, 1959, the U.S. Senate passed a bill making Hawai'i the 50th State. August 21, 1959 was officially declared Statehood Day. I heard this announcement when I was attending summer school between my freshman and sophomore year of high school. I did not hear anyone cheer. In fact, I saw everyone with a sad face. When I went home, my parents questioned why the people of Hawai'i, its citizens, were never given a chance to vote for or against it.

When I turned sixteen years old, I was legally able to work. I decided to apply for a job at the Kahului Mercantile Store that sold general merchandise. It was very convenient because all I had to do was catch the Kahului bus from school that dropped me off right in front of the store. I was a go-for; I cleaned bathrooms, swept and mopped floors, and small talked to the ladies who worked there.

Behind the store was a building where Mr. Lester Hamai sold his appliances. I got to know him well. In fact, he asked me if I wanted to make extra money delivering appliances. I definitely accepted the offer. The only problem was that I had to work past my quitting time of five o'clock.

After work, I'd walk home about three miles through dirt cane field roads and Tournahauler roads. During the winter, it got dark early that made it hard to see the road. There were a few times that I stepped on a rock or in a pothole and sprained my ankle forcing me to limp home.

Neighbors, who had known us for a long time, finally realized that our family was leaving to our new house within a few weeks, for good. They wouldn't get any more fish, limu, bamboo shoots, or any of nature's bounty that my father gathered to give them.

One day before we made the move, the mother of the girl I liked asked me to come into their kitchen. I told her that if her daughter gave me any kind of indication that she liked me, then I would pursue her to go on dates with me. I was open to see what would happen. Was I in for a surprise? I always thought that her mother liked me. She stated directly that I should never think about marrying their daughter. I was stunned and asked her why. She told me that I was not good enough for her; she was Okinawan, and I was not. She also said that once I left this place, I was to forget about her child. I was so hurt that I stood up, swung open the door, and slammed it behind me as I left. In a way, she was correct. There were no hints that her daughter seriously liked me. If there were, then I would be forced to see her secretly. All she had to tell me was, 'I like you,' and that would have changed everything.

At the beginning of August, in the summer of 1960, our new house was completed. By the end of summer, as planned, we had already moved practically everything into and outside of the new house in Kahului. What we did not need, we gave to friends and neighbors. What they didn't want, we took to the dump.

Reality struck when I gave my bike away to a friend. That bike meant everything to me while I lived there in the camps. Instead of walking, I'd ride it wherever and whenever I needed to go. Occasionally, I sanded off the old paint and brushed on a new fresh coat. Whenever I had a flat tire, I'd break out the flat tire kit and patch the tube. I did that numerous times. Whenever the spokes or the internal mechanism needed grease or oil, I served as its mechanic. I knew that bike inside and out. When I gave it away, it seemed as though I had lost a good friend who was very, very close to me. I really did talk to my bike before I gave it away. I told my constant companion that the next owner would take care of him well, that he didn't have to worry about a thing. I heard a few months later that the bike was broken, was never fixed, was left on the side, got rusty and, later, was thrown away.

Another concern with the move was the plants that my parents kept through the years. The anthuriums and orchid plants in their heavy concrete pots had to be carried one by one from the hot house to the truck that my father borrowed. There must have been well over a hundred potted plants so it took numerous trips to transport them to the new home in Kahului.

As we moved things to the new house, it dawned on me that I was beginning a new life at the age of sixteen. Although the new house had a toilet within the house, a bedroom I could call my own, and brand new appliances, there was something missing.

I had not seen or visited Mr. Choi for ten months between the ages of ten-eleven. I'd seen him before and after numerous times, too many times to count. Before leaving the camp for good, in the summer of my sixteenth year, I went to visit my sage for the last time as a camp resident.

There was a pause when we finally faced each other. Tears flowed from both of us, then he said in a quiet voice, "I wish you well, my friend." I also wished him well with a big hug. I had known him for six years, minus the ten months. In all of those years, I felt a very special bond. I often felt that he was my second father or my guardian angel. That day, I lost a very special friend. I felt like I was on my own now. I also felt that emptiness inside. How else can I describe it? Two days later we left the camp for good.

I would not be able to see my neighbors or my friends on a daily basis. I would not be able to walk to the camp store and buy cigarettes or candy. I would not be able to chew sugar cane on a regular basis, swim The Pump, or race my bike down Walker Hill with my friends. I would not be able to go to Sam Sato's frequently to eat saimin, or catch any more tropical fish for my aquarium. We were no longer residents of Camp Four any more.

A couple of months after we moved to Kahului, I asked my father if I could use the car to visit Camp Four at least one more time to see it and, hopefully, visit Mr. Choi.

I parked my parents' car close to the Camp Four Store and walked to the house where we once lived. The neighborhood kids had broken the windows. Having been away from the camps for a while made me realize that I definitely wasn't part of it anymore.

Some residents passed by, their conversation polite: 'How are you? How have you been? How is the family? How is school?' None of the personal things we once shared openly came up, and there seemed to be a lack of willingness to express one's self. The changes in my life reminded me of a story about Leonardo Da Vinci.

Early in his career, Leonardo Da Vinci was painting a picture of Christ and found a profoundly beautiful young male to model for his portrait of Jesus.

Many years later, Leonardo was painting a picture that included Judas. He walked through the streets of Florence looking for the perfect person to paint as the great betrayer. Finally, he found someone dark enough, evil-looking enough, to do the job. He approached the man to do the modeling. The man looked up at him and said, 'You don't remember me but I know you. Years ago, I was the model for your picture of Jesus.

Knowing that things were not the same anymore as Leonardo Da Vinci realized, I went to see Mr. Choi. As I walked up the small hill leading to the bridge, I saw the house that I visited over and over again. Excitement rose inside of me that I would get to see my spiritual sage again.

I reached the gate, swung it open and walked into the yard. As I walked along the sidewalk, I noticed something very different. All of the daisies that had flourished months before were now dead. I leaped the three steps to the porch and knocked on the door. A little girl of Filipino descent opened the door. I was totally shocked! "Who is this?" A lady in the background with a heavy accent asked what I wanted.

"I've come to see Mr. Choi," was my reply, as I peered into the living room hoping to see *goza* and a few *zabuton* on the floor. None was in sight. "What's going on?" I asked myself.

I heard what I didn't want to hear. "Mr. Choi no longer lives here. He died about a month and a half ago. The neighbors told us that he had been fighting stomach cancer for a year and a half. He never told anyone of his condition. The neighbors said that the

234

Japanese boy who once lived nearby and had since moved away should also be spared about the old man's affliction. We understand that the only person Mr. Choi talked about was the Japanese boy. Do you know this boy?"

I didn't respond, I was trying hard to hold back the tears inside. The woman continued, "I also understood that there was a large envelope found in the house for that Japanese boy." I was also told that the neighbor had the large envelope or has the knowledge of who possessed the large envelope. I never told the Filipino lady that the Japanese boy was I. I felt that later she'd put two and two together and realize it.

I quickly walked to the neighbors to find out who had the large envelope that Mr. Choi had left for me. The neighbor, Mr. Fujimoto, confirmed it. "Yes, Donald, this large envelope is for you. We found him dead in the house. He had been dead for a couple of days. We noticed a lot of flies on his screens, so we went to investigate.

A few of us decided to give away what he had, and took the rest to the dumpster. In fact, there was so little to dump. As we tossed his things, we noticed a large envelope addressed to you, as well as a small envelope containing instructions to send his valuables to a stepsister in California. There was also money in the small envelope for the postage. Would you believe that it was the exact amount needed to send his belongings to California?"

As I took the envelope from Mr. Fujimoto's hand, my inner self told me to go to the bridge where it all began, where I shoved my friend into the water, where I had my accident at the cane field, where Jimmy and I rode up a small hill, and where I saw a man standing by the picket fence who asked me, "Who learns more – a man who speaks or a man who listens?"

I sat on the bridge and proceeded to open the large envelope. Inside were pages and pages of hand written notes, written in black ink from a fountain pen on typing paper. What was totally amazing was that the hand written message to me was in a straight line, as though there were lines on the paper. He must have borrowed the pen and the paper because I never even spotted those in the house.

I opened the large envelope and started to read the pages and pages of hand written notes, but noticed something particular. The notes were hand printed and not free hand.

He wrote, "I know that you will be sitting on the bridge as you read these pages of my hand written letter. I also know that from the first time we saw each other eye to eye, we were destined to be good friends. When you left for your new Kahului home, I was sad at first. Then it dawned on me that you might be coming back to Camp Four to see me. As days passed to a week, I felt that I had to write this to you.

I never told you that I had stomach cancer because I didn't want you to worry about me. As time went by, it started to hurt more and more and I thought about you. No matter how much it hurt, I was determined to write you a letter. As you read this letter, please do not feel sorry for me. Believe me when I say, I am not fearful of death. Remember what I told you, that everyone has to die sooner or later. Well, my time has come up.

I want you to remember what I have written for the rest of your life. Although at times it seems that I've repeated things and also gone from one subject to another, believe me, my intentions were good. All that I have taught you reflects what I have been taught by my father, friends, experiences from living, and my true feelings toward life.

I can still remember the tree that grew along the dirt irrigation ditch outside my bedroom window. This tree did not need any watering to survive, since the water from the ditch and the rain always kept the soil around the tree damp. Although there are no real summers or real winters in these islands, this tree would go into a process of shedding its dead leaves, then sprouting new ones. This cycle continues year after year. Within a couple of years, this tree grew as high as a two-story building. Besides shading the area, this tree, like any tree throughout the world, converted enormous amounts of carbon dioxide into oxygen,

236

making the air purer to breathe.

One day, I returned home and noticed that there was something missing. There was so much sunlight coming from my bedroom. I noticed that the tree was gone. In the plantation haste, because the tree was too large, they decided to cut it down. This tree was no longer alive. After many years of growth, this tree was chopped and hauled away within a few hours. The hackers never realized its beauty, the cycle it had gone through for years, and the shade that the tree created. The tree was big so it took a few hours to destroy its beauty. This tree was started from a single seed, planted in a pot to create a seedling, and, when it grew bigger, that tree was transplanted to this area.

Are we not like the tree with our own character and the sense of being? Don't we go through cycles from childhood to adulthood that makes us as mighty as the tree? Do we not have the character that makes us individualists? Don't we individually have different concepts from our births? Are we eager to learn and grow to be pure in heart, with the total understanding of life, as we perceive it?

Like the tree, we start from a seed that our forefathers planted and nurtured a long time ago and grow to what we are today. We are formed from what we've been told and learned as we grew up. Whether right or wrong, our parents believed that they were the only people needed to bring up a child. There was no maybe. If there was a maybe, we might have had the right to think on our own and make our own decisions. As much as it was right then, it could be wrong today.

We have many preconceived notions. One is that the only way to success is to win, often at the cost of lives, hurt, and destruction. Hierarchy demands competition and not cooperation. We have learned from young that we have to be better than the next person. The best way to succeed is to be smarter than the other person. If you don't study hard, you'll never amount to anything. Look at the person next to you getting better grades. Why don't you study harder? With all these preconceived ideas, we have become numb to the idea that if we are not number one, then we are nothing.

Because of these notions, many of us have gone through life not caring whether our success was in the cards or not. Many times we tried as hard as we could and yet we got shot down because others thought that we didn't try hard enough. Trying hard sometimes got us to a point where we did not want to make mistakes and fail. Is it not enough that we try hard enough to be credited for what we are and not for what we are intended to be?

Like the tree, we have character of our own. We are individualists who believe that we are part of the whole process of life. As I have mentioned before, we are all meant to be here or we would have not been born. The purpose of life has not yet been revealed too many. When it is revealed, we will know our purpose. Until then, we will continue to live a life full of ups and downs, a life where prayers are answered and unanswered. It is this life that we must be thankful for each day, for our lives are a circle within a larger circle that we must understand and fulfill. For all things, we'll have an answer in the end.

What kind of people should we respect the most? It is people who can motivate, teach, encourage, and help bring out the best in other people. They give what they possess from the heart and are friendly, helpful, and loving. What is the purpose of a person who has knowledge and yet doesn't share it with the world? What is the purpose for a person who has spirituality and doesn't share it with the world? So many have died selfishly without sharing knowledge and spirituality. How many people could have benefited from their knowledge and spirituality?

Does this sound like something hard to achieve? There are people who are walking this earth today with the qualifications of Jesus or the Buddha. I have mentioned inner peace before. It is a matter of developing these qualities from within ourselves that gives us this inner peace.

My father told me a long time ago, "Be good and you will have little or no problems. Major or minor problems will disappear in a relatively short time. There is always a solution to the problem.

Whether the problem is big or small, spiritual people find solutions and not create problems.' Donald, there is one thing you should absolutely know and remember. That is not to lie. A person who lies has to have a good memory. He has to remember what he had said earlier. If you don't lie and tell the truth, there is nothing you need to remember. Is this not true?"

Another thing is, don't swear. If you swear around your family, your children will pick it up. You just add more fuel to the fire. You start swearing, your kids start swearing, then their companions start swearing, and it goes on and on. Don't start.

At this point, I'd like to end. My stomach is starting to hurt badly. I just coughed up blood. This is not a good sign. I don't think I have a week left in this world.

All I ask of you is that you'll remember me, but not for all the good times we had together. What I'll remember most till my last breath is your eagerness to learn. With this eagerness, I want you to remember all that I have told you and put that into practice. If you learn better things along the way, put that into practice also.

Do you understand everything that I have told you, Donald?" Signed, Mr. Choi.

Where had I heard that before? Yes, I heard it from my grandfather, my mother and now Mr. Choi. Isn't it ironic that all of them said the same thing, word for word? How can this be? What's happening?

One day, a question dawned on me. Could my grandfather; mother or Mr. Choi planned this together? I don't think so. Remember the time Mr. Choi talked about predestination? Could I have been predestined to bring together three life histories, including Mr. Choi's?

I figured out that there must be something much bigger than all of us somewhere out there. I believe that there is someone out there called God (Supreme Being). The Almighty works in mysterious ways, whomever that God might be to each individual. It is something that I cannot comprehend fully, though I'd like to.

One day, one of my sons had a two-page homework assignment that he had to turn in the following day. Well, you know how kids wait until the day before they have to do their assignments. He had a deadline and no chosen project. I suggested that he write about my camp days, especially our adventures and fun.

In about an hour, I gave him a brief history of my days in the camp. At the end of the hour, a strange thing happened. I asked him, "Do you understand everything that I have told you, son?" I didn't realize the importance of the words of my question until a few minutes later.

I've asked a few of my friends and all the people whom I interviewed, if they would like to go back to the days of the camps. Almost ninety percent said that they would choose those times over today's life. Although most of them suffered, a majority told me that they would rather have no money and a happy life than live a rich comfortable life but a meaningless one. The ten percent preferred not to ever relive that past, the suffering and pain was too much for them. One person told me that now he can choose to do whatever he wanted with his money. The camp days were then and today is now. Why go back?

I'll conclude by answering my own question. I, too, would return to the camp life right now. Those were the days. "Hey, you got sugar? May I borrow some?" "Hey, you got rice? I ran out." "Hey, you got coffee? I need some." And…on………..

CONCLUSION

As you know, everything happened years ago. Actually, I feel as though it happened in another lifetime. It's like I lived in two different eras during one span of existence. June 22, 1944 to late summer of 1960 was my first life. From late summer 1960 to the present is my second. I'm a sufferer from culture shock. I was pushed from an old lifestyle to a modern one. I had gone from one world to another in one day.

I believe in my heart that camp life was much more enjoyable. It's not that I don't enjoy life now, but back then, there was more love, freedom, trust, and togetherness among neighbors and friends. Cars and homes were unlocked; people trusted each other without fear of being robbed. No one talked about lawsuits or depended on government help.

I always believed that Pu'unene, Maui was a special place to live, as do many other residents. Earlier in life, I confirmed Maui's uniqueness. Even if I should decide to live elsewhere, I could and would always come back to My Personal Paradise, until recently.

Today, we rarely talk to our neighbors. Newspaper headlines note people on welfare and lawsuits by newcomers. In today's Maui, we must lock our houses and cars. Even with precautions, we can still get robbed of our valuable keepsake when we are not at home.

As years went by, I realized that everything seemed to change. Slowly, there was less and less freedom and more and more restrictions. Once there were beautiful sunsets. Today, smog occasionally accumulates along the horizon. Once there were beautiful beaches. Now there are floors and floors of beachfront high-rise condos, hotels, a concrete jungle, with little access to the ocean. As the population grew, roads turned into highways along which trash is thrown. Where there were once only three streetlights, now there are dozens.

New ideas and customs now clash, making Hawai'i what it is today. Contemporary society is in a hurry up mode with their

241

only destination – a point of no return. Sure there were clashes before. My grandfather, mother and I experienced it.

My grandmother (on my mother's side) told me that my grandfather was denied a supervisory position numerous times not because he couldn't do the job but because he was a *Jap*. When she heard that, she cried all night.

This is what my father told me a long time ago. During the start of the war, he was given a black rimmed badge with the word *restricted* written upon it. Even though he was an American, he was singled out among other nationalities at the work site. My father claimed that Japanese-Americans were also blamed for starting the war. He felt worse when he found out later that people who married Japanese were also issued these black-rimmed badges, confirming the suspicion that Japanese Americans were segregated.

I had realized long ago that the whites had all the big houses. The mansions had indoor flush toilets within their homes. Some even had tennis courts. Not a single *haole* lived in a plantation house as far as I know.

We were unaware that life in the camps was so harmful to our health. As I grew, I always had the philosophy that I should enjoy life and not worry about the future. Tomorrow was always another day. Now I am aware that many plantation workers who lived in the camps and worked in the cane fields passed away from throat, lung, and stomach cancer, including my father.

No one made a study or surveyed workers of the possibilities that camp worker deaths were linked to the smoke, dust, chemicals in the ground, water pumped from the ditch with the use of Durham bags to catch impurities, or sprayed chemicals close to drinking water facilities.

As Mr. Choi said, "We're all fools together. It's just that some of us know it, and others don't. The world is a puzzle and in that puzzle there are many people who make up the puzzle. The world out there is a school. Life is the only teacher. It offers many experiences. If experience alone brought wisdom and fulfillment, then elderly people would be happy, enlightened masters. But the lessons of experiences are hidden within the mind. Your mind knows it's true and yet your mind rebels. We've experienced much but we learned so little.

We are overflowing with preconceptions, full of useless knowledge. We hold many facts and opinions in our minds yet we know so little about ourselves, let alone the world. Before we can learn, we have to clear our minds of misconceptions. The world is a perfect place. It is the people who mess up this world. Many think they own this world. Remember, that when one dies he or she leaves this world, what he or she did here will determine heaven or hell. That person better believe there is reincarnation.

It is better for all of us to take responsibilities of our lives. As we open our eyes, we see that our state of health, happiness, and circumstances of our lives has been, in large part, arranged by our conscious or our subconscious.

All in all, the best thing that has surfaced from this mixed and often confused New Age Group is the consistently growing realization that the reason we are here is not to compete with one another for more and more wealth, power, or status, and to cause trouble to others, but to learn to love ourselves, others and the surroundings around us. We have to respect all living things, both plants and animals on this planet. Until we do, we will waste all good things on this earth. What has been destroyed can never be replaced.

We must heal our injured spirits, bodies, minds, hearts, relationships, and planet by enlisting this source of love and power. That power comes from within. It's listening to what your body is saying that creates this power."

If one believes that throwing rubbish, cans, or bottles out of windows from a moving car is great, wait until he or she sees how worse it is to go to hell. If you kill some one by running over, shooting, stabbing or punching a man, woman, or child at

243

will, then the Creator will take care of you. Remember, there is always someone wiser, taller, better looking, stronger, faster, and spiritually superior. I could mention more, but you get the drift.

Mr. Choi is not a fictitious character in this book. Mr. Choi's philosophy is my philosophy; his beliefs are my beliefs. Mr. Choi's home was an example of how simple life can be without all the clutter of material things. They are used for a while until new and better ones are added. Old material things are stored and usually never used again, given away, or simply thrown in the trash by your kids when you die.

How do I know this man, Mr. Choi? I had lengthy conversations with him. I presumed he was in his mid-sixties, although we never discussed his age for some odd reason. He stood about five feet, four inches, had receding salt and pepper hair, and dark wrinkly skin from working in the cane fields so long. He had a thin body structure and was a little bent over. He was a man with a round face and typically slanted brown oriental eyes. He always wore a white T-shirt and khaki pants well above his ankles. He is the only man, besides my father, that I truly miss in my life. They say that you never miss someone until something like death happens. I know Mr. Choi would not be living today, but believe that my father could have still been, if he hadn't died at the early age of forty-seven from stomach cancer.

I do know that if my father was alive today, he would be at the ripe old age of ninety-three. I am sure that he would have enjoyed playing with his grandchildren. I'm certain that he would have loved taking them to the beach much more than I did. He would have taught them how to swim and how to spear fish. Ah, but all of this is spilled milk and regretful. You just cannot have everything you want in life. Life goes on with regrets and happiness, hopefully with more happiness.

In conclusion, life must go on. I am a person that must tell the truth, no matter what happens. If telling the truth hurts someone, then so be it. If I tell the truth, I don't have to remember what I contrived. Mr. Choi said it well, "It takes a very smart man to lie. He has to remember everything he said. Some day, the truth will come out and the deceiver will be called a liar. The funny thing is that person is telling the truth in his own mind."

The church that I attend says it all. "The Golden Chain of Love" prayer during regular Sunday services, a portion of the Buddhist prayer is written, *"I will be kind and gentle to every living creature and protect all who are weaker than myself. I will try to think pure and beautiful words, and to do pure and beautiful deeds, knowing that what I do depends not only on my happiness or unhappiness but also on the happiness and unhappiness of others."* IS THIS NOT SO?"

"Do you understand everything that I have told you?".................

RESOURCES

<u>Maui News</u>   Maui Publishing Company   1902-1950
The Maui Publishing Company (*The Maui News*) made it possible to find information in the many newspaper articles published throughout the years. All newspaper articles are available at Maui County Libraries (Kahului), Maui College Library, and state libraries.

<u>The Museum of Japanese Immigration to Hawai'i</u>
Pamphlet acquired from the Museum of Japanese Immigration to Hawai'i contained information about my grandfather's voyage to get here and what happened the year my grandfather left for Hawai'i. Thank You to the Museum of Japanese Immigration to Hawai'i for its letter of permission to use the pamphlet word for word.

<u>Hawaii's Plantation Village in Waipahu</u>
Mahalo (Thank You) to Hawaii's Plantation Village in Waipahu on O'ahu for their approval of the use of photographs that I took while visiting there and for other pictures used in this book. Visitors will get a glimpse into plantation days. I highly recommend that if you are interested and want to learn more about camp life in O'ahu, please go and visit Hawai'i Plantation Village in Waipahu.

<u>Wayne Moniz</u>
Born and raised on Maui, he graduated with B.A.s in English and Communications from the University of Dayton, Ohio and received a M.A. in Theater Arts and Film from U.C.L.A. He has taught English and creative writing on the high school and college levels, named Maui Teacher of the Year in 1995.
Dubbed the "Dean of Maui Playwrights" for his 14 plays by the Maui News, he has published three books of his dramas and musicals and a collection of short stories, "Beyond the Reef": Stories of Maui in this World, for his company, Punawai Press. In 2009 Koa Books printed his book, "Under Maui Skies" and Other Stories. The collection of Maui Tales garnered the Ka Palapala Po'okela Readers Choice Book of the year in 2110. Maui Filmworks recently released the audio book for "Under Maui Skies". In 2005, he received the Cades Award for Literature, Hawai'i's most prestigious writing prize for his body of work.

Contract
Photos & Sketches

The Japanese Immigration Bureau Contract

This AGREEMENT made this ....day of ........A.D.
1899, by and between the JAPANESE EMIGRATION
COMPANY of Hiroshima, the KUMAMOTO EMIGRATION
COMPANY, and MORIOKA AND COMPANY, all emigration
companies organized and existing under the laws of Empire of
Japan and doing business together as partners for the purposes of
this Agreement, under the firm name of "The Japanese
Immigration Bureau" hereinafter called "The Bureau,* party of
the first part, and ....a corporation doing business under the
laws of the Hawaiian Islands, hereinafter called "the Planter,*
party of the second part.
    WITNESSESTH;
    1. The Planter hereby request the Bureau to furnish to it in
       Honolulu.....able-bodied male Japanese agricultural
       laborers and.....female able bodied Japanese agricultural
       laborers within..... months from the date hereof upon the
       terms hereinafter set forth.
    2. Upon the arrival of such laborers in Honolulu the Planter
       agrees to immediately cause them to be examined by a
       competent physician appointed by it for the purpose of
       determining whether they are able-bodied and fit to
       perform agricultural labor, and to accept as agricultural
       laborers all who shall be found to be able-bodied and fit,
       and to pay to the Bureau for each such male laborer so
       furnished by the Bureau the sum of thirty-five dollars
       ($35.00) United States gold coin, and for each female
       laborer so furnished by the Bureau the sum of thirty
       dollars ($30.00)
    3. Such payment shall cover all expenses of recruiting such
       laborers in Japan, their passage money to Honolulu,
       commissions for securing them all incidental expenses up
       to the time of arriving in Honolulu.
    4. The Planter shall pay all Hawaiian quarantine expenses,
       hospital tax, medical examination expenses and all local
       transportation and other charges after the arrival of such
       laborers in Honolulu.

5. The Planter hereby agree that it will furnish employment either of an agricultural character or other employment connected with sugar or coffee cultivation or production, to all of he laborers furnished to it by the Bureau, during the term of three years from the date of the arrival of such laborers in Honolulu, and will also provide for such laborers free of charge, unfurnished lodging, fuel, water for domestic purposes, medical attendance and medicines for the laborer and his family, and will pay all personal taxes of such laborers.

6. And also all that he will pay to each male laborer furnished by the Bureau under this agreement the sum of Fifteen Dollars ($15.00) per month, and to each female laborer furnished by the Bureau under this agreement, the sum of Ten Dollars ($10.00) per month as wages. The entire wage of such female laborers shall be paid to them at the end of each month, but the Planters shall at the end of the month deduct Two Dollars and Fifty-Cents ($2.50) from the wages due to each male laborer, paying the remaining Twelve Dollars and Fifty-Cents ($12.50) to the respective laborers entitled thereto. The Two dollars and Fifty-Cents per month so deducted from the wages of each male laborer shall be immediately remitted to the Bureau which shall hold the same in trust for each of said laborer. Out of the accumulation of the said Two Dollars and Fifty-Cents ($2.50) per month to the credit of each male laborer, there shall be paid by the Bureau at the experation of said term of three years, his return passage to Japan, if he desires to return, and surplus after the payment of such passage shall be paid to each such laborer in cash.

7. The Planter also agree that if any of such laborers shall work overtime each male Laborer so working overtime shall be paid therefore at the rate of Ten Cents ($.10) per hour and each female laborer shall be paid therefore at the rate of Seven Cents ($0.07) per hour.

8. It is hereby mutually agreed that, for the purpose of this agreement, one month shall consist of twenty-six (26) working days of ten hours (10) each actual work in the fields, or twelve hours (12) each actual work in and about

251

the sugar mill or sugar house.

9. And also that each of the said laborers shall work at night and rest during the day when so requested by the Planter.

10. And also that the following holidays shall be allowed to each of the said laborers, Viz: New Year's Day, Christmas, the 3rd of November, Sundays, and all United States National Holidays.

11. In consideration of the foregoing agreements of the part of the Planter, the Bureau Hereby agrees to furnish to the Planter within the said period of…..months….able-bodied female Japanese agricultural laborers at Honolulu upon the terms and conditions hereinbefore set forth, subject to the approval of the Government of Japan and Hawaii.

12. And also that each of the said laborers shall faithfully labor for the Planters for the term of three years from the date of their arrival in Honolulu as aforesaid, as agricultural laborers, or at other employment connected with sugar or coffee cultivation or production.

13. And the Bureau hereby further agrees that if any laborer furnished by it either as Laborer or as a substitute therefore shall discontinue his service for the said Planter or absent himself form his employment for a period of 15 days for other cause then sickness or death, or because of assault on the laborer by any agent or servant of the Planter, the Bureau shall within ninety (90) days after receiving notice from the Planter that such laborer has so discontinued his service or absented himself from his employment as aforesaid, provided it as possible to recruit additional laborers in Japan and to introduce the same into Hawai'i, replaced such laborer who has discontinued his service or absent himself from the employment of the Planters as aforesaid, by another laborer who shall pass a physical examination similar to the one hereinbefore specified for the original laborer, provided such examinations is required by the Planter, for which furnished of such additional labor no charge shall be made by the Bureau to the Planter.

14. In case the Bureau is unable for any cause to furnish the Planter with such additional laborer in the place of the laborer discontinuing or absenting himself from the

employment of the Planters as aforesaid, within the said period of ninety days, it hereby agrees to immediately pay to the Planter as liquidated damages for such failure to furnish such laborer, the sum or Thirty-Five Dollars ($35.00) for each male laborer and Thirty Dollars ($30.00) for each female laborer discontinuing service or absenting himself or herself as aforesaid from the employment of the said Planter.

15. It is hereby further mutually agreed that the end of the said period of three years The Planter shall have the option to re-engage the laborers furnished to it by the Bureau upon the payment by it the Bureau of an additional sum of Thirty-Five Dollars ($35.00) for each male laborer so re-engaged and Thirty Dollars ($30.00) for each female laborer so re-engaged, provided such laborers to cause them to pass a physical examination similar to that provided for above, and to reject any laborer who fails to comply with the physical conditions hereinbefore required concerning such laborer.

16. The Bureau hereby further agrees upon the execution of this agreement to give to.....as Trustee for the Planter and for other Planters who have entered or may enter into contract with the Bureau, similar to this one, a bond in the sum of.....conditioned for the faithful execution and observance by it of the foregoing agreements by it made, and within.....days from the date hereto to deposit with.....in said Honolulu the sum of.....which shall be held by the said.....subject to the conditions of this agreement, and of said bond.

Any payments which may become due by the Bureau to the Planter, under the terms of this agreement and of said bond, shall be paid by said.....to the Planter from the said deposit either upon the written consent of the Bureau as to each such claim, or, in case of refusal of such consent, upon the said.....being satisfied by proper investigation that said sum is due to the Planter under the terms of this Agreement and of said bond.

In WITNESS AND WHEREOF the said parties have hereto and to two other instrument of like date and even

253

tenor set their hands and seals the day and year first above written.

Executed and delivered)
)
in the presence of   )

Source: JFMAD 3.8.2.84 Hawaikoku keiyakuiman inyu
Nina hokoku zakken (July 1897- October 1899)

My father working in the soup kitchen

Sam Sing Camp
Camp Four

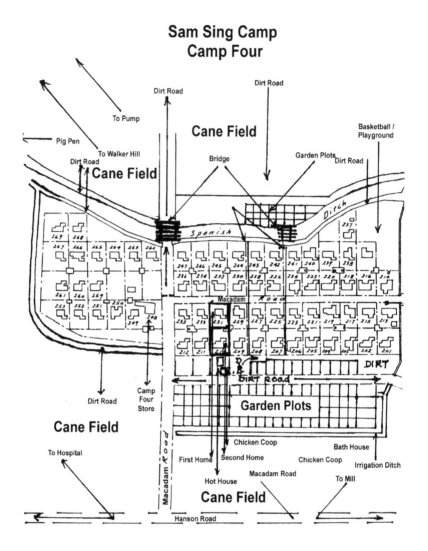

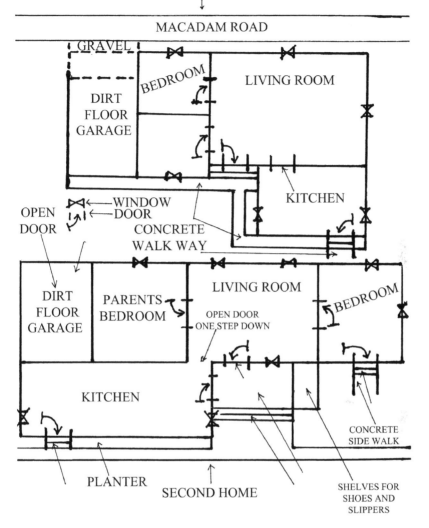

FIRST HOME

MACADAM ROAD

GRAVEL

BEDROOM

LIVING ROOM

DIRT
FLOOR
GARAGE

KITCHEN

OPEN
DOOR

WINDOW
DOOR

CONCRETE
WALK WAY

DIRT
FLOOR
GARAGE

PARENTS
BEDROOM

LIVING ROOM

OPEN DOOR
ONE STEP DOWN

BEDROOM

KITCHEN

CONCRETE
SIDE WALK

PLANTER

SECOND HOME

SHELVES FOR
SHOES AND
SLIPPERS

257

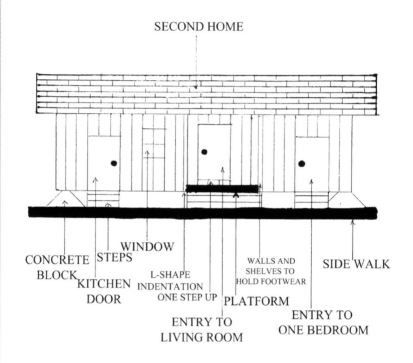

SECOND HOME

CONCRETE STEPS WINDOW

BLOCK
KITCHEN
DOOR

L-SHAPE
INDENTATION
ONE STEP UP

WALLS AND
SHELVES TO
HOLD FOOTWEAR

SIDE WALK

PLATFORM

ENTRY TO
LIVING ROOM

ENTRY TO
ONE BEDROOM

4 SEPARATE FAMILY BATHROOM
IN ONE BUILDING

WB- WASH
    BASIN

O-TOILET

⌐ DOOR
⌐ OPENING

WB   O   O   FURO

O   WB

FURO

O

FURO

2x4 ROFTERS   T&G WALLS

CONCRETE
WALL

HOLE TO
BURN
WOOD

HOLE TO
BURN KAIAWE
WOOD

DOOR ENTRY

CONCRETE
SIDE WALK

259

School's out — Forever at Puunene School as era ends

By ROBERT McCABE
Staff Writer

PUUNENE — The Stars and Stripes were lowered down the flagpole at Puunene School for the last time Friday afternoon.

Pu'unene School
Administration Building

Side Stairs of Administration Building

Kindergarten & First Grade

Second Grade

Cafeteria

Girls
Bathroom

HC&S Plantation

265

Crane picking up cane to process in mill

New type of turnahaulers

Old crane used to pick up cane in the fields

Old type of turnahaulers to haul cane to the mill

Sold meat to employees

Original Post Office still in operation

Front of boss' home

Side view of boss' home

Plantation Identification
Bango Number

Walker
Hill

Pump House

Haiku Ditch

Where I first learned how to swim

Kerosene Stove

Pots and Pans used in camp

Outhouse

Kerosene Lanterns used to light homes

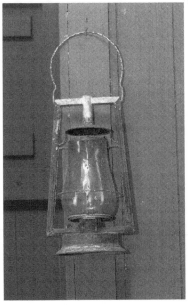

Windows in plantation homes

Inside view of rafters

Estimation on camp location

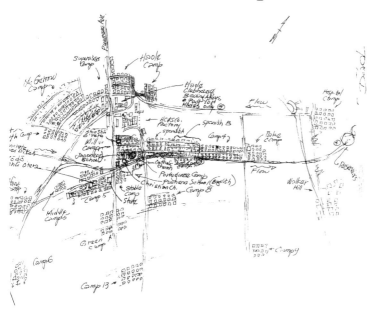

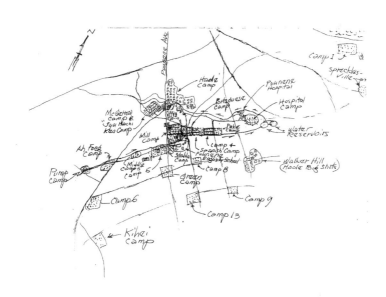

SAM SING CAMP

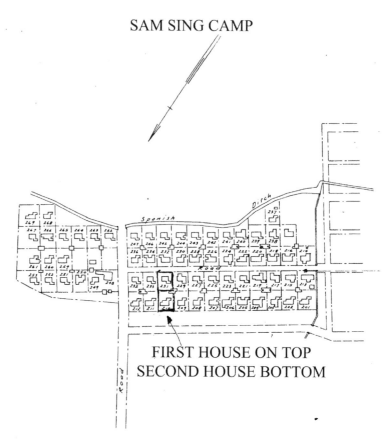

FIRST HOUSE ON TOP
SECOND HOUSE BOTTOM

LATER KNOWN AS CAMP 4

278

CAMP 4

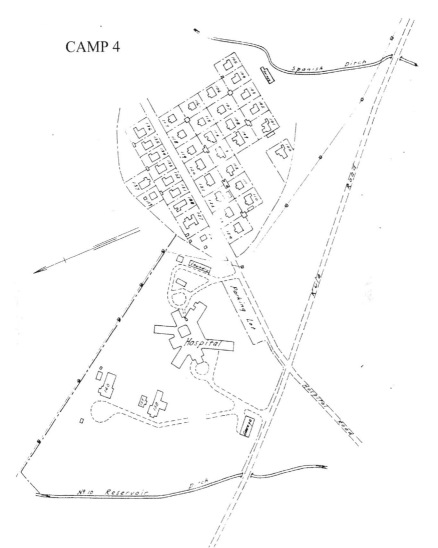

LATER KNOWN AS HOSPITAL CAMP

HAWAIIAN CAMP

CAMP TWO

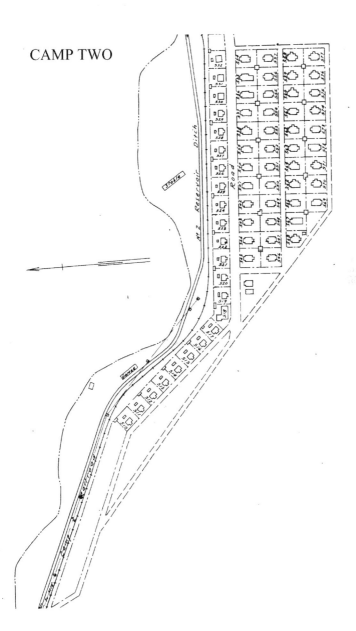

LOWER &
MIDDLE
CAMP THREE

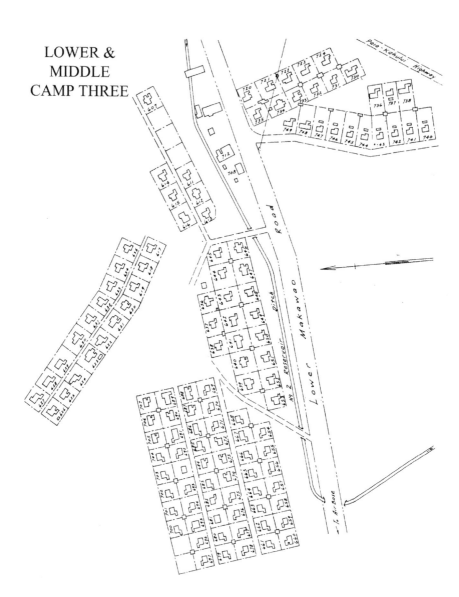

UPPER CAMP THREE

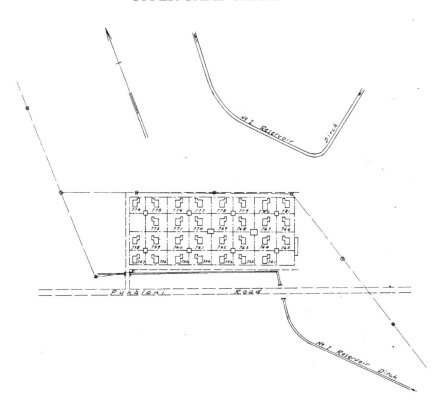

CAMP FIVE

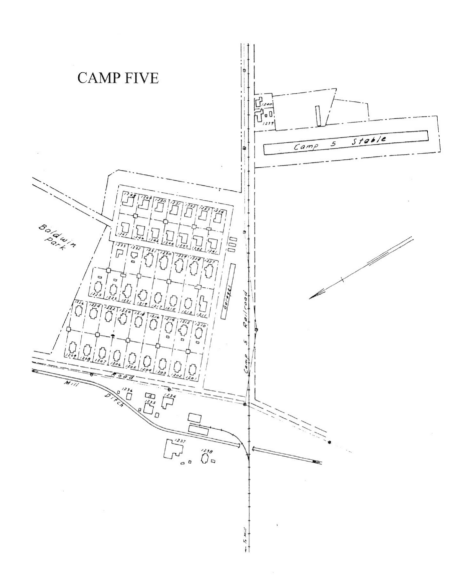

284

PUMP 5-6-7 CAMP

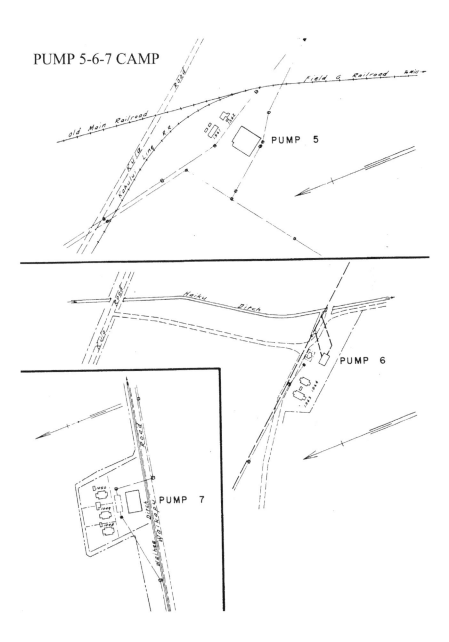

PUMP 5

PUMP 6

PUMP 7

285

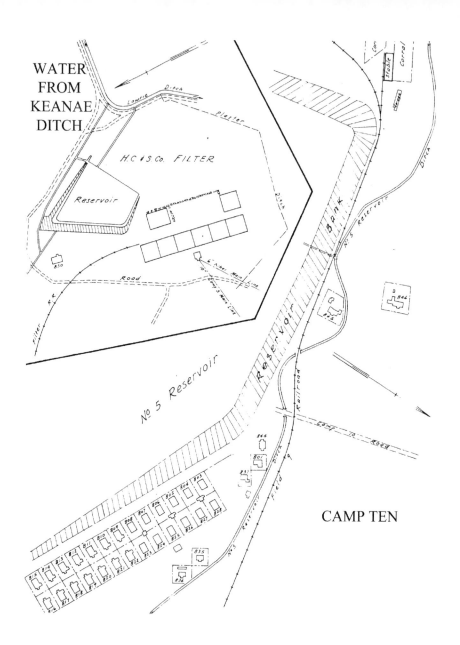

WATER
FROM
KEANAE
DITCH

H.C.& S.Co. FILTER

Reservoir

CAMP TEN

AH FONG CAMP

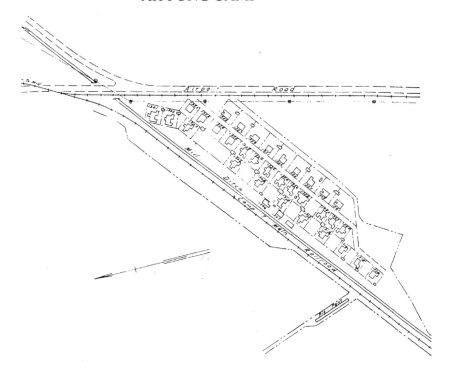

ALABAMA CAMP

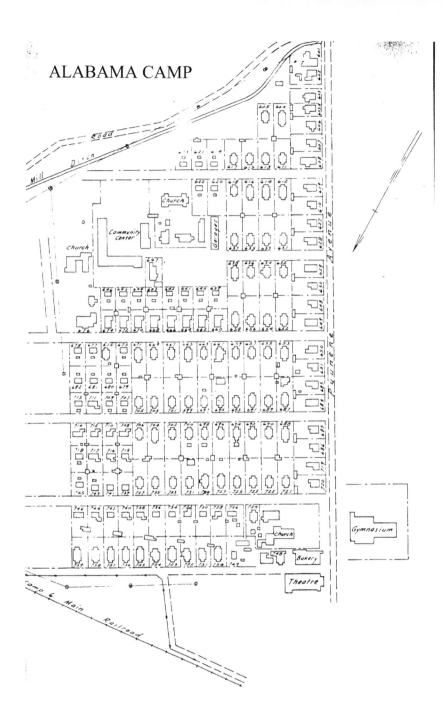

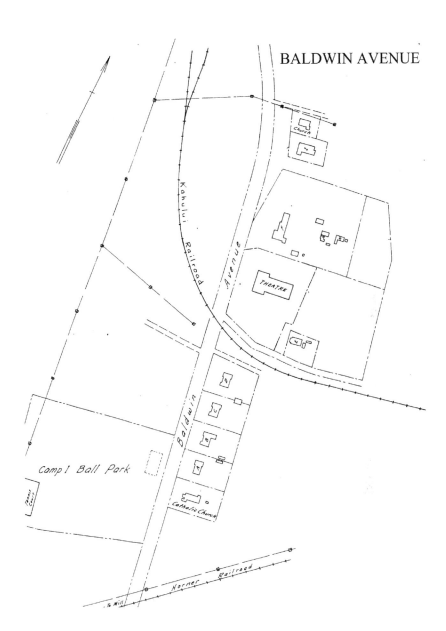

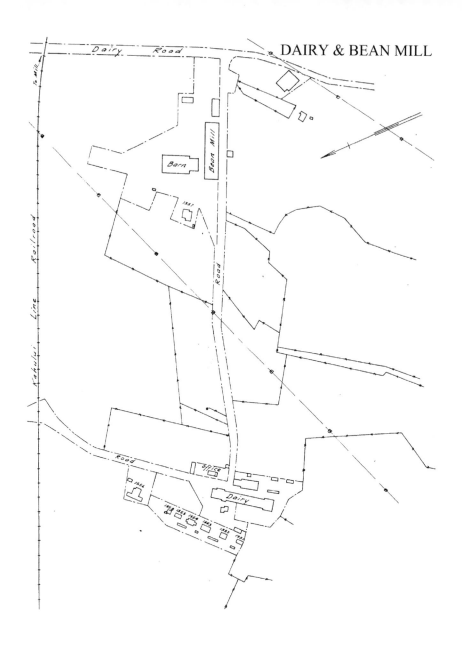

GREEN CAMP

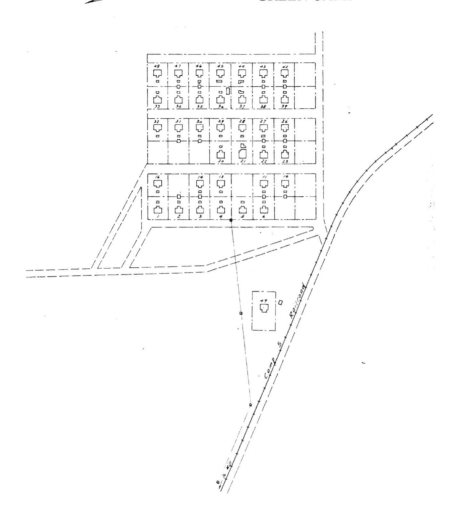

JAPANESE CAMP

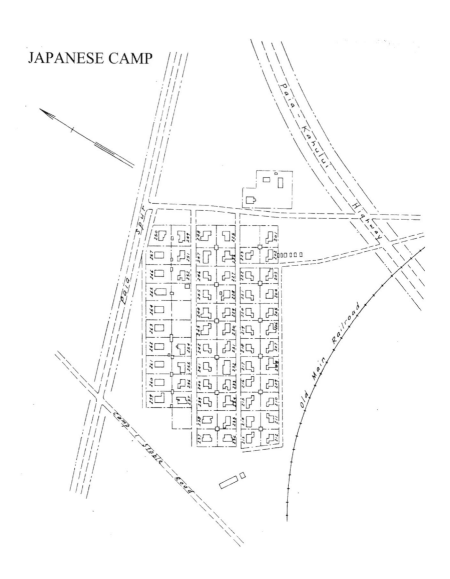

KAHULUI STORE CAMP

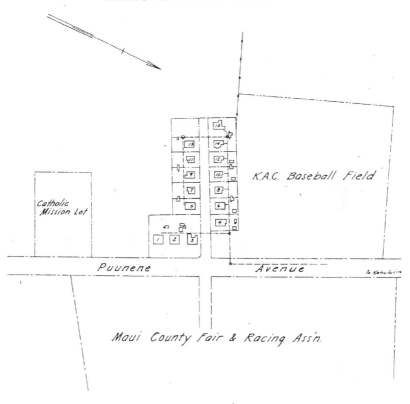

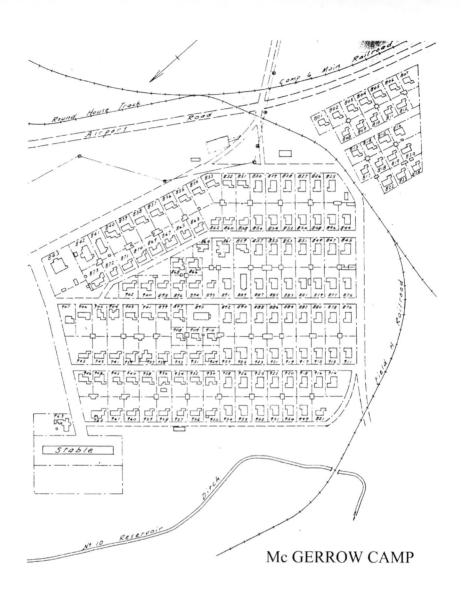

Mc GERROW CAMP

RUSSIAN CAMP

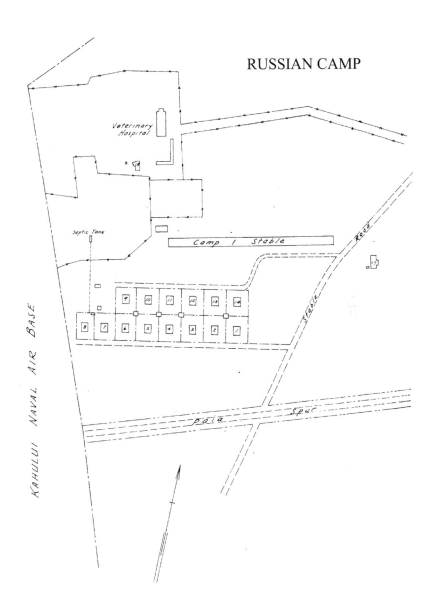

SPANISH A CAMP

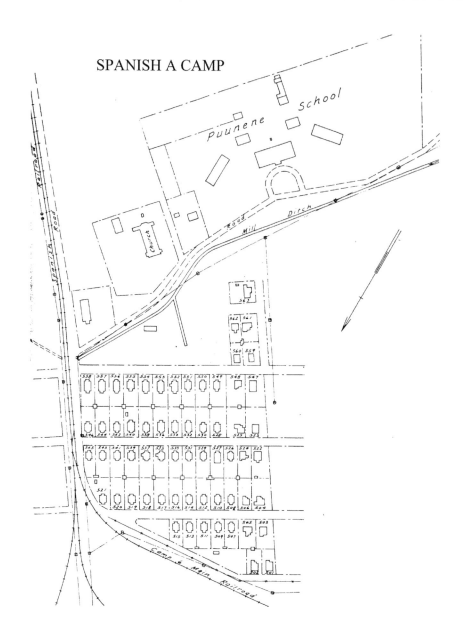

SPANISH B CAMP

WALKER HILL

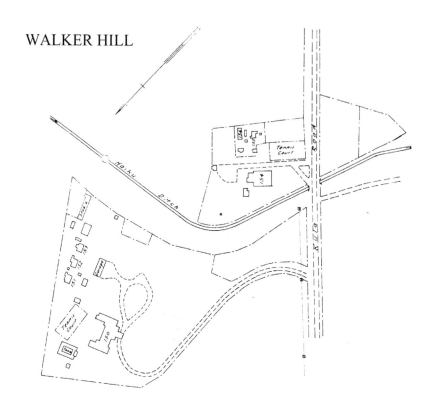

YOUNG HEE CAMP

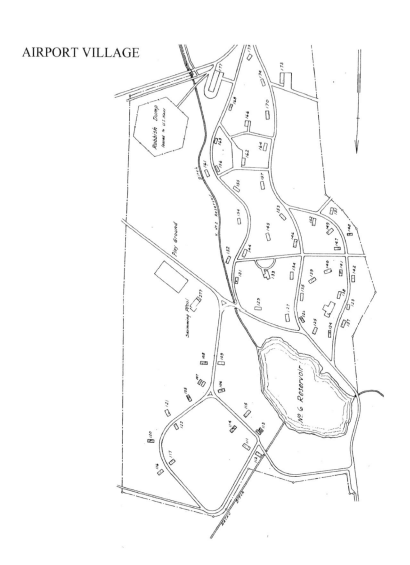

PUUNENE MILL

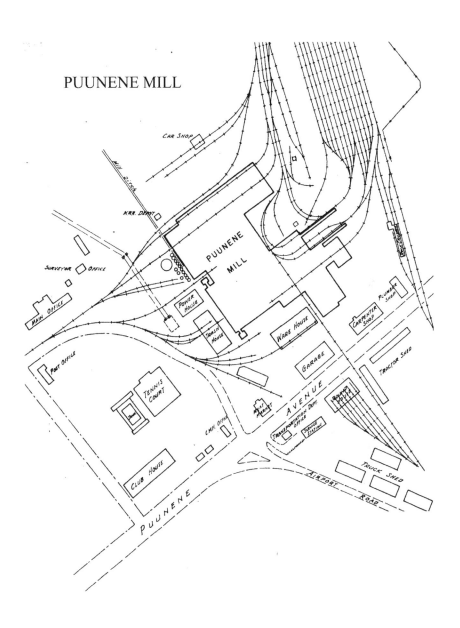

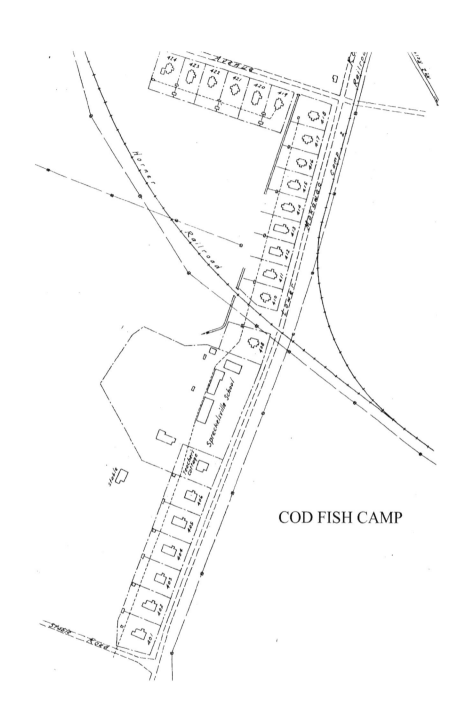

COD FISH CAMP

302

Made in the USA
San Bernardino, CA
22 April 2016